Distributing Health Care

ST ANDREWS STUDIES IN
PHILOSOPHY AND PUBLIC AFFAIRS

Founding and General Editor:
John Haldane
University of St Andrews

Distributing Health Care

Principles, Practices and Policies

Edited and Introduced
by Niall Maclean

St Andrews
Studies in
Philosophy and
Public Affairs

ia

IMPRINT ACADEMIC

Published in the UK by Imprint Academic
PO Box 200, Exeter EX5 5YX, UK

Published in the USA by Imprint Academic
Philosophy Documentation Center
PO Box 7147, Charlottesville, VA 22906-7147, USA

ISBN 9781845400514

A CIP catalogue record for this book is available from the
British Library and US Library of Congress

Cover Photograph:
St Salvator's Quadrangle, St Andrews by Peter Adamson
from the University of St Andrews collection

Contents

Notes on Contributors

Professor John Appleby joined the King's Fund in 1998 following senior lectureships in health economics at the Universities of East Anglia and Birmingham. After his masters in health economics at the University of York in 1980, John worked in the NHS for seven years in Birmingham and London. For five years he worked for the National Association of Health Authorities (now the NHS Confederation) as manager of the Association's Central Policy Unit.

Paul Carrick teaches philosophy at Gettysburg College. He is the author of *Medical Ethics in the Ancient World* (2001), and has published in the *Cambridge Quarterly of Healthcare Ethics, The Journal of Mind and Behavior*, and *Perspectives in Biology and Medicine*. He is a bioethics consultant for Pinnacle Health Hospitals and founding director of the Honors Program at Harrisburg Area Community College.

Dr Susan Cleary has recently been appointed as the Director of the Health Economics Unit at the University of Cape Town, where she has worked as a researcher and lecturer for the past 6 years. Her research focuses on equitable and efficient health care for HIV-positive people.

C.A.J. (Tony) Coady was formerly Boyce Gibson Professor of Philosophy at the University of Melbourne and is now Professorial Fellow in Applied Philosophy at the Centre for Applied Philosophy and Public Ethics (CAPPE) in that university. He is best known for his work in epistemology, especially his book *Testimony: A Philosophical Study* (Oxford University Press, 1992), and in applied philosophy where he has written extensively on issues to do with war and terrorism, much of which is further developed in his book *Morality and Political Violence* (Cambridge University Press, 2008). He was a foundation member of the Victorian Government's Infertility Treatment Authority from 1996 to 2001.

Margaret M. Coady is a foundation member of the Australian Research Council Special Research Centre for Applied Philosophy and Public Ethics, and a Senior Lecturer in the Centre for Equity and Innovation in

Early Childhood at the University of Melbourne. Her specialist areas, on which she has published widely, are professional ethics and children's and families' rights. She was a foundation member of the Victorian Child Death Review Committee, and is a current member of the Infertility Treatment Authority, of the Clinical Ethics Advisory Group of the Royal Women's Hospital, and of the Ethics Committee of the Victorian Association of Family Therapy.

Leonard Fleck, PhD is currently Professor of Philosophy and Medical Ethics at Michigan State University (East Lansing, Michigan). He is completing a book for Oxford University Press under the working title *Just Caring: The Ethical Challenges of Health Care Rationing and Rational Democratic Deliberation*.

Howard Glennerster is Professor Emeritus in Social Policy at the London School of Economics and Political Science. He has written widely on the finance and economics of health care and is a member of the English Secretary of State for Health's Advisory Committee on Resource Allocation.

Anthony Harrison is a Senior Associate in health policy at the King's Fund, where he has worked since the early 1990s after a career in the Government Economic Service.

Dr Niall Maclean is an Associate Fellow of the Social Market Foundation and was recently *Philosophical Quarterly* Research Fellow in the Centre for Ethics, Philosophy and Public Affairs at the University of St Andrews. He has also worked as a researcher in the Department of Public Health Sciences at King's College (University of London). His main areas of interest include moral, social and political philosophy, and health policy. His publications include articles in the *British Medical Journal* and *Social Science and Medicine*. Niall is currently training to be a barrister in London.

Di McIntyre is a Professor in the Health Economics Unit and the South African Research Chair in 'Health and Wealth' at the University of Cape Town. Her research focuses primarily on equity issues, particularly in relation to health care financing, resource allocation and the public-private mix.

Okore Okorafor has been working as a researcher and lecturer at the Health Economics Unit at the University of Cape Town for the past 5 years. His areas of interest include equity in health care financing, resource allocation and econometrics.

Michael Thiede is an Associate Professor of Health Economics at the University of Cape Town. He is conducting research on health care inequities, pro-poor strategies in health reform and the economics of pharmaceutical markets.

Niall Maclean

Introduction

Health Care Distribution
— What's the Problem?

'NHS can't afford drug that transforms lives'

(*The Times*, April 19, 2006)

'Cancer: There are life-saving drugs. So why can't we have them?'

(*The Independent*, April 2, 2006)

'MS drugs likely to stay off health service list'

(*The Guardian*, August 7, 2001)

Newspaper headlines such as these are becoming increasingly familiar, not only in the UK but in any society that operates a system of publicly funded health care. What is at stake is whether some new drug or surgical procedure ought to be included in the package of care that is purchased out of public funds. There is now a vast array of effective medical treatments, brought into existence by the startling rate of technological advance witnessed over the past fifty or so years. The current development of genetic technology means yet more novel treatments being developed in the near future. The sheer number of treatments, combined with their cost, forces even wealthy societies to pick and choose which subset they can afford to provide. Headlines like those reproduced above will continue for as long as the number of available treatments continues to outstrip available funds.

It would be a mistake, however, to think that cases involving cutting-edge treatments are the only, or even the archetypal, health care distribution questions. They certainly grab the most column inches, for readily comprehensible reasons. Novel treatments at the horizon of scientific knowledge are themselves intrinsically interesting, and the typical decision regarding these treatments—to fund, or not to fund—

possesses the kind of binary starkness that makes for a good newspaper story.

Far less dramatic but no less important are a range of distributive questions that concern forms of health care usually considered much more mundane, and where the decisions to be made are more subtle than 'to fund, or not to fund'. We might all agree that this more ordinary health care should be made publicly available, but questions remain about the *amounts* we are willing to fund. How many clinics and hospitals ought to be provided? How many medical professionals do we want to staff them? How many diagnostic tests do we make available? How many sessions of labour intensive treatments such as physiotherapy or psychological counselling? It is at least theoretically possible to fund a health care system to such a level that access to facilities is immediate for all classes of patient (the sick and the not so sick), where patients can spend an unlimited amount of time with the medical professional of their choice and be provided with unlimited amounts of ordinary health care. Of course, not even wealthy societies fund their health care systems to this level. Once again, the simple fact of resource constraints means that we must settle on a particular sub-optimal distribution.

But what does it mean to say that resources are limited? So far, I have been taking it for granted that not even wealthy societies can afford to fund what might be thought of as an optimal distribution of health care. We might define such a distribution as one in which all *kinds* of health care, both cutting-edge and mundane, are provided in such *amounts* as to provide the most amount of benefit to patients that we possibly can (i.e. spending a further pound, euro, or dollar would produce no further medical benefit). Some might question the assumption that not even wealthy societies can afford to fund an optimal distribution. It could be argued, for example, that sufficiently wealthy societies (e.g. the US, or Japan, or the developed countries of Europe) could afford to do so if they simply devoted more of their gross domestic product (GDP) than they do at present to the health care system. Several rejoinders could be mounted to this suggestion. It could be pointed out that the seeming inability of even wealthy societies to fund optimal distributions of heath care has persisted through a period in which they have, in the main, been devoting ever greater proportions of GDP to health care. Consider the UK. Since the creation of the National Health Service (NHS) the proportion of GDP spent on health care in the UK has more than doubled, from 3.5% in 1948 to 7.7% in 2002. The projection for the year 2013 is for the proportion to rise again, to between 10.3% and 11%.[1] Headlines like

---

[1]   These figures are taken from the 'Letter to the Chancellor of the Exchequer' section of the Wanless Report (HM Treasury, 2002). They represent *total* health spend in the UK (i.e. spending from public and private sources

those above have been commonplace throughout this period of continued investment.

"Well then devote *even more* of our GDP to health, until we secure an optimal distribution!" might be the reply. It is implausible to think that any society really has the appetite to follow through on such a spending pledge. The fact that many health needs are capable of consuming such vast resources were they to be treated optimally means that devoting 'as much as it takes' of our GDP to secure an optimal distribution would seriously hinder (and possibly render impossible) the pursuit of other valued social projects. The good protected and promoted by medical care — health — is just one good amongst many. It has rivals. Just as no individual person would allocate his personal resources in such a way as to make him optimally healthy if doing so would seriously hinder his ability to pursue any of the activities that give value to life, neither would any society consent to a similarly one-eyed allocation of resources to health care at the expense of education, job creation, cultural activities, transport, defence, policing, environmental initiatives, etc. While some basic level of health might be a necessary condition for leading a valuable life, it is certainly not sufficient. Any decision to pursue health at all costs seems analogous to that of a builder who blows his entire budget laying the best possible set of foundations he can afford, leaving no money to build anything on top of them.

But what if 'spending as much as it takes' to secure an optimal distribution would entail spending more than we do at present, but nowhere near 100% of GDP? We might still legitimately wonder if we would be willing to make the sacrifice. Consider the UK. We currently spend about 8% of GDP on health care, and yet we regularly seem to be confronted with the need to set limits to the care that is provided. At the same time, we also read news stories about how a lack of resources is hindering the education system, the transport infrastructure, policing, defence, etc. Even if an optimal distribution of health care could be achieved by spending more than 8% of GDP but less than 100% these other valued projects would still suffer. Given how far away we are at present from an optimal distribution of health care, it seems reasonable to assume they would suffer a great deal. It would of course be open to our insistent critic to claim that these other projects are of less importance than the health care system, and their suffering a great deal is a price worth paying if we thereby secure an optimal distribution of health care. But it is not at all obvious to me how this claim could be

---

combined), and cannot therefore be seen as indicative of the total spent on the NHS alone. The authors of the report assume that private spending on health care in the UK is around 1.2% of GDP, and likely to remain at that level in the short to medium terms.

established convincingly. I will have much more to say in my chapter in this volume about the difficulty of ranking different kinds of medical benefits as being more or less valuable. The points made there apply *a fortiori* to any attempt to rank medical and non-medical benefits as being more or less valuable. Nevertheless, it is still possible to make a modest suggestion: even if securing an optimal distribution of health care would require using somewhat less than 100% of GDP the cost to other social projects would be still be enormous, and it is very doubtful that health is *sufficiently* more valuable than these other projects to justify such a one-eyed policy.

We might, therefore, rightly be suspicious of anyone who suggests our seeming inability to fund an optimal distribution of health care is merely an artificial consequence of a reprehensible failure to commit sufficient of our GDP. Yet there are other ways to argue that the seemingly genuine need to set limits to health care provision is in fact artificial. One claim sometimes put forward is this: if we were to get tough on all the inefficiency and wastage in our health care system, sufficient resources would be freed up for us to fund an optimal distribution of health care, without having to inject extra resources into the system. Most publicly funded health care is delivered by large organisations. In the case of the UK it is delivered by a staggeringly large one – the NHS – that employs some 1.3 million people. There can be no doubt that in such large and complex organisations there will be considerable scope to bring about improvements in efficiency.[2] What is much more doubtful, however, is that the money saved thereby would (when combined with the existing total spend) be sufficient to fund an optimal distribution of health care. Of course, this is a complex question whose full resolution would require detailed empirical research. I can only appeal here to the following seemingly plausible argument, as it might apply to the UK's NHS: we currently seem to be *so* far from having an optimal distribution of health care that the extra resources required to create one would be very considerable; in order for resources of this magnitude to come from an 'efficiency drive', the NHS would currently have to be operating extremely inefficiently; it does not seem to be operating at this extreme level of inefficiency; therefore, it is unlikely that resources of the requisite magnitude would be freed up as a result of an 'efficiency drive'.

---

[2]   This is not to imply any kind of intrinsic tendency towards rank inefficiency in large organisations; rather, it is to make the (I hope) commonsensical point that the larger and more complicated an organisation the more scope there will be to *do* things with its structure. Hence, other things being equal, there will be greater scope to bring about *gains* in efficiency (which need not be the same as remedying rank inefficiency) in large and complex organisations than in small and simple ones.

It is worth considering one final argument in support of the idea that setting limits to health care provision is an artificial activity. Many observers are critical of certain of the business practices of the large private concerns that make up the health care industry: pharmaceutical companies are the obvious example, though we ought also to include companies that manufacture various forms of medical equipment. As businesses, it might seem unremarkable that these organisations structure their activities in such a way as to generate profits. However, it is sometimes argued that the quest for profits results in the prices of drugs and medical equipment being set unacceptably high. If we could get these companies to settle for smaller profit margins, thereby reducing the cost of the goods they bring to market, we would be able to afford something closer to an optimal distribution of health care without needing to put extra funds into the health care system. This is another difficult question demanding careful empirical analysis, and consequently I can once again only hint here at what I hope is a plausible sounding answer. We seem to be some distance away from having an optimal distribution of health care, and the extra resources required to take us there would probably be very considerable indeed. Even if we could persuade the member companies of the health care industry to settle for smaller profit margins, it is unlikely that this would reduce the price of health care to such an extent that resources of this magnitude would be freed up. This seems especially plausible when we take into account certain relevant background facts: the profits of many of these companies are already capped (in the UK, for example, the profits of pharmaceutical companies are currently capped at 21%); at least some of these companies do not currently generate large profits, and would be unable to maintain their performance were they to operate on smaller margins; and many mechanisms are currently in place to drive down the cost of health care goods (such as time-limited patents that render a drug 'generic' after a certain period of time has elapsed).

Even accepting that I have failed to give detailed answers to these empirical questions it is nevertheless highly plausible to think that the situation I described above — where even wealthy societies cannot afford to provide an optimal distribution of health care — is a genuine one. It is not, I contend, a mere artifice that would disappear were we to inject more funds into the health care system, or eliminate wastefulness, or get tough with the powerful commercial interests in the health care industry. However, even if my arguments are not found plausible, and the suspicion is retained that the need for limit setting is less genuine than it appears, we would still face the question of how to set limits to health care provision while we tackled the underlying causes that brought about this artificial situation. It would take a great deal of time to divert funds away from other ongoing social projects and towards health care. This diverting must of necessity be an incremental process in order to ensure the 'donor' services do not immediately collapse. Dealing with inefficiency and commercial interests would also probably be drawn-out processes, although for different reasons. As such, even those who stubbornly believe that the need to set limits is an artifice to be overcome will still face the question of how we ought to set such limits in the potentially lengthy period before the overcoming is achieved.

The essays in the present volume tackle different aspects of health care resource allocation. As befits the nature of the topic, and as the second part of the volume's title suggests — 'Principles, Practices and Policies' — a range of perspectives are brought to bear. The opening two chapters would fall most naturally under the umbrella label 'principles'. We begin with a historical overview of the various impulses, ideas and motivations that have underpinned the desire to use both private and public resources to provide medical treatment to the sick. Professor Paul Carrick of Gettysburg College argues that the history of collective medical care, from the Ancient Greeks through the middle ages and into the era of modern medicine, shows a range of distinct yet related motivating principles. These include the redemptive, utilitarian, prudential, and charitable motives. While our natural tendency might be to try to subsume these under some more general and fundamental 'master' principle, this would be an affront to the historical record, Carrick suggests. Just as the modern day problem of health care distribution has no single answer, the history of collective medical provision has no single, unified explanation. There may indeed be an instructive connection between these two facts. Nevertheless, as we look to the future in contemplating more equitable forms of allocation, Carrick identifies an ideal he labels the 'philanthropic imperative'. He believes adherence to this ideal could motivate reform, both nationally and internationally, in the decades ahead.

The second chapter remains within the broad category of 'principles', although its focus is more directly on the various philosophical approaches that can be applied to the question of health care distribution rather than on the various more or less principled approaches that have been brought to bear historically. In this chapter, I argue that it is possible to discern the forms these philosophical approaches can take by considering the kinds of arguments that can be mustered in support of a particular idea: that certain individuals in certain circumstances have a *moral claim* to receive health care. I group these arguments into two broad types — what I call 'basic benevolence' approaches (which are necessarily concerned with the importance or value of medical goods) and 'justice-based' approaches (which focus less on the importance of these goods, and more on our being *entitled* to receive them). I argue that the latter approaches are better suited to the task of justifying the kind of organised, large-scale health care provision found in modern societies. I go on to argue that justice-based approaches are also better able to generate determinate answers to the question of how health care resources should be allocated under conditions of relative scarcity, since they explicitly recognise and attempt to deal with the fact that modern societies are marked by reasonable and seemingly intractable disagreement about what are the most important kinds of medical goods. I end by setting out a particular model that avoids certain of the problems found in existing justice-based approaches.

The remaining five chapters of the book redeem our promise to deal with 'practices and policies', although the authors tackle the particular questions posed in specific countries in a way that is sensitive to relevant moral considerations. We begin with two chapters on the United Kingdom. In chapter three, Howard Glennerster, Professor Emeritus in Social Policy at the London School of Economics, describes the recent history and current reality of health care distribution in the United Kingdom. Thirty years ago most allocation decisions in the UK were inexplicit, unreasoned, and usually made at local level. Since then, Professor Glennerster argues, there has been a steady shift towards a more explicit, reason-governed, and centralised approach: overall spending priorities have been set using an accountable nationwide process; steps have been taken to ensure that all citizens, regardless of where they live, have an equal chance to access health care; common standards of treatment for various medical conditions have been set across the entire NHS; and, perhaps most controversially, there is an increasing focus on ensuring the NHS supplies only the most 'cost-effective' treatments. However, Professor Glennerster also argues that many of the most important distributive questions, including the question of how much should be spent on the NHS at the expense of other social projects, are still not debated openly in the UK. Moreover, many of the decisions that are formally supposed to be taken 'in the open' are still marked by a degree of inexplicitness: one important example concerns how the UK's National Institute for Health and Clinical Excellence (NICE) decides whether a particular treatment is 'sufficiently' cost-effective.

Chapter four is given over to discussing how the current system of health care allocation in the UK could be improved upon. Professor John Appleby and Anthony Harrison of the King's Fund argue that the focus on cost-effectiveness found in much current UK health policy should be rendered more explicit and followed through more rigorously. They argue that the total budget for the NHS—one of key issues Professor Glennerster argues is not currently debated in an open and transparent way—should be set by assessing the type and magnitude of the benefits that would accrue were the budget to be increased within various specific 'treatment programmes'. This would require much more effort in data gathering and analysis than currently takes place, but would secure the very considerable goal of increased transparency. Policy-makers would be able to set the global spend for the NHS by summing how much it costs to make each treatment programme maximally efficient (which might, for example, be reached when an extra pound spent on that programme would produce greater marginal returns if spent on an alternative programme). The same goal of greater transparency could also be secured when the global budget is allocated between treatment programmes, by prioritising those programmes that produce the greatest marginal returns. Appleby and Harrison recognise that the ethical assumptions built into this model will be found uncongenial by those sympathetic to less utilitarian approaches. They counter by arguing that their model is practically achievable within the context of current health policy, seems well equipped to promote uniform standards of care for the same disease condition, and does at least allow for the making of *explicit* trade-offs.

Our focus shifts in chapter five to a country whose health care system embodies some of the most striking moral issues, and whose political culture sites some of the most fiercely contested debate, found anywhere in the developed world: the USA. Professor Len Fleck of Michigan State University begins by examining the history of health care provision in the US, noting that this was driven in the post-1945 period by notions of individual freedom and economic liberalism. This has led to a health care system marked, Fleck argues, by inefficiency and extreme inequality of provision. The US is also the birthplace of most of the salient advances in medical technology, and health care costs within the country are escalating alarmingly as new treatments come to market in a seemingly endless stream. Fleck argues that while respect for individual liberty can form an acceptable *component* within a conception of health care justice suitable for the US context, it cannot dominate to the exclusion of other ethical considerations. He goes on to set out a pluralistic conception of justice that draws on several such considerations, and argues that it can be used to yield answers to the problem of health care distribution in the US that can be considered 'just enough': not perfectly just, but nevertheless a considerable moral improvement on the status quo. At the core of Fleck's approach is a commitment to a process of fair and rational deliberation that takes place in a 'moral and political space' which has its boundaries drawn by certain 'constitutional principles of health care justice'. This approach chimes well with the model of political discourse endorsed (and often revered) by US citizens.

Chapter six is devoted to discussing the particular ethical challenges faced within, and the lessons that can be learned from, the Australian health care system. Margaret M. Coady and Professor Tony Coady of the University of Melbourne explain how this system is marked by a relative absence of formal centralised control, and is further complicated by the mechanics of the Australian federal system of government. There is an interesting division of labour not found in many other health care systems, where the Australian states and territories organise hospital care and the Federal Government takes responsibility for out-of-hospital treatment. The Federal Government has sought to establish various centralised bodies to supervise the allocation of health care resources, most notably those involved in the Pharmaceutical Benefits Scheme which oversee the safety of drugs and ensure that approved medications are remarkably affordable. Nonetheless, it seems that many salient distributive decisions are still taken at local level. While recognising the strengths of this localism, Margaret and Tony Coady go on to argue that there is scope within the Australian system for a greater degree of moral deliberation than is found at present. Such deliberation will focus on certain 'animating ideals' found in Australian political culture. Foremost amongst these is a firm but not unqualified commitment to clinicians' professional autonomy, and a concern to ensure that all Australians, regardless of their social standing or geographical location, enjoy equal access to health care. Although it is difficult to predict the outcome of open and frank deliberations on the future of health care allocation in Australia, Margaret and Tony Coady end on an optimistic note regarding the willingness of contemporary Australians to support valued public services via progressive taxation.

Our final chapter concerns a country possessing a highly complex recent political history and a set of public health problems of a severity seldom encountered anywhere else in the world: South Africa. Susan Cleary, Di McIntyre, Okore Okorafor and Michael Thiede of the University of Cape Town describe how the legacy of apartheid remains etched into the South African health care system, with serious socio-economic differences in access to treatment and a resource split between the public and private health care sectors that is markedly disproportionate to the numbers of persons served. Although several comprehensive reforms were proposed in the immediate post-apartheid period the implementation of concrete policies has proven problematic, and the health care system remains without an explicitly reasoned overall vision. There are problems of inequity both within the public health care sector, and between it and the private sector. Were these inequities to be overcome, the health care system within South Africa could serve as a powerful vehicle for deepening social solidarity within the country. While it is far from straightforward to see how headway might be made with these inequities, important lessons can be learned from recent attempts to deal with the enormous burden HIV/AIDS has placed on the South African health care system. Although the latest national strategic plan in this area seems to harbour the possibility of implicit rationing in the future it nevertheless shows an admirable commitment to principles of procedural justice, and could serve as a useful model for further reform throughout the health care system.

Principled approaches to the problem of health care distribution can be formulated at a certain level of abstraction, and doing so is important both in guiding thought and in shutting out certain unhelpful forms of background noise: lobbying by interest groups for priority to be given to particular treatments, for example, is merely an exemplification of the problem rather than any kind of contribution to its solution. However, after becoming clearer on the kinds of principles we want to aid in the resolution, the next task is not simply to apply these principles in any kind of mechanistic way. By focussing on particular countries our aim in this volume has been to show how the problem of health care distribution, while capable of being framed in general terms, manifests itself in quite different ways in different contexts. Great care is required in constructing distributive models that both represent an ethical improvement upon the status quo in a particular country and are practically achievable within its social and political limitations. My final duty as editor of this volume is to thank the contributors warmly for undertaking this task with such skill.

Paul Carrick

The Public Funding of Health Care

A Brief Historical Overview of Principles, Practices, and Motives

Old age is a natural disease, while disease is an acquired old age. (Aristotle, *Generation of Animals* 5.49.784b.33)

Introduction

Nationally sponsored programs designed to fund health care for the general public are largely a twentieth century phenomenon. Yet a long glance backward at the medical and public health history of Western civilization, extending from the ancient Greeks to the twentieth century, reveals earlier periods when governments, religious institutions, and other groups provided some measure of medical relief for the sick, the poor, and the homeless. In this essay, I will provide not an exhaustive but rather an illustrative account of this oft forgotten fact. My objectives are threefold.

First, to remind us that the active concern of society for the health of its citizens is hardly a new development arising full born, as it were, out of the biomedical revolution and refined moral sensibilities of our present age. As I will suggest, our current interest in public health, and the related question of how to allocate medical resources fairly, is part of a larger evolutionary social process. Second, to conjecture that the impulse of caring for the sick and injured, using public or private resources,[1] is typically driven by a variety of sometimes overlapping

---

[1] The phrase 'public or private resources' is used advisedly. There are relatively few well documented cases prior to about 1850 when public funds alone went toward rendering medical care to the sick or infirm. More typically, such efforts

motivations, both religious and secular in origin. Third, to indicate that no single monolithic philosophy of providing medical care for the masses emerges from the historical record. That is, no unified pattern of health care organization or individual or communal motivation can plausibly account for this seemingly altruistic behavior, behavior which is putatively aimed at promoting the common good of all members of society.

Given the interdisciplinary scope of this discussion, my inquiry will weave together sociological, psychological, and philosophical strands of evidence. Constraints of length will limit us primarily to developments in Europe and the United States. In the end, a limited sampling of societal practices, individual or communal motivations, and philosophical considerations will indicate that no simple story can be told about the public or private funding of health care.

Proceeding more or less chronologically, I will introduce evidence demonstrating that redemptive, utilitarian, prudential, and charitable impulses (among others) are at work in the humane decision to use public or private funds to provide medical care for the benefit of the sick or infirm. While I do not claim that these four motivations constitute a complete list, they do emerge as a recurring and significant typology — helping to solidify the emerging modern public health movement in England, the United States, and elsewhere in the West by the late nineteenth century.

The Public Health Movement and Distributive Justice

Struggling to survive amidst the social upheaval of the Industrial Revolution from about 1750 and well into the next century, peasants, labourers, share-croppers and others migrated from rural to urban areas — first in Europe and later in America — in search of a better life and regular employment. Instead, workers were routinely paid subsistence wages and laboured twelve to sixteen hour days in grinding, suffocating factories and other industrial environments in cities like Manchester, Liverpool, Chicago, and Boston. What's more, the unwashed masses were frequently shunted into crowded, unsanitary tenements in major economic centres such as Paris, London, and New York. Not surprisingly, the poor, hungry, and homeless were usually the hardest hit by infectious (communicable) diseases and other debilitating ailments. In fact, their miseries were redoubled by overcrowded tenement housing in the larger cities by the end of the eighteenth century and throughout the nineteenth century as well. These squalid living and working conditions contributed to new levels of urban blight and the inevitable spread of

---

involved funds from both the wealthier classes, acting charitably, and from governmental sources, acting prudentially.

infectious diseases like cholera, diphtheria, tuberculosis, smallpox, yellow fever, and measles.

Indeed, the modern public health movement may be understood, in part, as a humane response to the collective misery brought about by the Industrial Revolution and its introduction of steam power to run the massive factory machines, and by the population shifts which it provoked as workers were lured from country farms and villages to, in effect, become willing cogs in those often dehumanizing machines. The public health ethos represents a response on the part of doctors, nurses, city officials, clergy, and governmental leaders who personally or professionally cared about the future of their cities and towns. Understandably, they cared, too, about the preservation of their own and their families' and their communities' health in the face of these profound demographic migrations and accompanying threat of the outbreak of epidemic diseases that left no one feeling secure. In addition, poor personal hygiene, foul drinking water, spoiled food, lack of sanitation, putrid air—these and other factors were also commonly thought to be involved in undermining the health of the masses. However prejudicial or misleading, the views of a growing cohort of public health officials held sway with the establishment as their opinions were echoed in newspapers and summarized in public health notices posted publicly during the 1800 and 1900s in both England and the United States, according to social historian Roy Porter (Porter, 1999, pp. 397–427 passim).

Hence, by the opening decades of the 1800s some reasonably helpful public health measures were deployed. These included educational tracts about the importance of personal hygiene (cleanliness, it turns out, really was next to godliness); church sponsored kitchens for the care and feeding of the displaced and the poor; and early feminist social campaigns that stressed the need for improved sanitation. These efforts culminated in the so-called 'sanitation movement' that lobbied for closed sewers, potable drinking water, and other important environmental reforms. In addition, many churches and other religious organizations sponsored sermons aimed specifically at the poor, widowed, and orphaned. These stressed the need for 'good work habits', 'clean morals', regular bathing or, if needed, de-licing, medical examinations, etc. To be sure, however mixed the overall results were in actually protecting lives against infectious diseases like cholera and smallpox, such public health measures did indeed cost the state and other sponsoring organizations money. While most of the revenues to cover these costs came from government treasuries, other funding derived from such non-governmental entities as churches, guilds, professional societies, and wealthy families. The latter tended to view their contributions as a civic or religious duty if not also as an insurance policy against class war-fare.

Furthermore, by the middle of the nineteenth century, what could be called the emerging public health movement and its tacit commitment to promote sound hygiene and public sanitation for all, began slowly to be codified into law. In England, this reform was embodied in three key pieces of legislation.

First, the (revised) New Poor Law of 1834. This was encouraged by the utilitarian reformer and founder of the Sanitary Movement in Britain, Edwin Chadwick (1800–90). Among other things, the law created a sin-gle scale of benefit to the poor across England, without local variations (Chave, 1984, p. 5). It also provided subsistence, medicine, work, and crude housing for the indigent but able-bodied poor who, unsurprisingly, suffered in disproportionate numbers from a variety of chronic and debilitating diseases. But Chadwick came to see that the revised workhouse conditions created by the New Poor Law, a law that was actually intended to reduce the number of families on public relief by creating harsh workhouse conditions involving the separation of families, long hours of employment, and the lowest possible pay, in point of fact increased the number of families seeking subsistence wages. This puzzled him. He studied the situation in great detail, culmi-nating in his monumental *Report on the Sanitary Condition of the Labouring Population of Great Britain (1842).* This report to Parliament documented, among other things, that not fecklessness or sloth (as he and others had heretofore ruefully claimed) but rather disease and disability were over-whelmingly the primary causes of poverty. In addition, to overcome these unhealthy conditions, actions needed to be taken by municipal governments to provide clean drinking water, rid towns and cities of cesspools and piles of garbage that bred disease, and eventually estab-lish oversight and enforcement mechanisms. Disturbingly, Chadwick's report showed that the average age of death for the poorest laborer in London's worst slums was 16, while the better-off laborer lived to about age forty-five. 'Poverty could not be abolished, but the poverty due to preventable diseases could be', Chadwick declared. Given his powers of persuasion and careful documentation, he convinced Parliament that the situation among the urban poor was indeed dire (Porter, 1999, p. 411).

Second, this sense of urgency led to the passage of the England's first Public Health Act of 1848. This act created a central governmental authority, the General Board of Health. It compelled all cities and towns to establish boards of health responsible for implementing and enforc-ing sanitary conditions for drainage, water, garbage removal, housing, waste disposal, and the regulation of 'offensive trades' like butchering, slaughtering, tanning, etc. Shortly thereafter, in 1849, an English physician and epidemiologist by the name of John Snow (1813–1858), tested this law. He published his controversial *On the Mode of Communication of Cholera.* 'Questioning [Chadwick's preferred] miasmatism, he argued that cholera could not be spread by a poison in the ambient air [as had been widely held], since it affected the intestines not the lung" (Porter, 1999, p. 413). In fact, Snow suspected that cholera was not a contagion at all but rather a water-borne disease. A significant breakthrough occurred in August of 1854, when Snow traced 93 local cholera deaths to a single source, namely, contaminated drinking water drawn from London's Broad Street Pump. Snow moved quickly. On September 7th, he persuaded the Board of Guardians in Soho to remove the offending pump. The Board was at first skeptical but reluctantly agreed. Within months, local cholera deaths in Soho dropped precipitously. Thus, Snow's theory was confirmed in no small measure due to his persistent detective work and the regulatory governing structure created by the aforementioned Public Health Act of 1848 (Porter, 1999, pp. 412–3). Interestingly, in France the work of Louis Rene Villerme (1782–1863) almost paralleled the statistical conclusions of Chadwick. In fact, Villerme's ' … morbidity and mortality statistics also demonstrated a close correlation between health and living standards, and led the French government to establish a national public health advisory committee in 1848' (Duffy, 2004, p. 2207).

Third, there was the further development in England of legislation leading to yet another consolidating piece of legislation designed to fortify public health regulations.

> The sanitary legislation developed since 1848 was consolidated in the codifying Public Health Act of 1875, requiring the appointment of a medical officer of health to every sanitary district in England and Wales, while the Poor Law and public health administration were amalgamated in 1872 in the Local Government Board. [Hence], the medical expert's role in public administration had been established, and local government had acquired extensive public health powers (Porter, 1999, p. 414).

And so the Public Health Act of 1875 formally and systematically acknowledged the role of government to provide minimal levels of sanitation and sound hygiene for all citizens. This astonishing moral, social, and scientifically informed commitment, based on the realization that the strength of society as a whole depends on the sound health of all its citizens, eventually paved the way in Britain to the establishment of the National Health Service by 1948, and in the United States to the establishment of the National Institutes of Health, during that same year. Coincidentally, the World Health Organization of the United Nations, dedicated to eradicating disease and stopping pandemics wherever they occur, was also established in 1948.

But compared to Great Britain, the rise of the public health movement in the United States developed at a somewhat slower pace. This was due in part to the fact that England was the first country in Europe to experience the displacing and dehumanizing social effects of the factory system. Then, too, the United States was a younger nation. Her westward expansion by rail from New York to California was not complete until about 1890, and steam power took a little longer than in England to be adapted for factory use. In due time, her major cities began to swell first with displaced labourers and farmers looking to improve their lot in the cities, and then with European and Asian immigrants seeking the greater economic opportunities promised by the American experiment. Hence, by the mid to late 1800s, this led to sanitation and related urban problems associated with overcrowding, squalid tenement conditions, and generally overwrought infrastructure. The rates of morbidity and mortality began to rise, especially in the larger cities. Medical historian John Duffy expands:

> The movement to remedy these conditions was initiated largely by physicians, most notably Benjamin W. McCready, whose 1837 essay drew attention to the deplorable health conditions in the workplace and the slum housing the workers, and [also] by John H. Griscom, whose 1845 report, *The Sanitary Conditions of the Labouring Population of New York*, laid the basis for establishing the first effective municipal health department in the United States. [Another] ... outstanding layman of the early health movement was Lemuel Shattuck of Boston, who pioneered in the collection of vital statistics and promoted sanitary reform ... As in England, the public health movement was both a humanitarian and moral crusade. A few reformers emphasized improving the morals of the poor. [B]ut most recognized that immorality and intemperance were closely associated with the crowded and brutally degraded living conditions of the poor (Duffy, 2004, p. 2206).

Thus, America's first National Board of Health was instituted in 1879. This occurred largely in response to the terrifying yellow fever epidemic of 1878 which spread like wildfire across state lines. In particular, yellow fever took its human toll up and down the Mississippi River. It was thought to be carried by commercial steamboats and their crews that plied the muddy waters from New Orleans to St. Louis. This outbreak killed over 50% of the people in some places. (Porter, 1999, p. 418) With the germ theory of disease (demonstrated in 1878 by Louis Pasteur, and expanded in 1882 by his arch rival Robert Koch) now equipping state-sponsored public health functions with a plausible new rationale for the scientific treatment and eradication of disease, 'the USA was active in setting up publicly supported bacteriological laboratories for disease diagnosis and control' by the last decades of the nineteenth century (Porter, 1999, p. 419). Partly as a result of this social upheaval and this revolutionary aspect of disease diagnosis, the role of the federal government expanded to include the coordination of state health boards. These entities typically consisted of a patchwork quilt of local and regional offices usually run by political appointees and overseen by at least one medical doctor. In 1912, President Theodore Roosevelt (1858–1919) acted decisively to bring these bodies into greater harmony with each other and with the public they aimed to protect. Specifically, he transformed the Marine Hospital Service, then under the limited authority of the surgeon-general, into the more powerful United States Public Health Service.

From this point forward, there was no turning back politically or philosophically. The federal government would increasingly play a critical role in monitoring and regulating health care standards throughout the United States. It would use public funds to achieve these goals and, at the same time, work in consultation with one of the most powerful professional lobbies ever established on the American scene, namely, the venerable American Medical Association (first established in 1847, and followed in 1872 by the establishment of the American Public Health Association).

What's more, during the 'New Deal' reforms of President Franklin D. Roosevelt (1882–1945) in the 1930s, a series of public health laws were adopted that further expanded the federal government's responsibility for the health and welfare of its citizens.

> From June 1933, the Federal Emergency Relief Administration promoted rural sanitation and participated in schemes to control malaria and other diseases. Also, the Public Works Administration built hospitals and contributed to other public health projects. In 1935 the Social Security Act authorized the use of federal funds for crippled children, maternity and child care, and the promotion of state and local public health agencies (Porter, 1999, pp. 646–7).

But in 1945, John Duffy recalls that when President Harry Truman (1884–1972) proposed a national health insurance program, he ignited the ire of the powerful AMA which promptly denounced it as 'socialized medicine', something mainstream Americans felt skittish about since, at worst, it smacked of Soviet-like state control of people's lives and seemed to threaten their personal privacy. Moreover, in 1948, when Truman again made national health insurance a campaign issue, the AMA hired a powerful public relations agency and activated a speaker's bureau to defeat this measure—dubiously claiming that national health insurance would lead to a failure of medical services similar to Britain's bureaucratic behemoth. Nevertheless, the AMA reluctantly ceded to the Kerr-Mill bill, 'providing limited federal funds to help states pay for medical costs of the aged' (Duffy, 1993, p. 322).

In addition, during President Dwight Eisenhower's (1890–1969) administration of the 1950s, a central cabinet level office—the Department of Health, Education, and Welfare—was established. It brought greater order and accountability to what had hitherto been only a loose association of multiple federal and state agencies. Collectively, these regulatory and enforcement agencies would now be anchored in Washington DC. They would continue to carry out their growing responsibilities, including public health services such as public education programs aimed at curbing alcohol abuse and cigarette smoking, along with the regulation of health and safety conditions in schools and factories, and the oversight of the safety and efficacy of food and drugs.

Later on, by the mid-1960s, the Democratic Party renewed its drive for a national health insurance program that Truman had earlier championed but failed to implement. John Duffy recalls that although the AMA was unsuccessful in blocking this second effort, it did manage to weaken its scope. So, in 1965, the Social Security laws were amended and Medicare and Medicaid became a reality. Medicare, which took effect in 1966, provided hospital and medical services to citizens who reached the age of sixty five. In contrast, Medicaid allocated federal assistance to state medical programs for the indigent poor. In sum, while Medicare made no attempt at a wholesale restructuring of the American healthcare system, it more than symbolized 'that the public would henceforth have a voice in determining the nation's health policy' (Duffy, 1993, p. 322.).

To be sure, just how one defines 'public health', or the allied concept, 'medical care', is of critical importance. Let's pause to clarify these key concepts.[2] By 'medical care', I mean the use of any diagnostic, therapeutic, or prognostic tool, treatment, or service adopted by qualified healers in a given society. Although the therapies of these healers may change over time, it is essential that they are believed to be conducive to the restoration or preservation of health. For example, in 400 BC Athens, the use of leeches to stop bleeding from a wound or infection would qualify as medical care on this definition. But merely supplying to a soldier a well fitting saddle for his horse, would not. For in this latter case there is no medical treatment involved per se, no real therapy — even though the saddle doubtlessly does contribute to the health and safety of both rider and horse.

In contrast, 'public health' may be more broadly defined. John Duffy calls it '... the collective action by a community or society to protect and promote the health and welfare of its members' (Duffy, 2004, p. 2206). Note that under this definition, the supply of a properly fitting saddle may very well qualify as a public health measure, assuming this was made available to other citizens, too. In addition, physician and public health historian George Rosen observes that

---

[2]   In some cases, these concepts overlap in actual usage even though they retain their distinct meanings. Such ambiguities are usually resolved by paying attention to the contexts of use.

the major problems of health ... have been concerned with community life, for instance, the control of transmissible disease, the control and improvement of the physical environment (sanitation), the provision of water and food of good quality and in sufficient supply, the provision of medical care, and the relief of disability and destitution. The relative emphasis placed on each of these problems has varied from time to time, but they are all closely related, and from them has come [the notion of] *public health* as we know it today (Rosen, 1958, p. 25, my emphasis).

Given Rosen's orientation, which I am inclined to adopt, what are some related guiding principles or perspectives regularly associated with the field of public health today? At least three elements deserve our special attention.

First, *the community health perspective* is a key element in helping us understand the history and political influence of this field. It states that the health or disease of an individual citizen is, to some degree, the proper concern and responsibility of the larger community or government within which he or she lives and works. Notwithstanding the swaths of evidence from previous centuries that we will be exploring, the acceptance by many progressive governments during the twentieth century of some level of responsibility for the health of citizens constitutes a significant social and political commitment not matched in earlier epochs. Consider two examples: Plato, from antiquity, and Thomas More, from the Renaissance. They envisioned nothing even approaching a comprehensive community health perspective in their writings. Granted, in his *Republic*, Plato (427–347 BC) did criticize physicians who futilely treated their terminal patients, thereby implicitly bilking them and draining the medical resources of the state. But he nowhere systematically tackles the question of distributive justice in connection with the allocation of medical resources (Carrick, 2001, p. 7). Nor would such a question have naturally occurred to him: it was just assumed in ancient Greece that matters of personal health were not subject to interference or regulation by the state.

Similarly, Thomas More (1478–1535), in his imaginative treatise *Utopia*, advocated a limited public role for physicians in the lives of his citizens. He, too, implicitly emphasized that each person needed to accept responsibility for the state of his or her own health. Granted, More did advocate the option of voluntary euthanasia so that the terminally ill or decrepit could find some appropriate end to their suffering in the inglorious winter of their lives. But, again, neither Plato nor More entertained anything like a government directed public health ethos of the sort we are investigating.

Ironically, that formidable vision issued, with mixed results, from the pen of the nineteenth century social revolutionary Karl Marx (1818–83), and his capitalist backer, Friedrich Engels (1820–95). It is easy to forget that in Marx's provocative *Communist Manifesto* he held out the hope for social equality for all workers. He implied too that when the bourgeoisie and capitalism were overthrown by violent revolution, then the class distinctions that created double standards and inadequate systems of education and possibly health care would also be a thing of the past (Marx, 1848, pp. 47–50 passim). Hence, the Marxist-inspired institutions of pre-1992 Russia under the former Soviet Union, arguably administered the most extensive state-controlled public health care system in medical history. By most accounts, this resulted in a notoriously uneven, impersonal, and sometimes inhumane system of medical services for Soviet citizens (particularly in the areas of psychiatric, maternal, and geriatric medicine).[3]

Second, returning to our central discussion, I find that beyond the community health perspective just mentioned there is something that could be called *the holistic health perspective*. This constitutes another essential element in the field of public health. It states that an individual's health properly concerns not simply her personal factors like exercise, diet, or genetic heritage. It also involves much larger societal factors such as adequate sanitation, decent housing, workplace safety, clean air and water, and a host of related external environmental factors. Holistically considered, these external, non-personal factors that contribute to a citizen's overall health are seen as the government's responsibility to develop and regulate, in accord with what is judged to be in the best interests of the people.

Third, philosophers, theologians, social reformers, and public health professionals, among others, will recognize the contentious role that the philosophical principle of '*moral legalism*' has sometimes played in attempting to promote a healthier society. This is the third element of the public health movement. In many ways, it is the most controversial and contentious. Moral legalism is a liberty-limiting principle. It states that there is a moral duty on the part of governments to enact laws that would prohibit objectionable behaviour, especially behaviour that, if left unchecked, would pollute, harm, or disgrace the larger community.[4] Anthropologically, moral legalism is said to have its root in the ancient human tendencies to label, ostracize, or banish members of a society as

---

[3]   For more on medical abuses within the Soviet Union see Bloch and Reddawy (1984).

[4]   This principle may be seen as an expansion of the *harm principle*, according to which individual liberty is justifiably limited only if it prevents harm to others. According to John Stuart Mill (1806-73) in his *On Liberty*, this is the sole legitimate principle that would warrant government to restrict the liberty of citizens. Mill would resist any expansion of the harm principle, and would view the principle of moral legalism as going too far by authorizing the state to engage in paternalistic practices which it has no business doing (Mill, 1859, 1971).

'outcasts' who break taboos or allegedly pollute others by carrying out behaviours deemed harmful to the tribe (Beauchamp, 2004, p. 2231.)

In the United States, as in the United Kingdom, such behaviours as the over-consumption of alcohol, cigarette or marijuana smoking, and homosexual or inter-racial marriage have, at various times, been judged 'morally objectionable' and been proscribed — in part, by appealing to the principle of moral legalism. Moreover, this liberty-limiting principle is sometimes also in the air when legislators and other architects of public policy try to ascertain what commonly held moral intuitions of their constituents, supplemented by the best scientific insights, would plausibly justify laws aiming to promote the public health and common good of society.

Consider an example: would requiring food handlers to thoroughly wash their hands every thirty minutes constitute a sound public health law? Or is this requirement too stringent and ultimately unenforceable? Obviously, any such deliberation within a democratic framework needs to be carefully balanced. On one hand, there is the constitutionally guaranteed (and potentially reckless) liberty-right of the individual citizen to be left alone to pursue life, liberty, and happiness (even if, in some cases, the citizen does things that are technically legal but offensive to others). On the other hand, there is the paternalistic (and potentially overzealous) duty and responsibility of the state to protect its citizens and affirm its vision of the common good. In this capacity, it may of course proscribe behaviours it deems harmful to the body politic. Therefore, concepts and schemes for promoting public health intersect in natural ways with higher order moral issues such as 'distributive justice'. For example, in a public health situation, consider this question: who ought to receive life prolonging heart or lung transplants when there may not be enough donor organs to go around for all those in need?

Lastly, what standards of social harmony and fair play ought we as philosophers, politicians, public policy analysts, legislators, and informed citizens to use when determining precisely what a just health care system should look like? Obviously, this is both a moral and legal question — and a question of great political and humanitarian intrigue in the United States where, astonishingly, nearly 20% of the population carries no health insurance whatsoever.

These and related social justice topics are taken up with considerable energy and insight in the ensuing chapters of this volume. It is my contention that almost all such medically-related social justice questions are either rooted in, or can be shown to be anticipated by, the public health movement we are examining. But before proceeding any further, I would like to affirm Daniel Beauchamp's instructive list of four goals that any sound philosophy of public health must aim to accomplish.

1. A philosophy of public health must give a central place to the unique approach and method of public health, with its distinctive emphasis on community, and on the central role of the scientific method in formulating courses of action for social improvement.

2. A philosophy of public health must give priority to prevention, and must challenge and revise explanations for health problems with the community perspective, which is essential to effective prevention.

3. A philosophy of public health must set out and defend an adequate definition of the common good, taking into account public health's pursuit of the common well-being—measured in terms of rates of disease and early death—as the object of group or common action.

4. While the philosophy of public health must acknowledge the claims of individual autonomy and justify actions that limit liberty and autonomy, it must do so in a way that leaves the community perspective and the common good intact (Beauchamp, 2004, p. 2211).

Let us turn, then, to some of the more significant pages of that long history. Our goal will be met if we locate and analyse several distinct occasions when redemptive, utilitarian, prudential, or charitable motives worked to provide a measure of funding aimed at helping to preserve or restore the general health of citizens.

The Redemptive Motive and Funding Hospitals

Today, we may rightly think of major hospitals as largely secular institutions; as showcases of scientific medicine aimed at restoring or prolonging human life by using the latest high tech therapies against the ravages of disease or hardships of injury; and, in America and elsewhere in the developed world, as largely public institutions receiving large portions of their revenues from government grants, matching funds, or reimbursements.

But among the earliest hospitals in the West were religious institutions and these were decidedly low tech. Their funding was generally not from governments, and their caregivers and sponsors were animated, at least in part, by the redemptive motive to care for the sick and suffering as God had ordained. By 'redemptive motive', I mean that an agent is acting in such a way that he earnestly believes that his action will elevate his soul in the eyes of heaven. This occurs by cancelling a personal sin or earning merit from the deity in accord with the specific prophesies or rituals of a particular religious tradition.

To illustrate, early Christian hospitals arose largely within the social milieu of religiously minded men and women who, in their personal acts of attending to the sick, were also seeking to fulfil God's word. Was not Christ portrayed in the Gospels (see especially *Luke*) as a healer of the poor, one who restored sight to the blind, purged devils from the insane, and miraculously raised Lazarus from the dead? In fact, the first hospital serving the general public was founded in 390 AD by a wealthy Christian woman, Fabiola (d. 399). As a new and spirited convert, she decided to sell all her worldly possessions to provide medical care for the sick and poor (Carrick, 2001, p. 224; Porter, 1996, p. 208) in an organized institutional setting. Hence, caring for the sick, lame, and hurting within a redemptive framework of belief created a pathway for the religious individual to simultaneously redeem herself from sin and also attend to 'the least of these', as the Christian Gospels command (e.g., *Matthew* 25: 31–46).

As for the funding of these early Christian hospitals, we know that by the fourth century they were supported by various bishops and other operatives from within the early Christian church in addition to some members of the landed aristocracy (Miller, 2004, pp.1184–5 passim). Moreover, prior to the establishment of these first hospitals, by the fourth century AD Christian guest houses, also called 'hospices', were founded (Miller, 2004, p. 1184). These places of refuge were usually overseen by nuns or assistants who were dedicated to the care and sustenance of the poor, sick, or weary traveller. But hospices were not specifically providers of medical care. This fact distinguishes them from the later Christian hospitals which were generally overseen by at least one doctor *(iatros)* Yet hospices and later hospitals were both supported by the church and by donations from wealthier Roman families, and by others who were able to contribute something for their life-affirming services and care. Hence, it is fair to conclude that the redemptive impulse was a leading motivational factor for those who established, supported, and administered both hospices and hospitals during the late Roman Empire.

But was there an even earlier forerunner to both the early Christian hospital and its institutional predecessor, the hospice? Indeed so, the pagan temples of the Greek physician-god, Asclepius. A famous example still stands in ruins at Epidaurus on mainland Greece; it was built around 450 BC and operated until at least 395 AD. These religious temples *(asklepieia)*, of which over 400 were built during Pre-Christian antiquity, once dotted the ancient landscape from Olympia to Constantinople (modern day Istanbul). Funding for the Aesclepian temples generally came from one of two sources: patients and their families seeking the hypnotic dream-sleep cure *(incubation)* for one of their own; or wealthy families seeking to fulfil their felt sense of civic virtue. In addition, there were probably occasional contributions from nearby sponsoring Greek city-states.

The physician-God Asclepius, son of Apollo, was said to have had the power to rescue the sick from the jaws of death, and make whole the ill and lame. But from the rational, non-superstitious perspective of traditional Hippocratic medicine — grounded on the humoral theory of disease according to which a proper balance of the four humors assured the patient's good health — these Aesclepian temples were at best last ditch centres of care for those judged to be incurable. Therefore, hopeless, terminally ill patients often turned to supernatural Aesclepian remedies when the Hippocratic physicians judged that there was nothing more they could reasonably do. Can anyone doubt that these often desperate, religiously inspired patients, and their similarly inspired, well intentioned Aesclepian priests — who sometimes dressed in flowing robes in imitation of the god — both experienced some redemptive grace as they sought heaven's divine cure? Whatever the outcome of this mystical God-centred therapy, votive offerings and payments were received by the Aesclepian healers from the suffering patient and her family. Thus, it is safe to conclude that a sense of redemption (and a wished-for spiritual and bodily wholeness) was involved in the funding and support of these renowned pagan health care centres, too.

The Utilitarian Motive and Funding Military Medicine

Alongside religious temples and related medical sites associated with the Greek god Asclepius, the Roman Empire saw fit to erect special infirmaries (*valetudianaria*) dedicated exclusively to soldiers. For example, it was well recognized by the Roman Senate that soldiers who were wounded in battle or faced other potential health emergencies needed immediate care. 'A standard military hospital plan evolved', according to Roy Porter, which had '… individual cells off a long corridor, a large top-lit hall, latrines and baths' (Porter, 1999, p. 78). In contrast, the more affluent Roman citizen would usually receive medical care not in a hospital but at the private house of his physician. Yet the poor and destitute would be lucky to hobble or drag themselves to a religious shrine hoping for some sort of miracle. Thus, for all but the military, the medical marketplace of the Roman Empire was strictly speaking a laissez-faire situation and most uneven in its distribution of medical services to the hoi polloi.

Furthermore, the warrior-centred infirmaries were especially crucial in helping to fortify the military strength of Rome's legionaries stationed along the northern borders — where barbarians began to take a deadly toll beginning in the fourth century especially (Miller, 2004, p. 1184). But if so, how could one fairly describe the political and strategic motivation of Rome (and later, many other countries) in creating and funding such strategically placed military hospitals?

In essence, I would argue that this motivation may be fairly called 'utilitarian.' That is, a person, group, or institution is carrying out a particular action or plan because, at bottom, it is believed to be helpful to securing the common good of all.[5] So here generals and politicians, under pressure from repeated waves of barbarian attacks, came to see that their society as a whole would benefit if soldiers (injured, or threatened in battle, or otherwise at risk of losing their strength in war) were provided competent medical care (relative to those times). Hence, these soldiers could be restored to the task of defending their communities as rapidly and efficiently as possible. What I am suggesting, then, is that Rome funded military infirmaries (as did the French during the Napoleonic Wars, as did the federal Congress during the American Civil War — the examples are endless) precisely because Rome realized that trained and experienced soldiers were valuable state assets. These human assets could do more effective work for the greater glory of the whole society if they had doctors and other medical assistants at their disposal when weakened or threatened by disease or wounds. In short, publicly funded military infirmaries had social utility: they were useful and productive medical institutions operated for the optimal benefit of the state, its soldiers, and its citizens — all things considered.

Furthermore, centuries later in the modern British Isles, the English medical doctor James Lind (1716–94) observed that 'armies had lost "more of their men by sickness than by the sword", especially through unsanitary camp conditions' (Porter, 1999, p. 294). In addition, the Scotsman and physician-general of the British Army, John Pringle (1707–1782), scientifically corroborated Lind's insight by publishing *Observations on the Diseases of the Army* (1752). In it, Pringle stressed methods by which troops could adopt practical measures of hygiene in order to prevent the most common battlefield diseases such as typhus, dysentery, bilious fever, scabies, etc. Porter gives this estimate of the impact of Pringle's *Observations*:

> While not strikingly original, it captured the Enlightenment concern for hygiene, public health, and the value of life. Pringle is also remembered for developing the idea of the neutrality of the military hospital. At the battle of Dettingen (1743), he proposed to the French commanding officer that the hospital tents on each side should be immune from the attack. The idea stuck (Porter, 1999, pp. 294–5).

Are there other instructive examples of the utilitarian motive driving state policy in favour of medical care or medical experimentation — especially for those in the military? Examples abound: it is well established that medical insights and innovative surgeries, procedures, and therapies are often invented and tested in the crucible of war. For

---

[5] By using the term 'utilitarian', I mean this in the pre-philosophical, naïve sense of that word. I am not here referring to classical utilitarianism associated with the hedonic calculus famously authored by the nineteenth century English social reformer, Jeremy Bentham (1748–1832), and his philosophical disciple, J.S. Mill (1806–1873).

example, in the late nineteenth and early twentieth centuries, military personnel were among the first to benefit from programs of mass inoculations. These followed discoveries by Jenner, Pasteur, Koch, and others that such techniques could be effective in protecting against a myriad of infectious diseases. Indeed, this was one of the more humanitarian and dramatic benefits of discovering the germ theory.

For example, during the Boer War of 1899–1902, the British army suffered many disease-related casualties. Immunisation against typhoid was discovered by Almroth Wright (1861–1947) in 1897. Yet few British soldiers received the vaccinations due to irregular state policies that were in place at the time. This was tragic. Porter clarifies that in the South African theatre of the Boer War, 13,000 soldiers were killed by typhoid, whereas 8,000 actually died in battle (Porter, 1999, p. 443). As a result of this emergency, the British government formed a special commission to study diseases related to war casualties. Thereafter, in 1913, it adopted a policy of vaccinating all soldiers sent abroad against infectious diseases, including typhoid fever. In point of fact, during the Boer War, the incidence of illness from typhoid fever was around 10%. In contrast, after being vaccinated, the incidence of typhoid among British troops during World War I (1914–18) dropped to around 2% (Porter, 1999, p. 443).

Also, tetanus was known to be a particularly dangerous disease for soldiers, with the death rate of those infected usually standing at above 40%. So, by the beginning of World War I, decisive public health measures were taken to protect the troops against tetanus. In general, this disease had been especially hard on soldiers. The causal agent, later identified as tetanospasmin, is a toxin secreted by the bacterium *Clostridium tetani* which lives in the soil. Hence, when a soldier was wounded, very typically 'the bacillus entered the body through gaping shell wounds. [But] from 1915 [on], practically every wounded soldier received the antitoxin, and so tetanus was dramatically reduced' (Porter, 1999, p. 443). Again, the utilitarian motive to provide competent and immediate medical care for the military is seen to produce the best outcomes by helping to fortify the defences of a nation as a whole, whether at war or at peace. And there were other social dividends. Civilian populations in Britain and elsewhere were eventually protected by vaccinations, too, in medicine's fight against the ravages of typhoid, tetanus, and other lethal diseases.

The Prudential Motive and Funding Quarantines

History records few things to be as frightening, alien, and disorienting to human communities and their governments as the large scale public health scourges known as epidemics. Epidemics may be defined as 'concentrated outbursts of infectious or non-infectious disease, often with unusually high mortality, affecting relatively large numbers of people within fairly narrow limits of time and space' (Evans, 2004, p. 789). The most catastrophic epidemic in the entire history of Europe occurred during medieval times, spreading from rats to people, between 1347–51. I am referring to the Bubonic plague. It is also called the Black Death due to the telltale dark blotches that appeared on the faces of the doomed just prior to their deaths. Shockingly, in just over three years, this pestilence wiped out approximately twenty million people, about one quarter of the entire population of Europe and the Mediterranean (Porter, 1999, p. 123). It appeared episodically thereafter, too, arousing great fear and consternation, but never with such sweeping force.

The Black Death likely originated in China. Then, from central Asia, it spread via the Tatars to Italian merchants who were fighting the infected Tatars for preferred trade routes in the Crimea. In returning to their native Italy, the plague travelled with these Italian merchant-soldiers, breaking out first in Messina and then in Genoa. So virulent was the plague that most died within three days of being infected. Typically, the most vulnerable included peasant families and the indigent poor. Even without contracting such catastrophic epidemics, their average age at death in 1400 was not much over 30 years (Porter, 1999, pp.122–127 passim). And the unenviable truth is that these unfortunates were often left to rot in their own bodily fluids when they were ordered to be involuntarily quarantined. This happened in towns including Milan and Vienna during the most deadly outbreaks of the plague. Moreover, relatively few townspeople were lucky enough to flee in advance of these scourges: there was little advance warning and few alternative destinations seemed safe. Hence, in trying to survive this fourteenth century public health catastrophe, governments acted to protect themselves and their citizens in ways that were barely rational (by contemporary standards) and, from hindsight, often tragic, heartless, and futile.

To be sure, there were many factual misunderstandings about the true nature of the plague that made most medical and governmental responses ineffective. For one thing, the prevailing theory of health at that time was still the Hippocratic humoral theory, with significant refinements by Galen (AD 129–c. 216). This theory stated that if a person becomes ill with an epidemic disease or any other malady it was at least partly his or her own fault. Such vulnerability to disease was likely due to some weakness or imbalance of one's four humors over which individuals have some rational control through proper diet, exercise, and sound hygiene. Following this logic, healthy people did not normally get sick; and if they did they were probably responsible for it on some level.

In addition, alongside the humoral theory there was a correlative environmentally-based theory known as the miasmic theory of disease (miasma was considered to be foul or polluted air). It held that contagions arise from the stench of swamps, waste, and other rotting organic debris. Humans breathed in this putrid air and so it tended to make us sick — disturbing our internal humoral balance. More alarmingly, it was widely held that once a person becomes infected with the plague, others can acquire the disease just by touching that person or by standing in his immediate vicinity. In addition, besides this pair of naturalistic theories of disease (humoral and miasmic),[6] there was still the influential supernatural theory of disease held by Christians and other mystics. This theory construed illness, and especially pestilence, as something sent by God to punish sinning humanity. Therefore, this supernatural view of disease only exacerbated the public's personal sense of panic, guilt, self-loathing, and despair.

As a result of these theories of disease, citizens were sometimes advised by local governmental authorities to evacuate their cities and towns in advance of the relentless plague which, in fact, was caused (we now know) by flea-infested rats.[7] In addition, local governments in Italy, France, Germany, and elsewhere enacted involuntary 'quarantines' (this term derived from the Biblical *quarantenaria* meaning forty days) against all those travellers and ships known to have originated from ports or cities already infected by the plague (Porter, 1999, p.126). Local governments also set up health boards in cities including Milan, Florence, and Lucca. Also, they closed their borders if at all possible against outsiders thought to be infected. In some cities, like Milan, they involuntarily quarantined and sealed their own plague-infected citizens in their own homes, leaving them to die. Both doctors and priests, who were entrusted to care for the sick or perform Last Rites, also sometimes fled for their lives in sheer terror of what might happen to them if they remained behind to perform their official duties.

Therefore, as we have just seen, one of the most commonly used, publicly funded methods of restoring health and preventing disease, was the state's deployment of the quarantine. Typically, this restrictive measure could be applied to seaports or roads, halting shipping or commerce; or to individuals and their families, limiting their freedom to come and go as they pleased in their homes or neighbourhoods. Hence, the method of quarantine — however unfairly, unevenly or unnecessar-

---

[6]   One recalls that the humoral theory, according to which disease occurred when one of the four humors (yellow bile, black bile, blood, phlegm) became excessive, was completely overtaken by the germ theory by around 1880. The competing miasmic theory held sway even later, until gradually losing ground to Koch's bacteriological model of disease by the late nineteenth century.

[7]   The bacterial cause of the Black Death was subsequently discovered in 1894 during the Hong Kong epidemic by Japanese scientists A.Yersin and S. Kitasato. By 1898, the French epidemiologist P. L. Simond showed that the transmission of the bacillus, *Yersinia pestis,* was communicated from rats to humans via fleas: a single bite from an infected flea could be fatal (Rosen, 1958, p. 324).

ily applied in the fourteenth century—arguably embodied a prudent method of rationally imposing preventive medicine measures on citizens (and strangers) with the goal of stopping the spread of this unforgiving Black Death. (Again, the plague was thought to be a disease transmissible by contact with the miasmic breath, or through touching the open sores or even normal-looking skin of real or imagined victims who were thought to be exposed to the contagion).

In sum, I think it is fair to conclude that a 'prudential motive' was almost certainly at work in the decision to use state funds in deploying the restrictive measures of quarantine. These funds were needed to mount naval blockades of docks and ports, and to pay those workers involved in identifying, apprehending, and enforcing involuntary restrictions and other *cordone sanitare* for those suspected of being infected. In general, a person, group, or institution may be said to be acting from a prudential motive when their resulting behaviour shows evidence of skilful selection, adaptation, or use of an appropriate means to a desired end.[8] Here, the desired end was halting the spread of the bubonic plague by skilfully using a means that conformed to the best medical thinking of the day. Unlike the 'utilitarian motive', cited earlier, the prudential motive does not require the actor to contemplate the more universal consideration of what constitutes the common good of society. Instead, prudential acts merely involve a scaled back, lower-order focus on what seems more or less appropriate to the situation at hand here and now. Thus, the scope of awareness (what I call the 'epistemic scope') of a prudentially motivated act is somewhat less encompassing than its utilitarian counterpart in the long run.[9]

The Charitable Motive and Funding Inoculations

Who can doubt that a fourth type of motivation, what I am here calling the 'charitable motivation', is also involved in carrying out humane acts of medical care? The charitable impulse has deep historical roots. We observe the author of the Hippocratic treatise *Precepts*, who practised medicine in Athens during the first century BC, admonishing his fellow physicians thusly: 'And if there be an opportunity to serving one who is a stranger in financial straits, give full assistance to all such. For where there is love of man, there is also love of the art' (*Precepts* 6; quoted in

---

[8] My definition is modified slightly from the *Webster's Third New International Dictionary* (1965, p. 1824), to include the Aristotelian notion of 'appropriate' choice. Hence, the prudent motive leads to actions that are moral, not merely clever. Such actions, following Aristotle (384-322 BC), ultimately involve the larger issue of determining what is good for man. See also Copleston (1962, Vol. 1, Part 2, p. 86).

[9] The possible objection that this scope of awareness may be more a matter of degree than kind is discussed in the penultimate section of this paper, below.

Carrick, 2001, p. xviii). Indeed, one can hear in these distant words a commitment to the importance of empathy and charity in the treating of the outsider, the sick, and the destitute. What's more, the Homeric tales of Zeus, Dionysus, and Artemus, among other Olympians, fostered an awareness in the pagan mind that the gods themselves could appear incarnate as human strangers in need. So it would be wise to greet the stranger in need carefully but never meanly.

Nor can one ignore that a selfless response to the suffering of the stranger is affirmed both in the Hebrew Bible and the Christian Gospels. While charity is a Christian virtue endorsed in the parable of the Good Samaritan, Jewish tradition also affirms the importance of compassion toward those in need, as the story Jonah and the whale affirms. This type of other-centred, charitable motivation is characterized by a deeply felt impulse to extend a helping hand: to succour the sick and broken with a saving, caring touch.

Formally defined, 'charitable motivations' are those evidenced by a kindly and sympathetic disposition aimed at rendering aid to the needy or suffering.[10] Such acts typically involve freely giving to others goods or services of value that could otherwise have been withheld. In addition, it is interesting to recall that the eighteenth century German philosopher Immanuel Kant (1724–1804) regarded acts of charity as *imperfect* duties.[11] That is, properly speaking, such acts may never be morally *required* of another as would, by comparison, such *perfect* duties (in Kantian language) as the repayment of a personal loan. Again, perfect duties are always obligatory duties for Kant, never optional. And so, for Kant, as for most of us living in the twenty-first century, charitable acts such as sending money to the International Red Cross for food relief in Sri Lanka are praiseworthy but strictly speaking optional. They cannot in the ordinary sense be morally required.

But is this really a fair description of charitable acts in the context of contemporary medical care? Yes and no. For while one may not require a physician in private practice in the United States, say, to donate his or her medical services to the needy poor, there are acknowledged limits to the exercise of such professional options. For example, it is a recognized medical and moral duty not to cause (or allow by acts of omission) someone who is penniless to die on the front door of one's clinic just because they cannot afford emergency medical services. Again, if life-saving aid

[10] Webster's Third *New International Dictionary* (1965), p. 378, hereafter WID. 'Charity' derives from the Late Latin word 'caritas', meaning Christian love. *Webster's* defines the latter as: 'the virtue or act of loving God with a love which transcends that for creatures; *loving others* for the sake of God' (WID, 1965, p. 378, my emphasis).

[11] Kant, I. (1875, 1964) *Groundwork of the Metaphysic of Morals* (New York: Harper Torchbooks).

that could have been rendered was in point of fact withheld, would this heartless inaction not be widely and justifiably condemned? Moreover, since for Kant charitable acts also conform to the moral law (what he called the 'Categorical Imperative') — according to which persons ought to be treated as ends in themselves, never as mere means — charitable acts are in any event exemplary and praiseworthy.

To summarise, we may observe in these persistent religious, scientific, and humanistic traditions — from Hippocratic precepts, to Judeo-Christian scriptures, to Enlightenment thinkers such as Kant — an implicit affirmation of the importance of the charitable impulse as a necessary condition for membership in the moral community. I dare say this humane tendency to consider the safety and welfare of the other is one of the enduring legacies of our ancient and modern past embodied at least in part in our own age by social workers and health care professionals, plus the government agencies and taxpayers who tacitly agree to fund and facilitate their good works.

In addition, within the ethos and norms of the public health movement as it arose from roughly the eighteenth century to our own day, charitable acts may include providing bandages, prescription medicines, crutches, inoculations, surgical procedures, pure drinking water, fresh linen, etc., at little or no direct cost to the recipient. Indeed, with the gradual acceptance of Louis Pasteur's (1822–96) germ theory by about 1875, and the gradual adoption of Robert Koch's (1843–1910) bacteriological model of disease about twenty-five years later, doctors, medical researchers, and public health officials were increasingly encouraged by the promising social and health implications of these stunning scientific breakthroughs. Hence, during the nineteenth century when it came to using public or private funds with the end in view of restoring or preserving the health of the masses, government officials began to push for a variety of preventive medicine measures. Perhaps chief among the more controversial of these measures was the deployment of public inoculation programmes. To be sure, inoculations were attempted, at various times, to thwart a variety of deadly diseases including cholera, smallpox, diphtheria, and malaria. (Inoculations were later called 'vaccinations', once specific vaccines were developed containing the immunising antigens or micro-organisms which were then injected). In fact, Rosen states that the method of inoculation was known to healers throughout the world at least since the early 1700s, and probably earlier in the East and Orient (Rosen, 1958, p. 184). As a technique, it became established in medical circles under the simple-sounding principle, 'Like cures like.'

For example, it was known to some midwives and others that exposure of a non-infected person to a series of weakened (attenuated) doses of a pathogen, say, measles, somehow had the power to render that 'inoculated' person immune from the very disease to which she had been intentionally exposed (Rosen, 1958, p. 183). While inoculation was an extremely useful method,[12] many in England and elsewhere during the seventeenth and eighteenth centuries were sceptical. They worried, not altogether without justification in the early days of the technique, that those exposed to excessive or corrupted doses of the allegedly life-saving pathogens might somehow grow ill and die. As we saw in our earlier account of the bubonic plague, these horrific epidemics were capable of wiping out whole generations: labourers, farmers, merchants, craftsman, sailors, the landed gentry—none were spared. Philosophically, most adults came to realize that all people were in some sense true equals before the onslaught of these unyielding scourges. Predictably, as the techniques of inoculation and vaccine development became more efficient and reliable—thanks to the early efforts against smallpox by researchers like Edward Jenner in 1796, and over a century-and-a half-later against polio by researchers like Jonas Salk in 1953—the public's scepticism and resistance against inoculation programs slowly gave way to guarded acceptance.[13]

Of course, these inoculation programs were actually not free but were usually funded by governments or, in some cases, supported by the emerging health care professions, or by monies donated by pioneering medical researchers and their sponsoring labs and institutes. Such programs were initially, at least, cast as charitable programs for the improvement of the health and welfare of the poor. This preventive medicine trend gradually spread across Europe as the method of inoculation became perfected, and as the science and clinical evidence backing it up gradually won both scientific and popular acceptance by the middle of the nineteenth century.

In fact, it was in England, with the publication in 1798 of Edward Jenner's paper, 'An Inquiry into the Causes and Effects of the Variolae Vaccinae ... [Known as] Cow pox', that the efficacy of using vaccines in the process of inoculation was established. Jenner, a country doctor and clergyman's son who studied in London under John Hunter, was one of the first medical scientists to endorse the widespread use of inoculations in his fight against smallpox (Rosen, 1958, p. 188ff; Porter, 1999, p. 274ff.). To Jenner's remarkable achievement we now turn.

---

[12] Specifically, smallpox inoculation was known as 'variolation', although the term is now rarely used.

[13] Even now, this acceptance is somewhat fragile and wont to slip: witness the suspicion of the combined measles, mumps, and rubella inoculation in the UK in the late 1990s, that grew from a study linking the vaccine to serious side-effects. Despite the study being roundly and openly discredited at the time by the broader scientific community, these suspicions lingered for some time.

Rosen reminds us that, during Jenner's lifetime (1749–1823), smallpox was one of the most feared diseases in Europe and America – a leading cause of death. 'It smouldered endemically in city and town, flaring up recurrently into epidemic outbreaks ... According to William Douglas, writing in 1760, smallpox was a chief cause of the high infant mortality in Europe' (Rosen, 1958, p.184). Porter adds: ' "The speckled monster" had become virulent throughout Europe, responsible in bad years for perhaps a tenth of all deaths; Queen Mary of England (1662–94) died of it, as did Louis XV (1710–74) of France' (Porter, 1999, pp. 274–75). Thanks largely to Jenner's experiments, inoculation caught on as a protective measure against smallpox in England, along with preventive medicine programs against other deadly diseases, by 1900. Even so, there were still those who held out. For example, some of the Calvinists in Scotland resisted inoculation on grounds that rendering a patient immune through human intervention interfered with Divine Providence. In contrast, the *philosophes* in France, including Voltaire (1694–1778), endorsed inoculations as a boon to mankind; the practice was officially endorsed by the French government in 1750.

Back in England, Lady Mary Wortley Montagu (1689–1762), the wife of a British consul in Constantinople, was a forceful early advocate. In fact, she decided to have her five-year-old daughter inoculated against smallpox in London, in 1721. This she did after having observed a few years earlier a somewhat cruder form of the technique used by peasant women in Turkey (Porter, 1999, p. 275; Rosen, 1958, p. 186). Across the seas, in Colonial America, the clergyman Cotton Mather (1663–1728) was also a strong advocate of inoculation. '[H]e knew about suffering, having had to watch as two wives and thirteen of his fifteen children succumbed to disease' (Porter, 1999, p. 175).

To clarify, the immediate aim of smallpox inoculation was to induce a mild dose of the disease in a non-infected person, thereby conferring lifelong immunity without causing unsightly pock-marking or any other harmful consequence (Porter, 1999, p. 275). Before he began his experiments that led to the groundbreaking development of an effective smallpox vaccine, Jenner was familiar with traditional inoculations. In performing them, he aimed to infect his subjects with weakened doses of the smallpox material in order to confer immunity. In the process of performing traditional inoculation, Jenner noticed something odd: those subjects who had earlier contracted cowpox – a disease of cattle occasionally contracted by humans – had evidenced no reaction whatsoever to his traditional smallpox inoculation. That is, they appeared to be immune to smallpox.

But Jenner did not feel confident with his observation. So, remembering the challenging words of his professor, John Hunter, 'Why not ... experiment?', Jenner decided to test his hypothesis. What if the cowpox had properties that could be developed into a vaccine that would render subjects immune to smallpox?

> In 1796, an opportunity to try out this idea presented itself. Jenner inoculated a boy, James Phipps, with cowpox matter taken from the hand of a milkmaid, Sarah Nelmes, who had acquired the infection naturally. Then after several weeks he inoculated the boy with smallpox, but it failed to take—James Phipps was immune to smallpox. (Rosen, 1958, p. 188).

Ironically, when Jenner first tried to present the result of his experiment to the Royal Society, he was refused. Soon thereafter, however, his results were accepted in 1798 under a more modest title. Within just three years, his 'Inquiry into the Causes and Effects of the Variolae Vaccinae' received widespread attention in Continental Europe and America. In fact, it was published in a third edition by 1801, and went into Latin, German, French, American, Dutch, Spanish, and Portuguese editions by 1803 (Porter, 1999, pp. 276–77).

To the layperson, the often missed epidemiological significance of Jenner's contribution is that while smallpox was fatal to humans, cowpox was benign. Therefore, if Jenner were able to develop a vaccine from the cowpox material, the inoculation process would in this case be measurably safer. Moreover, if his hypothesis proved correct, a successful cowpox vaccine could then be developed in larger quantities, and dispensed to more subjects more cheaply and efficiently than the traditional inoculation. For the latter technique did not strictly speaking require vaccination at all; mere exposure, through whatever medium, would do. In addition, things could run amok using traditional inoculation. For one thing, the inoculated person could sometimes contract the full disease from the attenuated dosage if the quantities were too potent or the exposures were too frequent, and die. Second, if the aim was to inoculate large numbers of people there was a substantially greater risk that something could go wrong with the quantity and quality of the *materia medica* of the dosages themselves since the chemistries were not that well understood.

No doubt a lasting hallmark of the practical significance of Jenner's discovery of the smallpox vaccine is the greater confidence it inspired toward the medical community itself among the people whose lives he and others helped to save through the deployment of massive and often charitable vaccination programs. At first, this was the case for smallpox but later for a long list of deadly diseases that were defeated or resisted via the vaccination process which Jenner helped develop and perfect. In so doing, Jenner may also be said to have laid the initial groundwork for the science of immunology. Indeed, once Jenner's vaccination techniques gained currency, his discoveries were further confirmed in 1800 by Harvard Medical School's first professor of physic, Benjamin Waterhouse (1754–1846). Waterhouse published his own confirmation under the title, 'A prospect of exterminating the smallpox" (Rosen, 1958, p. 189). In addition, President Thomas Jefferson (1743–1826) became an active supporter of Waterhouse, arguing forcefully for public vaccination programs as a civic imperative (Rosen, 1958, p. 189). Connecting the motive of charity to Jenner's scientific breakthrough, Rosen states that a benefactor by the name of Valentine Seaman was the first advocate of mass vaccination in America. In 1802, Seaman originated in New York the 'Institute for Inoculation . ." the main purpose of which was to furnish inoculations free of charge to the poor (Rosen, 1958, p. 189). In England, over 5000 individuals had been vaccinated by 1799 alone. The practice was deemed so important in Sweden that it was made compulsory. In contrast, compulsory vaccination was resisted for a time in England for fear the rights of individuals would be trampled by the state (Porter, 1999, p. 277; Rosen, 1958, pp. 189–90). The situation in Germany was arguably even more progressive.

The German government briefly explored the idea of 'Medical Police', a term meant to convey the need for a government administered program of health protection for all citizens. Its principal proponent was Johann Peter Frank (1748–1821) who wrote a six volume work on this topic which was published between 1779–1819. But the project never really reached fruition until after 1871 when a central department of public health came into being. By 1883, Chancellor Otto von Bismarck (1815–1898) introduced for the first time a system of medical social insurance. 'Bismarck's system became a model for other European countries, including Britain' (Chave, 1986, pp. 8–9). In France, Napoleon (1761–1821) was so taken in by the seeming miracle of defeating smallpox by Jenner's technique that he ordered his entire army vaccinated. He is further reported to have said: 'Anything Jenner wants shall be granted' (Porter, 1999, p. 277). Not to be outdone, in 1802, the English Parliament awarded Jenner a prize of £10,000. Just a year later, in 1803, the Royal Jennerian Society was founded. Its prime aim was to promote vaccination for the masses as part of a charitable and humane program. Indeed, by the beginning of the nineteenth century, rulers in Europe and elsewhere embraced the general dictum that the promotion of health was essential to a well functioning state (Porter, 1999, p. 277).

Summary: Four Motives Supportive of Public Health

I began this paper by conjecturing that any effort to pursue a unified psychological, sociological, or philosophical explanation for that most remarkable of human practices, namely, the decision of governments, institutions, or groups to use public or private funds in order to succour the sick or make whole the injured, would almost certainly face treacherous seas. Based on the evidence gathered here, I submit that this conjecture has so far been confirmed.

But while a unified, monolithic account of the public or private funding of health care has eluded our capture, what we have discovered during this voyage has in some ways proved more instructive. We have discovered a broad, multifaceted account that accommodates a wider range of historical periods and governing philosophies than any single explanatory principle would likely do. Why would a single explanatory principle not fly? Because, as should be evident from the present sketch drawn from 2500 years of social history, things are just not that tidy in the chronicles of Western governments and in the diaries of the common people over which they ruled. Hence, despite the fact that no unifying raison d'etre has emerged to account for the seemingly altruistic behaviour that lead to the public or private funding of health care, this result is hardly cause for despair.

In point of fact, we have identified and characterised at least four critically important human motivations that are often involved in preserving, restoring, or enhancing the health and well-being of citizens. These action-guiding elements include the redemptive, utilitarian, prudential, and charitable motives. Furthermore, any one or more of these motives qualifies as *sufficient conditions*. That is, when present they tend to function as contributing causes psychologically and morally in almost any decision-making process that leads individuals, groups, institutions, or governments to actually fund health care for the masses (at whatever level of funding). Thus, by being made more aware of the necessary conditions involved in this decision-making process, we have come closer to a fuller understanding of the tableau of human impulses, volitions, and choices that encourage such other-directed, socially conscious projects as those associated with what is now widely called the public health movement.

Objection and Reply: Oversimplifying Choice and Action?

Nevertheless, some may object that the picture I have just painted commits the fallacy of oversimplication.[14] This it allegedly does because the four motives which I have explicated as more or less discrete concepts in our four central illustrations — the funding of hospitals, military medicine, quarantines, and inoculations — may sometimes overlap with each other. But, as I will show, this objection is hardly fatal. In fact, properly understood, it reminds us that some apparent impediments from the logical point of view turn out to be little more than instructive mirages when viewed from the right angle, i.e., with a deeper understanding, in this instance, of how language and thought actually work together.

---

[14] An earlier version of this objection was suggested to me by Niall Maclean. The core fallacy is of course committed when one takes a complex thing and construes it to be much simpler than it really is.

So let us suppose, for the sake of discussion, that the preceding objection is correct: our four motives do sometimes overlap in their action-guiding capacities. Hence, suppose that what I have described as the 'charitable motive' to give aid to the needy by funding inoculations, may at times overlap with the 'redemptive motive'. Thus, the redemptive motive, too, may impel an actor to accomplish the same end out of (in this case) a basic love of God. Does the fact that one or more of these motives may overlap undermine all that we have come to understand so far?

Not at all. If anything, the fact that these four motives may occasionally overlap invites us to ask a critical question, one with illuminating implications for how the human mind, choice, and volition shape individual or institutional conduct in what some call the phenomenology of action. Is it realistic to assume that the diverse impulses and motives at work as we experience ourselves and others in the world, and as we act on things in the world to accomplish desired ends, are in fact as rigidly distinct as we sometimes imagine them to be? In short, is the existential and psychological process of deliberation and decision-making messier than we imagine?

In my view, the only honest answer is yes. We often talk *as if* concepts and motives are more rigid and discrete than they really are. But why? We do so, I suggest, mainly as a short-hand technique by which we may more conveniently and efficiently negotiate the world. This technique includes, at the highest deliberative levels of government, the orchestration of the collective motives and agendas of diverse political constituents needed to build a consensus aimed at establishing sound health care policies within democratic societies. As a result of these practical insights, social habits, and collective capacities, we do not have to spell out everything that we are experiencing in tedious, time-consuming detail in order to get things done in our households, communities, or nation states.

In addition, I conjecture that neither the worlds we regularly mediate and describe through the multiple lens of language, nor the higher-order concepts that anchor our action-guiding motives and impulses within the common ethos of our natural languages, behave in the artificially rigid and inflexible ways we sometimes imagine. In fact, based on my own observations, I would argue that the discrete, action-guiding motives we have been exploring (the redemptive, utilitarian, prudential, and charitable motives) do, in fact 'give'; that is, they do indeed 'overlap' and 'interpenetrate' in the mind of the actor. Again, this happens especially when they converge on common ends that are deemed worthy of execution by citizens, institutions, or governments. Furthermore, our four central motives behave in this flexible, overlapping manner precisely because, at bottom, they turn out to be conceptually related in an interesting, suggestive way. That is, they bear what could be called a family resemblance to one another.[15] If so, as members of the same loosely related conceptual family (to be named below), is it so surprising that our four leading motives may overlap in various contexts?

So again, to admit that there is this occasional overlapping of concepts hardly spills the wind from our sails. Instead, it usefully serves to remind us that as actors, whether legislators, kings, or citizens, our motives may sometimes work in concert but also manifest in 'mixed', creative, and even contradictory ways. It hardly follows from this that the four motives in question have no distinct characteristics, or no proper limits of usage. Indeed, as I have suggested, they may be flexible, overlapping, yet more or less discrete — without conceptual embarrassment or loss of explanatory power in any robust theory of human action.[16] Hence, the objection from oversimplification need not foul the lines of our analysis any further.

Conclusion: Philanthropy and Funding Public Health

What, then, is the name of the parent concept to which the four central motives under investigation may be said to bear a family resemblance? One gets a bold hint, I suggest, by reflecting further on the now familiar passage of the Hippocratic author of *Precepts*.

> And if there be an opportunity to serving one who is a stranger in financial straits, give full assistance to all such. For where there is love of man (*philanthropia*), there is also love of the art.[17]

If my intuition is right, our four motives, properly speaking, are related to the higher-order concept of 'philanthropy'; at its root, it literally means 'loving mankind' (derived from the Greek *philia* = love, and *anthropos* = mankind). In contemporary usage, philanthropy may be defined as: (1) 'good will toward one's fellow man, especially as expressed through active efforts to promote human welfare'; or (2) 'an

---

[15] By using the phrase 'family resemblance', I am adapting Wittgenstein's terminology. My simple point is that these four motives — the redemptive, utilitarian, prudential, and charitable — may, in fact, share no easily identifiable common characteristic. Yet, like members of a human family who may not look much like one another individually but are nevertheless recognisable as bearing a similar family resemblance or orientation, we likewise notice the shared relatedness of these four motives. This we do because they often appear in similar contexts and behave in similar ways (often moving us toward acts or programs that assist others). See Ludwig Wittgenstein (1953), section 67.

[16] A complete theory of action, while outside the scope of this paper, may be found in L. Davis's *Theory of Action* (Davis, 1979).

[17] For a different take on the Hippocratic tradition of philanthropy, which construes occasional pro bono medical care as a clever way for doctors to improve their reputations, see Edelstein (1967).

act or instance of deliberate generosity: a contribution made in the spirit of humanitarianism' (Webster's Dictionary, 1965, p. 1697).

I submit that actions arising from the *redemptive motive*, which seek to benefit mankind out of a love of God and so lead quite naturally to the funding of hospitals, bear a family resemblance to this parent notion of philanthropy (as defined above). So, too, actions arising from the *utilitarian motive*, which seek to optimise the balance of well-being over misery and so lead quite naturally to the funding of military medicine for the better defence of the community, also bear a family resemblance to our notion of philanthropy. As for the *prudential motive*, was it not predicated on selecting appropriate means to desired ends? Can anyone doubt that, even today, the funding of medical quarantines is sometimes the desirable thing to do — in order to reduce human suffering and benefit those citizens not yet infected? This last consideration also links the prudential motive in a familial way to our core notion of philanthropy: however difficult to enact and enforce, quarantines can and do serve humanitarian purposes, too. Lastly, there is the *charitable motive*. This encourages actions aimed at aiding the needy or suffering and so lead quite naturally to the funding of inoculations designed to prevent the spread of communicable diseases like smallpox. It also bears an obvious family resemblance to our preceding notion of philanthropy.

My final conjecture is that our notion of philanthropy loosely unites and subsumes each of our four central motives in at least two interesting and parallel ways. First, it interfaces with the redemptive and charitable motives by helping us notice that these both aim to generate good will and promote human welfare — the former for the glory of God, and the later for the sake of the poor. Second, it interfaces with the utilitarian and prudential motives by helping us notice that these both aim to promote the health of citizens by restoring the national defence and by blocking the spread of epidemics — the former for the sake of balancing optimal outcomes, the later for the sake of finding appropriate means to wise ends. If so, 'philanthropy', as here defined, may be said to constitute a basic concept which both links and illuminates the fuller meanings and potential psychological powers of the redemptive, utilitarian, prudential, and charitable motivations as we experience the effects of these forces in our lives.

But if this is the case, then I must modify an earlier important claim. While it is still true that no monolithic philosophy or care-giving principle emerges from the historical record to account for why governments, religious institutions, or other groups may have decided, over the centuries, to support the funding of health care, it would now be false to conclude that there is no unity at all in the four leading motives we have identified. What unites them is precisely the humanitarian vision that good will toward one's fellow man involves consideration of a higher-order philanthropic imperative. The imperative in question asserts that we ought to work to reduce human suffering and promote, as generously as possible, the well-being of all citizens. I am calling this imperative *the philanthropic imperative*.

Consider further: If this philanthropic imperative were wholeheartedly endorsed by the international community of nations, what would happen? If these nations worked openly together to achieve humane medical care through cooperative arrangements with each other and with such groups such as the World Health Organization, would not the funding of sound public health programs tend to flourish on a more responsive and extensive global scale than they do today?[18]

In my judgment, the answer is yes. At bottom, the international endorsement of the philanthropic imperative — which I have here reinterpreted as a core value at the heart of any humane program of public medicine — would go a long way toward building and sustaining sound programs of global health for planet Earth and its many inhabitants well into the twenty-first century.[19]

---

[18] Consistent with at least part of my conclusion, it is interesting to observe that the world's largest private philanthropic institution, the Bill and Melinda Gates Foundation, has christened their 'Global Health Initiative' as a current top priority. See www.gatesfoundation.org for details.

[19] I owe a debt of gratitude to Professor Philip Wilson, a medical historian at Pennsylvania State University's College of Medicine, Hershey, PA, for helpful criticisms of an earlier draft of this paper. Thanks, too, to Professor David Hufford, Chair, Department of Humanities, and the staff of the George T. Harrell Medical Library at Hershey, for arranging guest scholar privileges during the 2006 summer term.

Niall Maclean

Philosophical Approaches to The Problem of Health Care Distribution

Health Care Distribution—What's the *Moral* Problem?

The problem of health care distribution, as I set it out in the general introduction to this volume, is this: there is a genuine mismatch in even the wealthiest societies between health care resources and what is available to purchase, and this means that *limits* must be set to health care provision. This certainly looks like a problem, but why should it be thought of as a moral problem?

Clearly, not all resource allocation problems are moral problems. When we think about how to spend our personal incomes, assuming we are in the standardly unhappy position where our funds are insufficient to buy all that our heart desires, we face a resource allocation decision—but not, it would seem, a moral question. However we choose to spend this money will be irrelevant from a moral point of view, and we can do as we please unburdened by the demands of morality. Since not all resource allocation questions are moral questions, simply pointing to the health care problem and claiming it is an instance of a resource allocation question will not be sufficient to establish that it is a moral question.

So what is it that makes some resource allocation questions *moral* resource allocation questions? Aside from scarcity, what is the added ingredient? One way in which resource allocation questions can take on a moral dimension is when some persons have a *moral claim* to receive a portion of the resources in question. Consider again the example of my personal income. If it were the case that I had promised to pay a debt that I owe to you at the end of the month, then when it comes to the end of the month and I am deciding how to spend my disposable income I *am* burdened by the demands of morality: how I spend my income has become a moral question. If I spend all of it on myself and cannot meet my promise to you I will have acted immorally; if I spend only so much on myself that I can (and do) pay my debt to you in full I will have acted morally. If I am right that this is one way in which some scarce resource allocation questions can become moral questions, it might be sufficient to show that the question of health care allocation is a moral question by showing that some persons have a valid moral claim to receive health care. How might this be done?

There are two broad kinds of argument that can be marshalled to this effect. Call the first type *arguments from basic benevolence*. The common element running through these is the idea that we have, under certain circumstances, a moral duty to bestow certain kinds of goods upon our fellow human beings. Important work is done by the two qualifications 'under certain circumstances' and 'certain kinds of goods'. Consider the second qualification. It would seem that I am not morally obliged to bestow *any and all* kinds of goods upon others — we would consider this to be overly demanding. I am certainly not, for example, morally bound to entertain you to stave off boredom. Having fun is a good, but it is not the kind of good that levies moral obligations on others to ensure we enjoy it. Only certain kinds of goods impose such obligations — goods that are sufficiently important. One example is the good of life. If I see you lying face down unconscious in a puddle, I am morally obliged to flip you over so you can start breathing again. But if I see you lying face down on your hammock with a bored expression on your face, I am not morally obliged to lift your spirits. The reason a moral obligation is levied in the first case and not the second is because of the importance of the good at stake.

Now consider the first qualification. As with the second, its purpose is to give expression to our intuition that the demands of basic benevolence ought not to be too onerous. Imagine you are lying unconscious face down in a puddle, but you are on the other side of a very treacherous river. I can only get over to you to flip you over by swimming across the river, which carries the near certainty I will drown. Your drowning is guaranteed if no one flips you onto your back. If I try to swim across the river, my drowning is a mere almost certainty. Few would argue that in not diving into the river I am neglecting a moral obligation. No such obligation *exists* in this case: even though the good at stake is sufficiently important, the costs to the benefactor are so serious as to mean that no moral obligation to assist arises under these circumstances. I could be accused of lacking superhuman courage or swimming skills but not of failing to act in accordance with a moral duty.

So, the argument from basic benevolence states that whenever we are in a position to bring about a relevantly important good to some needy person without thereby suffering a relevantly serious harm to ourselves (or undertaking the grave risk of such a harm occurring), we are morally obliged to do so. How might this argument be used to justify moral claims to health care? Consider the first qualification in the argument: in order to fall under the remit of obligations from basic benevolence, a good must be sufficiently important. It certainly seems plausible to think that many forms of health care would satisfy this condition. There is no relevant difference *in terms of the good received* between being flipped over by a passer by when lying face down unconscious in a puddle and having a sceptic appendix removed before it ruptures by a sufficiently skilled surgeon. Both activities are essential to the continued enjoyment of life itself. Now consider the second qualification: supplying the good in question must not be too onerous to the potential benefactors. In the various publicly funded health care systems that abound in the developed world we have ready examples of how it is perfectly possible to supply health care to those in medical need without thereby levying unaccceptably onerous burdens on any specific individual. These systems are financed in such a way as to leave no particular individual seriously out of pocket (often they are funded from progressive income taxation), and they are staffed by individuals who have freely chosen to undertake the work and are adequately paid for doing so. So, in this way — by focussing on the importance of health care goods, and how it is possible to supply such goods to those who need them without thereby unacceptably burdening any particular individuals — it might be possible to ground valid moral claims to health care in considerations of basic benevolence.[1]

What, then, of the second type of argument that could be used to justify such claims? Call these *arguments from justice*. Their focus is not on ensuring the enjoyment of fundamental goods, but on ensuring that individuals receive that which they are owed in justice. The distinction between providing a good and doing justice is porous, for the obvious reason that things owed in justice can usually be identified as kinds of goods. It is not necessary here to go into the complex and long-running debate about what precisely distinguishes obligations of justice from those of benevolence. For my purposes, it will be sufficient to mark out the difference between arguments from basic benevolence and those mounted from justice as follows. In arguments from basic benevolence,

---

[1]   The so-called 'Rule of Rescue' is a particular, and fairly strong, example of a principle grounded in considerations of basic benevolence that has been applied in medical contexts. McKie and Richardson (2003, p. 2411) see this rule as stemming from the strong 'psychological imperative' we feel to save identifiable individuals (i.e. those we are in some sense exposed to, and who are not faceless) from death or very serious harm, an imperative which is often accompanied by what they call 'shock-horror' reactions to the plight of those in danger.

the relevant moral obligations emerge partly because of the nature of the good to be bestowed: it is a necessary condition for the existence of moral obligations rooted in basic benevolence that the good in question be sufficiently important. Moral obligations rooted in justice are not tied in this necessary way to the importance of goods. It is sufficient for the existence of a moral obligation in justice that the potential recipient of a good be *entitled* to receive it. The moral force of the entitlement can exist quite independently of the good's importance, and it is thus perfectly possible to have a claim in justice to receive some relatively trivial good.

An example will help to clarify this distinction. Imagine I run a business which employs both men and women. I choose to pay the women 5% less than the men for doing exactly the same work, simply because they are women. We would very naturally describe my pay policy as unjust, since the women employees are entitled to receive the same pay as their male colleagues for doing the same work. This is so even though the good in question — a small sum of money to be paid on top of a salary that is already sufficient, let's suppose, to fund a comfortable standard of living — could not be considered very important or fundamental. Certainly, it is nowhere near as fundamental as the sorts of goods I described above that fall under the purview of arguments from basic benevolence. Nevertheless, the women have a valid claim in justice to receive this sum of money irrespective of its relative unimportance as a good.

How might the concept of justice be used to ground moral claims to receive health care? The philosopher who has done the most influential recent work on the concept, John Rawls, has suggested that the relevant principle of justice is that of equality of opportunity: he claims that '[health] care falls under the general means necessary to underwrite fair equality of opportunity' (Rawls, 2001, p. 174). This approach has been most fully developed by Norman Daniels in his book *Just Health Care* (Daniels, 1985). Following Rawls, Daniels believes that the principle of equality of opportunity can be construed narrowly or broadly. Under the narrow construal, sometimes called 'formal equality of opportunity', the principle is a close analogue of the old idea of 'careers open to talents': jobs and offices ought to be distributed on merit alone to the best qualified candidates. Features of the candidates other than their qualifications must play no part in the decision. The broad construal of the principle is sometimes called 'fair equality of opportunity'. Under it, the principle is taken to call not only for jobs and offices to be distributed solely on the basis of merit, but for everyone in society to have a fair chance to *develop* qualifications. We all possess what might be called 'raw talents': skills and abilities that exist prior to our receiving any education or training. Under the principle of fair equality of opportunity, it is a matter of justice that we have a fair chance to transform these raw talents into marketable qualifications.

Daniels attempts to flesh out what it might mean to provide this kind of fair chance to all by introducing the concept of a society's 'normal opportunity range' (Daniels, 1985, p. 33). This is the complete set of activities and life plans that are pursued by reasonable persons within that society. Obviously, this set will be affected by the society's background culture and level of material development — the normal opportunity range for the UK will be similar to that of Sweden, but very different to that of Somalia. Individuals will have a particular portion of their society's normal opportunity range rendered open to them by the raw talents they possess: the greater the range of talents, the wider will be the portion of the range available. The particular portion of the normal range rendered open to an individual by his or her raw talents is described by Daniels as their 'fair share' of the range. It is a matter of justice that these individuals have the opportunity to pursue any of the activities within that portion. As such, it is also a matter of justice that they have the chance to convert their raw talents into the kinds of qualifications needed to pursue any of these activities. *Anything* that shrinks the portion of the normal range rendered open to individuals by their raw talents — be it an overt act of discrimination by another person, or the want of an educational good that would allow a raw talent to be transformed into a qualification — ought in the name of justice to be rectified.

Daniels links his thoughts on fair equality of opportunity to health care in the following way. When we are free of ill health, Daniels believes we attain what he calls 'species-typical normal functioning'. This kind of functioning includes all the sorts of activities, both mental and physical, that are characteristic of members of the human race. Episodes of ill health hinder this normal functioning and give rise to medical needs. When ill health means we are incapable of species typical normal functioning, the portion of the normal opportunity range rendered open to us by our raw talents will almost always be restricted: because we are in a state of medical need, we will be unable to pursue at least some of the activities within our portion of the normal range. It is a matter of justice that *any* such restrictions are lifted. As such, it is a matter of justice that individuals suffering ill health receive the medical care required to restore them to a state of species typical normal functioning.[2]

---

[2] Daniels's focus on opportunity does not mean his framework is biased against those who are not in a position to take advantage of opportunities for jobs and offices e.g. the very young or very old. The normal opportunity range for a society includes *all* the activities reasonable persons take up at various stages in their lives, not just during those years when opportunities for jobs and offices are typically most prized. It includes activities valuable

So here we have two broad kinds of argument in support of the idea that there can be valid moral claims to receive health care: arguments from basic benevolence, and arguments from justice. It is not my purpose here to attempt to show conclusively that one or both general forms, or some particular instances of them, can withstand all the various counterarguments that might possibly be mounted. This would be an extremely extensive task, and I lack the space here to embark upon it. It might, however, be worth mentioning one task of particular importance in developing these arguments: namely, to make good sense of the correlative *duty* to supply health care. Who exactly do these duties fall upon? It is worth getting a clear idea from the outset of what we mean by 'supplying' health care. There is a narrow and a broad way to construe this term. Under the narrow construal, we supply health care when we actually provide care to the sick ourselves; that is, when we physically perform the role of care-giver. Under the broad construal, we supply health care when we help and support third parties to perform this role. Clearly, when we are thinking about the obligation to 'supply' health care in the modern world it is the broad construal we have in mind: usually, we are thinking about the putative obligations of citizens to help fund a health care system. Can we make good sense of these obligations?

Consider firstly arguments from basic benevolence. If I encounter you face down in a puddle, we are straightforwardly related to one another in a way that levies a moral obligation specifically on *me*. It is clearly up to me to help you: only I can help in time, and if I fail to perform the necessary act you will die. Moreover, I can perform this act at no great cost to myself. But am I, as a run-of-the-mill member of a political community, under an identical kind of obligation to help fund a health care system? As I suggested above, if the funding system is suitably progressive I will be able to contribute in a way that is not overly burdensome, and so at least the concern about costs to would-be helpers can be met. But it is clearly false to say that *only* I can fund this system. It is also hard to see how, if I fail to pay whatever sum would not be overly burdensome to me, that I will thereby cause some serious harm to befall some specific individual. The funds I personally contribute to any kind of large-scale modern health care system will be negligible. Any shortfall caused by my withholding these funds will, it seems highly plausible to assume, be easily absorbed. Basic benevolence arguments seem to apply more readily to the narrow construal of 'supply'. If I have the skill to remove your sceptic appendix and can do so at no great cost to myself, then when I find you writhing in the agonies of life-threatening appendicitis I am under an obligation of basic benevolence to offer to perform the nec-

---

at any stage of life, such as being able to pursue leisure activities, form meaningful relationships, etc.

essary surgery. Some extra work might need to be done to show how identical or relevantly similar obligations to 'supply' health care in the broad sense fall upon individuals in general (e.g. the set of tax paying citizens) who are not as intimately related to the recipients of health care.[3]

Proponents of justice-based arguments seem to face a somewhat easier task in making sense of obligations to supply health care in this broad sense. If we, the members of some political community, recognise that some group within our boundaries has a claim in justice to receive something, and where this claim is not taken to be a demand for compensation levied against some identifiable individual or group (e.g. when thieves are obligated in justice to return stolen goods to their rightful owners), then the obligation to supply the good in question is usually distributed fairly among all the members of the community. When we are prepared to recognise valid claims in justice to receive certain things, then we are usually quite ready to accept that there ought to be a set of social institutions in place to ensure that those in possession of the claims receive the things to which they are entitled in justice, and that there is an obligation in justice that falls upon citizens in general to help maintain these institutions. In this way, obligations in justice to supply certain things seem less tied to identifiable individuals who stand in immediate relationships to one another than do obligations rooted in considerations of basic benevolence.

It might seem, then, that justice-based arguments in support of the idea that there are valid moral claims to receive health care have, in this respect at least, a comparative advantage over basic benevolence arguments. Nevertheless, proponents of justice-based arguments might still be attacked by those who choose to go right to their root in claiming that while there might be obligations of benevolence to assist the needy there simply are no such things as obligations in justice to supply goods to others. The best known recent argument to this effect is set out by Robert Nozick in *Anarchy, State, and Utopia* (Nozick, 1993).There he argues that the ownership we each enjoy over our persons and justly held property is absolute, and leaves no space for enforceable obligations in justice for our talents or justly held property to be used in externally prescribed ways, even to assist those in dire situations (including the medically needy). It may leave space for obligations of benevolence, such as might arise when individuals encounter others in situations of dire need. However, the only obligations in justice Nozick recognises are purely nega-

---

[3]   Certainly, McKie and Richardson (2003) argue that the 'Rule of Rescue' is marked by a 'focus on *identifiable* individuals' (p. 2408, my emphasis). This does not mean that there cannot be other, perhaps less demanding, considerations of basic benevolence that could justify obligations to supply health care in the broad sense I have set out.

tive ones: justice demands we refrain from interfering with other persons or their justly held property, without their consent.[4] Anyone who wishes to argue that there are obligations in justice to supply health care might owe an argument to those sympathetic to such strong views of the rights we enjoy over our persons and property.

I hope to have done enough in this section to give some indication of the kinds of arguments open to those who wish to defend the idea that there are valid moral claims to receive health care. While I haven't dealt with all the various counterarguments that might be marshalled, I hope also to have suggested that these arguments do at least possess prima facie plausibility. In what follows, I shall be proceeding on the assumption that, were we to conduct a full investigation of the kind I lack the space to undertake here, at least one particular instance of a basic benevolence or a justice-based argument would prove successful in resisting counter-arguments. I will therefore be assuming that we ought to accept the existence of valid moral claims to receive health care. Moreover, I will be assuming that these claims give rise to obligations to 'supply' in the broad sense set out above: that is, obligations that fall upon the citizenry as a whole to support social institutions that provide health care to those that need it.

Earlier, I used the simple example of a cash debt to illustrate the point that when individuals have a moral claim to receive some portion of a set of resources then the question of how those resources are to be distributed becomes a moral matter. If we are justified in assuming that there are such things as valid moral claims to receive health care, and also justified in assuming that the obligation to supply this care (in the broad sense of 'supply') is to be viewed as attaching to the members of the community taken as a whole, then how resources in the community are distributed matters from a moral point of view. However else they are distributed, morality demands that some resources are diverted to meet the needs of those suffering from ill health. However, unlike in the simple case of the cash debt, where it is clear exactly *what* morality demands (the repayment of the debt in full), it is a good deal more difficult to see exactly what is morally demanded in the case of health care. If we accept the points I made in the general introduction to this volume concerning the nature and extent of resource constraints, it is not possible to 'pay' everything we might conceivably 'owe' to those suffering ill health, where this means doing absolutely everything we can within a given level of technology for each and every sick person in the community.

[4] The closest Nozick comes to recognising a positive obligation in justice to supply others with certain things is his principle of 'justice in rectification', which requires those who have unjustly acquired resources from others to compensate them for the injustice (Nozick, 1993, pp. 152–3).

This would destroy the community's ability to pursue almost any other valued project.

Nevertheless, morality does demand that there are such things as 'health care resources', and since the prospective recipients of these resources have valid moral claims it clearly matters from a moral point of view *how* these resources are allocated. But how ought we to distribute these resources under conditions of scarcity? If we cannot do everything we can for the possessors of these claims, to what sub-optimal kinds and amounts of health care are they morally entitled? How do ethical considerations guide us under these non-ideal conditions? This is, of course, the central question to which this chapter is addressed. It might seem natural to assume that we can make progress on this question by thinking more closely about the kinds of moral considerations that led us in the first place to accept the existence of moral claims to receive health care. Given this, setting out the broad shape of basic benevolence and justice based arguments will prove useful for the rest of this chapter. In the next section, I will consider how proponents of basic benevolence arguments might develop these arguments to justify particular distributions of health care.

Basic Benevolence and Health Care Distribution

As I have explained, obligations in basic benevolence only arise (if they do so at all) with regard to the provision of goods that are sufficiently important: there is a threshold level of importance below which these kinds of obligations will not apply. Given this concern with sufficiently important goods, it might seem that an obvious way to tackle the problem of which sub-optimal distribution of health care to prefer lies open to those sympathetic to basic benevolence approaches — we ought, they might claim, to provide *only* those treatments that confer sufficiently important kinds of medical benefits, in the amounts required to produce these benefits. All treatments that confer benefits below the threshold of importance should not receive public funds.

This obvious approach masks a host of potentially difficult questions. Perhaps the most fundamental is this: what exactly are 'sufficiently important medical benefits'? Where do we set the aforementioned threshold? In making headway with this question, we might be tempted to focus our attention on the distinction between needs and wants. We are familiar with politicians justifying both the existence and the scope of publicly funded health care arrangements by reference to the importance of meeting the 'medical needs' of the population. And we can easily see the powerful rhetorical work done by the word 'needs' by imagining how much weaker these pronouncements would sound were they to contain phrases like 'medical wants' or 'medical preferences'. But rhetorical power aside, is there any *meaningful* distinction to be drawn between medical needs and medical wants or preferences? When we use the phrase 'medical needs' are we merely adding lustre to a sentence, or does the phrase actually serve to pick out some class of things in the world?

Certainly, at a very abstract level it is easy to see a clear conceptual separation between needs and wants. Being in possession of one does not necessarily entail being in possession of the other: It is possible to need something but not want it (think of a severely depressed person who needs but does not want food), and to want something but not need it (think of Imelda Marcos in a shoe shop). Needs seem to be independent of our mental states (they exist whether we are aware of them or not), whereas wants just seem to *be* mental states. However, this tells us nothing about whether there actually are such things as *medical* needs, as opposed to mere medical wants dressed up in the language of needs.

It is also worth stating from the outset that, if there are medical needs, these can't be the kinds of things I shall call 'instrumental needs'. These are frequently expressed in everyday speech, and signify the speaker's requiring something in order to achieve a goal: thus, 'I need a light' signifies my requiring a flame in order to achieve my goal of smoking a cigarette. While the need here is genuine enough—in the sense that its being satisfied is a necessary condition on my smoking a cigarette—it would be perfectly natural for an observer to question whether or not I need to achieve the goal in question. This line of questioning would seem bizarre and out of place when directed at the kinds of needs with which we *shall* be interested. Call these non-instrumental needs. When a starving man says 'I need food', it is certainly true that there are some very basic structural similarities between what he has said and what I have said when I ask you for a light. But it would seem odd to subject his claim to an instrumental analysis to isolate the 'goal' for which he requires food (the 'goal' being simply to stay alive), and even stranger to question whether he needs to achieve that goal. While it is *possible* to render non-instrumental need-claims structurally identical to instrumental need-claims, the difference between the two kinds of claim is plain: it never makes good sense to question the 'goal' sought in the former claims, whereas it often does so with regard to the goals sought in the latter.[5]

The reason it does not make good sense to question the states aimed at in non-instrumental need claims is because these seem to be of such

[5]   David Miller provides a useful discussion of the differences between instrumental and non-instrumental needs in his *Principles of Social Justice* (Miller, 1999, pp. 206–7). While some such as Brian Barry argue that need claims must *always* be rendered instrumentally in the form 'A needs *x* in order to Ø' (Barry, 1965), many remain committed to the idea that our ordinary language is a reliable guide to the existence of a non-instrumental sense of 'need'. For an influential statement of this view, see David Wiggins's essay 'Claims of Need' (Wiggins, 1987).

overwhelming importance. If the starving man does not get the thing he needs—food—he will lose perhaps the most valuable state of all; namely, life. Clearly, many medical need claims are also claims for goods that are required in order to stay alive. If we accord needed status to food when this is required in order to stay alive, then it might seem that we ought also to accord needed status to medical goods when these are also needed in order to stay alive. However, many will feel that non-instrumental needs extend beyond needs for those things that are required merely in order to stay alive. There are a set of benefits that are less fundamental than life itself but which are nevertheless so important that needs for these things ought to be considered non-instrumental. Examples might be the need to engage in human relationships, or to perform some kind of meaningful work. Similarly, many will feel that the set of medical needs ought to extend beyond needs for those goods required merely in order to stave off the ultimate harm (namely, death), to include needs for goods required to avoid certain less fundamental but still serious harms—such as being in great pain, for example.

So, in order to identify a need as being non-instrumental, we are forced to think about the kind of benefit that will be brought about when the need is satisfied (or, conversely, the kind of harm that will ensue if the need goes unsatisfied). Earlier I said that those who wished to work within a basic benevolence framework in tackling the question of which sub-optimal distribution of health care to prefer had to be able to identify what are 'sufficiently important' medical benefits. I then suggested that one seemingly very natural way to make headway with the latter task might be to identify the set of medical needs (as distinct from medical wants), as exemplars of these sufficiently important medical benefits. However, it now seems that this would be to put the cart before the horse: we cannot hope to make headway on the question of what are sufficiently important medical benefits by referring to a set of medical needs because identifying the members of any such set requires prior thought about the importance of different kinds of medical benefits. I have said nothing to here to doubt the *existence* of non-instrumental medical needs. All I have done is suggest that in deciding whether or not something counts as such a need we cannot do without the more fundamental concepts of benefit and harm.

But surely, it could be objected, it is possible to construct an account of medical needs that makes no reference at all to these concepts and which focuses instead on the biological functioning of the human organism? When working properly, this consists of a set of interdependent physiological processes. Perhaps we can define a 'medical need' as arising whenever one or more of these physiological processes goes awry. However, thinking about things in terms of deviations from normal physiological processes does not mean we can sidestep questions about the

52   *Distributing Health Care*

nature of different kinds of medical benefits and harms. The physiological processes in our bodies are conducted more or less efficiently at various times, and most of the time we are totally unaware of these
fluctuations in performance. For example, my lungs will not at all times
possess exactly the same level of efficiency at processing oxygen. Their
efficiency at any given time will vary according a host of factors, including how much exercise I take (this improves lung capacity), how anxious
I am (this leads to shallow breathing), and whether I managed to get a
light for my cigarette. It is only certain *kinds* of fluctuations in physiological processes that would seem to give rise to medical needs. A 1%
reduction in the efficiency of my lungs that has no impact at all on my life
would not seem to give rise to a medical need. A 90% reduction that
means I will become hypoxic and die if I don't get administered with
pure oxygen would. In short, it is only fluctuations that cause some kind
of *harm* to befall the 'owner' of the physiological process in question that
would seem to give rise to medical needs. So, thinking about things
purely in terms of physiological processes will not allow us to demarcate
a set of medical needs. Once again, the concepts of benefit and harm are
required.[6]

So, proponents of basic benevolence arguments must confront
head-on the task of deciding what are 'sufficiently important medical
benefits' without expecting to get any help from the concept of medical
need, since this is parasitic on the more fundamental concepts of benefit
and harm. How, then, are they to decide on what are sufficiently important benefits? We do have a secure sense that at least some kinds of
goods are sufficiently important. In illustrating basic benevolence arguments, I have usually focussed on the extreme case of obligations in
basic benevolence to prevent individuals from suffering death. Extreme
cases have the advantage of making points clearly and powerfully, and
few would dispute that life itself is an example of a 'sufficiently important good' which will in certain circumstances give rise to obligations of
basic benevolence. As such, it might seem that all life-saving medical

---

[6]   Norman Daniels's account is a good example of how our thinking about health
        care needs must marry together two things: first, a recognition of the fact that
        health has a physiological underpinning; secondly, some substantive *non-
        physiological* concepts. While Daniels does not explicitly make use of the concepts
        I mention—benefit and harm—it is clear that something like these concepts is
        lurking in the background. He claims that humans have a 'species-typical
        [physiological] apparatus' that allows them to engage in the broad set of activities
        that partly define us as the type of creatures we are: he calls this 'normal species
        functioning'. With this in mind, he defines health care needs as those things we
        need to correct problems with our species typical apparatuses that give rise to
        certain kinds of *harms*: namely, an inability to engage in one or more of the
        activities that make up normal species functioning. (Daniels, 1985, pp. 29–32, my
        parentheses).

treatments should be considered to confer 'sufficiently important goods', and ought to be provided in any publicly funded health care package in the amounts required in order for the treatments to save lives.

There is a problem with this seemingly commonsensical approach, however. Blanket supply of all medical treatments that can save life, in the amounts required in order for them to have this effect, to all patients who might thereby benefit, would nowadays be a very expensive undertaking. Medical technology is such that we can now stave off death in a great many instances: patients in deep comas can be kept alive indefinitely on life-support machines; patients with terminal cancer can be given extra months of life via the administration of chemotherapy or radiotherapy; patients with hopelessly diseased organs can have replacement donor organs transplanted in them, and have further transplants if necessary be; and so on.[7] And these are just patients with dramatic medical problems: think also of the vast swathes of elderly patients dying of 'natural causes' who could be kept alive a little longer by having doctors on standby twenty-four hours a day to administer heroic last-ditch measures whenever required.

Most people would feel that we ought not to take absolutely *every* opportunity to save life. Typically, the reasons adduced for declining an opportunity to use health care in this way will be that the quantity of life secured will be very small (a few hours, days, or weeks, perhaps), or that it will be of low quality (marked by great pain, or mental confusion, etc). Crucially, these reasons will be framed within the context of resource constraints. It is not simply that the goods supplied in these instances are trivial in themselves—small amounts of life, even life of pretty poor quality, are still undeniably goods, and if we had unlimited resources we might think that there was an obligation in basic benevolence to supply such goods to those who would otherwise die. Think of the man face down in the puddle again. If he has terminal cancer that will kill him in a week we would still think I am under an obligation in basic benevolence to flip him over. A week of life is still a significant good, and my flipping him over is virtually costless to me or anyone else. We baulk at using health care to provide very small amounts of life or life of very low quality not because of the intrinsic triviality of those goods, but because we have a sense that resources consumed in supplying those goods would be *better spent* elsewhere.

This problem does not deliver a knockout blow to basic benevolence approaches to health care distribution, but it does levy certain challenges. It would seem that proponents of these approaches cannot

---

[7]   A useful discussion of the ethics of organ retransplantation can be found in Ubel et al (1998).

expect to make much headway with the problem by operating with an absolute standard of 'sufficiently important goods'. There are now a vast range of medical treatments, all of which deliver benefits that would seem to fall on the right side of any threshold of importance (e.g. treatments that can provide very small amounts of life). Unfortunately, we cannot afford to fund all such treatments. Moreover, funding any particular treatment in a context of relative resource scarcity levies opportunity costs: doing so means will have to forego funding at least some kinds of other treatments. Given this, it would seem that basic benevolence theorists must find some way of capturing our sense that even within the set of medical benefits that would be considered 'sufficiently important' some kinds of medical benefits are *more important* than others. They must, in other words, arrive at a ranking of the relative importance of medical benefits that fall above the threshold.[8]

As I have already suggested, it is easy to agree on rankings of medical benefits in extreme cases. Almost all of us would agree that several years of good quality life is a more important kind of good than the absence of very minor pain and discomfort. However, the great majority of ranking decisions will not be as straightforward as this. We might have an idea of the sorts of benefits that would be at the top of the ranking — perhaps a full lifespan of perfect quality would be at the very top — but we will quickly encounter very tough choices further down the scale. How are we to rank partial gains in lost eyesight against partial gains in mobility, for example? Or several years of low quality life against several months of perfect health? It seems very likely that individuals will disagree markedly over these kinds of tough choices, for comprehensible reasons: we all have our own ideas about what kind of life we want to lead, and some kinds of medical benefits will advance our favoured kind of life better than others. How ought proponents of basic benevolence approaches to proceed in the face of this seemingly inevitable disagreement?

One possible line of response is to downplay the significance of the disagreement. People disagree about all sorts of things, but the mere fact of disagreement does not in itself show there is no fact of the matter that

---

[8]   The 'Rule of Rescue', according to McKie and Richardson (2003), cannot be bent or modified to incorporate cost considerations: 'Perhaps the most conspicuous feature of the [Rule of Rescue] … is the tendency to disregard opportunity costs when the life of an identifiable individual is visibly threatened. There is a tendency to 'act first and ask questions later'. Considerations about costs are pushed into the background' (p. 2408, my parentheses). However, the rule is but one example of an approach grounded in considerations of basic benevolence. It is possible to construct other, less intransigent basic benevolence approaches which can take into account the issue of opportunity costs. It would seem that these approaches are more likely to make satisfactory headway with the modern problem of health care resource allocation.

could settle the issue at stake. Not all disagreements are intractable, and perhaps disagreements about the most important medical benefits are, despite appearances to the contrary, in fact resolvable. People might well have their own ideas about how they want to lead their lives but perhaps there are, nevertheless, certain kinds of improvements in health status that are objectively more valuable than others. If someone references their own ideas about how best to live in reversing aspects of this objective hierarchy, then they have simply made a mistake.

It might seem that some support for this kind of objective approach to ranking medical benefits could be gleaned from the so-called 'capability' models developed in recent years by Amartya Sen (1982; 1992; 1993) and Martha Nussbaum (2000).[9] These philosophers have worked largely independently, and there are salient differences between the models developed by each. Nevertheless, the core idea remains the same: we ought to evaluate how well an individual's life is going in terms of his actual (not merely potential) capability to do certain valuable things, or to be a certain way (i.e. attain certain valuable states). Both Sen and Nussbaum refer to these valuable doings and beings as 'functionings'. Both also seem to view capabilities to pursue functionings as having a kind of objective value: Nussbaum refers to 'those human capabilities that can be convincingly argued to be of central importance in any human life, whatever else the person pursues or chooses' (Nussbaum, 2000, p.74).

Unfortunately, the approaches of both Sen and Nussbaum lack the kind of fine-grained specificity that would help with the task described above: a full and objective ranking of all the currently vast range of medical benefits as being more or less valuable. Both Sen and Nussbaum recognise that health is a very important kind of 'functioning', but neither develops a capability approach sufficiently detailed to do this kind of work. Sen describes 'good health' as a 'very elementary' kind of functioning, but he does not specify the components of good health in such a way as would allow for a ranking as detailed as this (Sen, 1993, p. 31). While Nussbaum's capability approach is more fleshed out than Sen's—unlike Sen, she does at least 'take a stand on what the central capabilities are' (Nussbaum, 2000, p. 70)—she too does not unpack the functioning of 'health' in anything like the degree of specificity required

[9]   It is worth stating from the outset that both Sen and Nussbaum are generally concerned with issues of *justice*, and not benevolence. This does not mean that those interested in the latter issues could not legitimately borrow elements of their work in constructing an objective ranking of goods. Such a usage would only be problematic if the elements borrowed undermined or were otherwise in tension with important aspects of the borrower's theoretical commitments. I do not think the particular elements of the capability approaches I set out here would clash in this way with the central aspects of basic benevolence approaches to health care distribution.

to derive a ranking of this kind. She claims that '[b]eing able to have good health, including reproductive health' is one of the 'central capabilities', but she does not unpack 'good health' in anything like the requisite degree (Nussbaum, 2000, p. 78).

When we consider the nature of the tasks the authors of these approaches set themselves, it should come as no surprise that neither approach can help with the problem of deriving a full and objective ranking of medical benefits. Sen's goal is a fairly abstract one: to describe the conceptual space within which quality of life comparisons ought to be made, i.e. a space filled with the concepts of 'capability' and 'functioning', and not rival concepts such as 'welfare' or 'resources'. Nussbaum's aims are more concrete: she wants to move beyond this 'merely comparative use of the capability space' to specify what the central capabilities are, and to argue for the existence of obligations falling upon governments to supply all citizens with a certain minimum 'threshold' level of these capabilities (Nussbaum, 2000, p. 12). Nevertheless, she concedes that fleshing out the nature of these capabilities takes place 'in accordance with local beliefs and circumstances' and she allows 'room for a reasonable pluralism in specification'. She also accepts that the setting of the threshold level for each capability 'will need more precise determination', a process that also takes place within, and draws upon, distinct social and political traditions (Nussbaum, 2000, p. 77).

It is no surprise, then, that Nussbaum does not unpack 'good health' very precisely — this is a process that must take place on the ground, amongst people who might disagree 'reasonably' about exactly what 'good health' is. Even the minimal 'threshold' level of good health must be specified in this way; moreover, even if this wasn't the case, I take it that many of the health care distribution questions facing modern developed societies will concern advanced treatments that provide benefits far above any basic threshold of 'good health'. While Nussbaum asserts there are 'constraints' on which specifications are acceptable, and on where thresholds can be set, these are nowhere near determinate enough to allow for the creation of a complete ranking of all the vast range of benefits that can now be delivered by medical science (Nussbaum, 2000, p. 83). At best, Nussbaum's capability approach might provide some amount of guidance on the absolute minimum amount of health care that ought to be provided by any decent society. Since she is very clear that her model is supposed to apply to pretty much all existing societies, including those that could not afford to fund anything like the kinds of health care routinely provided in the developed world, this lends further support to the idea that the model will provide little if any guidance on the kinds of health care resource allocation questions encountered in affluent societies.

So, neither of these capability approaches seem able to offer an 'objectivist' way around the problem outlined above. Only a small amount of reflection is required to see that this outcome is not surprising. While it is certainly true to say that not all disagreements are intractable and that many are underlain by a fact of the matter that could bring all parties to agreement, disagreement about what are the most important medical benefits *do* seem to fall into a category we might call 'currently intractable'. If there *are* facts underlying the disagreement that would allow for a full ranking of all the current vast range of medical benefits, then we are certainly not at the moment in a position to discern their content. Note that this is not to make the stronger claim that there are no such facts. It is not even to say that we cannot, perhaps after many years of trying, discern something of the content of such (putative) facts. Frances Kamm's work (Kamm, 1993) is one attempt to find hidden sources of agreement regarding the ranking of medical benefits through the use of hypothetical examples that abstract greatly from the current reality of health care resource allocation. She claims, for example, that we would not select between patients for life-saving treatment on the basis that choosing one of them means we can provide a very trivial benefit (e.g. the curing of a sore throat) to another patient. We might, however, select between candidates for a very minor treatment (e.g. an earache cure) on this basis. When considering more significant benefits, Kamm also claims to have uncovered some hidden agreement. Since losing a leg is a far more significant loss than suffering a sore throat, we would give more weight to saving a life and a leg than saving a life alone. We clearly accord significant value to the saving of a leg, which might imply the existence of a point at which we would prefer to save a large number of legs rather than a small number of lives.

However, even if Kamm's work can be seen as constituting at least some amount of progress towards to an agreed-upon ranking of all medical benefits, the progress as it stands is fairly limited. The kinds of hidden agreements she uncovers (assuming they are genuine) are rather modest in nature. Moreover, her methodology for uncovering these agreements does not meet with universal approval (see for example Daniels, 1998). Given this, we might make a conservative claim: even if a contestable case can be made for thinking that we are making at least some amount of progress towards a full ranking of medical benefits, we are still a great distance away from completing the task, and further progress (if it happens at all) is likely to be slow. Here and now, we are left with no option but to characterise disagreements over what are the most important medical benefits as *reasonable*: since we currently lack the kinds of reasons that can bring individuals to agreement on these issues, adopting any particular ranking is no more or less reasonable than adopting any other.

So, the prospects for arriving at an objective ranking of medical benefits in anything like an acceptable time frame — we need to distribute
health care *now*, since some people are already seriously ill — seem very
slim. How ought basic benevolence approaches to respond to this? One
possible response is to give up on arriving at an objective ranking, and to
take some kind of purely subjective approach such as asking members of
a society to vote on what they take to be the most important medical benefits and then constructing a ranking from the preferences of a majority
of voters. It would seem, however, that subjective approaches sit uneasily with the essence of basic benevolence arguments. These arguments
are premised on the idea that some kinds of goods are more important
than others, with some goods being so important that we are (under certain circumstances) morally obligated to supply them. The value these
goods possess must be considered objective at least in the sense of existing independently of the approval or disapproval of particular individuals, including those who find themselves subject to obligations of basic
benevolence. Anyone who attempted to shirk their obligation to flip
over an unconscious man face down in a puddle by saying that, as far as
they were concerned, life is simply not important enough a good, would
be told by basic benevolence theorists that their view was mistaken — it
does not accurately reflect just how important, as a matter of fact, life is.
The same response would await anyone who took a more comparative
approach to the shirking, e.g. someone who said that possible damage to
his expensive manicure was a sufficiently grave risk that he ought not to
be obligated in basic benevolence to flip the man over. Again, the
response would be that the shirker has made a mistake: he has seriously
overestimated the good of neat fingernails, or seriously underestimated
the good of life.

The kind of threshold found in basic benevolence approaches
between sufficiently and insufficiently important kinds of goods evi-
dences a commitment to the existence of objective differences in the
value of goods. It would seem rather ad hoc for basic benevolence theorists to claim that there was only one kind of objective difference, i.e.
between goods that are 'sufficiently' important to generate obligations
of basic benevolence, and those that are not. A far more natural claim
would be that this threshold is simply one part of a general objective
hierarchy of values, with objective differences in value obtaining
between goods that fall above and below this threshold. And, if it is
more natural to accept an objective hierarchy of goods above the threshold, it might seem that basic benevolence theories ought to eschew subjective approaches to the ranking of medical benefits that fall above the
threshold. The problem with subjective methods such as majority voting
is that they can serve as no reliable guide to what are the facts of the mat-

ter: even the preferences of a majority of individuals with regard to the importance of a medical benefit could well be mistaken.[10]

So, proponents of basic benevolence approaches seem to be left in an uncomfortable position: they must arrive at some kind of objective ranking of medical benefits, yet the reasonable disagreement that pertains over the relative importance of such benefits will not be overcome in anything like an acceptable timeframe. The problems for basic benevolence approaches don't stop here, however. Even if a full and objective ranking of medical benefits could be arrived at in an acceptable timeframe, basic benevolence theorists would still face the question of what to *do* with the ranking. I argued they had to construct such a ranking because they would get nowhere with a simple absolute threshold approach, i.e. where some treatments were considered 'sufficiently important' and others were not. Such an approach can provide no guidance when we must pick and choose between the current vast swathe of medical treatments that all provide benefits above the threshold. However, constructing a full ranking of treatments above the threshold would not settle all the outstanding questions. For example, having constructed such a ranking are basic benevolence theorists committed to what we might call a strict priority view? On this view, we devote resources in such a way as to ensure that all patients eligible for treatments that can produce the most significant kind of benefit receive these treatments in the amounts required to receive that benefit. After we have spent maximally on this patient group, we then take the remaining money and move on to patients eligible for treatments that can produce the second most significant kind of benefit, and so on until the money has run out. Or are basic benevolence theorists committed to a more utilitarian approach? The aim here is to distribute available resources in such a way as to maximise the *total* amount of benefit produced.[11] This

---

[10] The so-called 'Quality Adjusted Life Year' method—an attempt to construct a unitary metric for measuring the amount of benefit a treatment produces by summing together the effects it has both on extending life and on improving its quality — is another subjective method that would sit uneasily with the essence of basic benevolence approaches. The particular 'quality adjustments' made as part of the method—that is, judgements about how valuable it is to be free of certain disease symptoms—are typically constructed from the preferences of a putatively representative sample of individuals posed specific 'trade-off' or 'gamble' questions. There is a great deal of technical debate surrounding the soundness of these ways of striking quality adjustments (see for example Duru *et al*, 2002). Even if these technical debates were to be resolved in favour of the QALY method, its focus on the simple preferences of individuals would, for the reasons I have set out above, pose serious challenges for any potential incorporation into basic benevolence approaches.

[11] This kind of utilitarian reasoning seems very close to hand in the 'cost-effectiveness' allocation policies of many countries; including, as Howard Glennerster and John

could lead to a distribution that diverges sharply from that advocated by the priority approach: it might demand, for example, that we preferentially fund many cheap treatments that produce moderately important benefits (that, say, fall just above the threshold of 'sufficiently important') for large numbers of people rather than a small number of very expensive treatments that produce very important benefits (that fall well above this threshold) for a tiny number of people, since favouring the former treatments will produce more benefit overall.

Since I have argued that proponents of basic benevolence approaches ought to accept the existence of an objective hierarchy of goods above the threshold, it might seem that they ought to give some amount of priority to the most important goods in that hierarchy. However, it is far from obvious that *absolute* priority should be given. Imagine I encounter ten people face down unconscious in puddles, nine of whom are very close to me and one who is very far away. The nine close to me are middle aged, the one far away is an infant. Because time is very tight (all ten individuals are close to drowning), I can choose either to save the nine middle aged persons close to me or the infant who is far away. On the strict priority view, I ought to save the child, since a full lifespan is a more significant benefit than the partial lifespans each of the middle-aged persons will enjoy. But these partial lifespans are still very significant goods, and are clearly above the threshold of importance required for obligations of basic benevolence to arise (since we would consider ourselves under such an obligation were we to encounter a solitary middle-aged person face down in a puddle). Even if a full lifespan is more valuable than a partial one, it is not obvious that it is *so* valuable that I should provide one full lifespan at the expense of nine partial ones.

If it is not clear that basic benevolence theorists are committed to according absolute priority to treatments that can confer the most important kinds of benefits, exactly what level of priority short of this ought they to accord? At what point can we justifiably forego providing a more important benefit to a small number of patients to provide a less important one to a greater number? Where exactly on the spectrum between the absolute priority view and the pure utilitarian view ought basic benevolence theorists to locate themselves? There are a vast number of intermediate positions between these two extremes, and the core logic of basic benevolence approaches — that certain fundamental goods ought to be provided to those who need them — seems to give scant guidance on which to adopt. Moreover, disagreements about which intermediate position is best seem to resemble disagreements about

Appleby and Tony Harrison argue in their chapters in this volume, the United Kingdom. For a detailed summary and critique of the ethical underpinnings of cost-effectiveness methodologies see Brock (2004a).

what are the most important kinds of medical benefits, i.e. they are *reasonable* disagreements. We currently seem to lack the kinds of fine-grained reasons that would allow us to say with certainty that one particular intermediate position is to be preferred from the vast range of possible candidates. Given this, no particular intermediate position seems any more or less reasonable than any other.[12]

None of the arguments in this section serve to show that basic benevolence approaches to health care distribution are irredeemably flawed, though they do give an indication of the kinds of problems and challenges facing those who would seek to develop such approaches. One of the attractive aspects of basic benevolence arguments — their drawing upon our intuitive sense that some kinds of goods are more important than others — turns out, in the context of health care distribution, to be the very feature that renders such approaches problematic. There is now a bewildering array of medical treatments vying for limited public funds, and they all seemingly provide benefits that would fall above any threshold of 'sufficiently important'. The challenge for those who would take a basic benevolence approach to health care distribution is to find some way of choosing between these treatments while both acknowledging the current seemingly reasonable disagreement over the relative importance of different medical benefits and remaining true to the core idea of basic benevolence theories: that some kinds of goods are objectively more important than others. A related and no less demanding challenge is to justify some kind of intermediate position between the according of absolute priority to treatments that provide the most important kinds of benefit and the adoption of a pure benefit-maximisation approach.

These are stern challenges. Yet there are many forms that basic benevolence arguments can take, and it is certainly conceivable that some version could make reasonable headway. However, it is surely likely that any such progress will be slow, and basic benevolence theorists will face the problem of how to allocate health care here and now. One interim option that may be preferable to resorting to a subjectively derived ranking of the relative value of different medical benefits (e.g. one constructed from voting) is to use a distributive mechanism that involves no ranking whatsoever. The obvious candidate would be some kind of lot-

---

[12] Norman Daniels and James E. Sabin (2002) make something like this point when they claim that 'general principles give no guidance' regarding where exactly we should strike the balance between absolute priority and absolute benefit maximisation. They also cite the empirical work of the economist Erik Nord (1999) as showing the considerable societal disagreement about which intermediate position is to be preferred, and the range of seemingly reasonable considerations that people bring to bear in support of their particular favoured position.

tery. We would make a judgement about where the threshold of 'sufficiently important' lies and list all the treatments that confer benefits that fall above this threshold. If I am right, this set of treatments will be very large, and not even the wealthiest society will be able to supply all of them. Having worked out how much it would cost to supply each treatment to all eligible patients, we would then select treatments randomly by lottery and stop when resources were exhausted. Such a method would at least reflect the core commitment within basic benevolence theories to the existence of a threshold of 'sufficiently important', and would also reflect the currently impoverished state of our knowledge regarding the relative value of medical benefits that fall above the threshold. Instead of operating with a subjectively derived and possibly erroneous ranking, we instead concede our state of present ignorance and give all 'sufficiently important' treatments a fair chance of being funded.[13]

Justice and Health Care Distribution

What, then, of arguments from justice: how do these fare with the problem of justifying particular distributions of health care under conditions of resource scarcity?

Let's begin with the particular example of a justice-based argument I set out above: Norman Daniels's fair equality of opportunity approach. It will be recalled that the purpose of health care according to Daniels is to correct deviations in 'normal species functioning', since these generally stop individuals from pursuing at least some of the opportunities rendered open to them by their native talents, i.e. they 'shrink' an individual's particular fair share of his or her society's 'normal opportunity range'. It might seem that a very simple distributive principle is implied by this: we ought to supply all kinds and amounts of health care required to restore individuals to a state of normal species functioning. Indeed, Daniels himself seems to embrace something like this simple principle when describing how his approach can 'characterise' the sorts of treatments that ought in justice to be publicly funded:

> [T]he fair equality of opportunity account provides a principled way of characterising the health care services that fall in the socially guaranteed tier.

---

[13] John Broome (1991a) has argued that a 'fair' chance is an *equal* chance, and so lotteries such as these must be genuinely random. In contrast, Dan Brock (1988) has attempted to justify 'weighted' lotteries that give a comparatively greater chance of being selected to treatments that can produce the greatest amount of health benefit. Since basic benevolence theorists would be forced to embrace lottery procedures precisely because they currently lack reasons for ranking treatments above the threshold as being more or less valuable, it is difficult to see how they could construct any kind of weighted lottery.

> They are the services needed to maintain, restore, or compensate for the loss
> of normal species-typical functioning ...(Daniels, 1985, p.79).

This 'characterisation' is very bare, and it masks an important and by
now familiar problem. It would seem that not even the wealthiest societies can afford to provide all medical treatments in the amounts required
to 'maintain', 'restore', or 'compensate' *optimally*. Some deviations from
normal species functioning can be perfectly maintained or completely
restored relatively cheaply, but for other conditions this optimal result
can be secured only at very great cost. Similarly, for some devastating
and incurable medical conditions we can only maximally 'compensate'
(i.e. provide the best possible approximation to normal species functioning we can) at very great cost, and even then the approximation might be
a pale imitation of the real thing. In short, we run into the fundamental
problem of health care distribution: not even wealthy societies are able
to do as much as is currently technologically feasible to maintain,
restore, and compensate for all deviations from normal species functioning. The question, then is this: exactly what sub-optimal level of mainte-
nance, restoration, and compensation is required by justice?

Daniels does not give anything like a full answer to this question in
Just Health Care. While he does at times seem to concede the relative thin-
ness of his account, admitting that it is 'abstract' and in need of a good
deal of 'moral judgement' in its application, he also claims somewhat
more optimistically that it 'provides a basis for argument' about which
treatments should receive public funding (Daniels, 1985, p. 79).
Although he is not explicit about how this 'basis' should be developed,
he does at one point hint that we ought to focus on his concept of the
'normal opportunity range': he claims that '[i]n general it will be more
important to prevent, cure, or compensate for those disease conditions
which involve a greater curtailment of an individual's share of the normal range' (Daniels, 1985, p. 35). Given this, it might seem that the way
Daniels would extrapolate from his theoretical 'basis' in specifying a just
set of medical treatments is to *quantify* 'curtailment' of the normal opportunity range, and to devote resources preferentially towards those conditions that cause a greater curtailment of the range.

In the quote I have just presented from Daniels, he focuses on how
severely disease impacts on '*an individual's share*' of the normal opportunity range. Obviously, the same disease will have different effects on
the particular portion of the normal range possessed by different individuals. This portion varies from person to person, since differently talented individuals have different kinds of opportunities rendered open
to them: for example, diseases that affect cognition will have a more serious impact on those persons whose raw talents are mostly intellectual in
nature, rather than physical. Given the vast range of different portions of

the normal range that will abound in societies made up of differently talented individuals, it would seem practically impossible to distribute health care on the basis of how severely diseases impact on the portion of the range held by *particular individuals*. The process of working out whose portions are currently worst affected by disease would be staggeringly complex. Even assuming it could be accomplished, this would be very unlikely within any kind of acceptable timeframe (some individuals are seriously ill right now). There would also be the problem of changing health states: the measurement process will be so onerous that by the time it is completed the medical condition of many of those who had been surveyed will change (they will either get better or worse), thus rendering inaccurate the prior assessment of how seriously disease impacts on their portion of the normal range.

Given these difficulties, it might seem that we ought to take a 'societal' rather than an 'individualistic' perspective; that is, we ought to focus on the impact of diseases on the normal opportunity range taken as a whole, rather than on the particular portions of the range possessed by individuals. Recall that Daniels defines the normal opportunity range as 'the array of life plans reasonable persons [in a given society] are likely to construct for themselves' (Daniels, 1985, p. 33, my parentheses). If some way could be found to estimate the extent to which a disease impacts upon this total set of life plans, we could then preferentially direct resources towards those diseases that have the greatest impact. How, then, might we decide which diseases have the 'greatest' curtailing effect?

It would seem that in making this decision we must consider both the number of reasonable life plans that a disease frustrates, and also how severely a disease 'curtails' opportunity (ranging, one assumes, from those diseases that make the pursuit of some set of plans slightly more difficult, to those that make it impossible to pursue a set of plans). We must consider both these elements because there seem to be problems with focussing exclusively on one or the other. Consider focussing exclusively on the number of reasonable life plans that a disease curtails, in preferentially directing resources towards those diseases that curtail the greatest number of life plans irrespective of the severity of curtailment. At some point in the resource allocation procedure, this could mean that a disease that slightly curtails opportunity to pursue n number of reasonable plans will receive more resources than a disease that severely curtails opportunity to pursue n-1 number of plans. This seems unacceptable. If opportunity is to be the driving concept in how we distribute our health care resources, it would seem that at least *some* attention must be paid to the severity of opportunity curtailment.

Now consider the strategy of focussing exclusively on the severity of curtailment, in directing resources preferentially to those conditions that cause the severest curtailment of opportunity. Taken in isolation, this approach fares no better. Such an approach would devote more resources to treating diseases that render it impossible to pursue some small set of reasonable plans (e.g. throat conditions that render opera singing - and only opera signing - impossible) than to those that might make it very difficult (but not impossible) to pursue *any* reasonable life plan. Again, this seems unacceptable: if opportunity is to be the driving concept, at least some attention must be paid to the number of life plans a disease curtails.

So, it would seem that any attempt to quantify the impact of disease on the normal opportunity range must be sensitive to both these considerations. But, even adopting this double focus, considerable additional problems will emerge. First, we can raise some serious problems of precision, both with regard to quantifying the number of life plans a disease frustrates, and with regard to assessing how seriously it frustrates them. Consider the former problem first. We might doubt whether we possess the kind of clear and non-arbitrary criteria for deciding where one life plan ends and another begins that seem necessary in order to *count* life plans. For example, consider these plans: the plan of being good at the breaststroke; the plan of being good at the front crawl; the plan of being good at the backstroke. Ought we to consider these to be separate plans, such that a keen swimmer with a broken arm could claim to have three plans curtailed? Or ought we to lump these activities under the general life plan of being a good swimmer, such that this individual can only claim to have one plan curtailed? If we take the former option, what stops us from breaking these life plans down into smaller and smaller component plans (such that the life plan of being good at the front-crawl breaks down into the plan of being good at the initial dive, the plan of being good at the leg-kick, the plan of being good at rolling one's body in time with the stroke, etc.)? If we take the latter option, what stops us from subsuming the life plan of being a good swimmer and other similar plans under more and more general descriptions, such that we would describe someone with a broken arm who is a keen swimmer, rower, and mountaineer as really only suffering from the frustration of one life plan, e.g. the life plan of being physically active? There seems to be no uncontroversial way of proceeding here.

The latter precision problem seems no less intractable. Judgements about the degree of difficulty a disease places on the performance of a particular set of activities will surely always just be 'guesstimates', and in many instances it will be impossible to choose rationally between different judgements. Individuals will disagree about how difficult a disease makes it to pursue a particular set of activities, and there seems to be no rational way to resolve their disagreements.

Secondly, while there might seem to be a good case to be made for being sensitive both to the number of plans a disease curtails and to the severity of curtailment, it seems far from clear how we are supposed to 'sum' both considerations into an overall assessment of the impact a disease has on the normal opportunity range. Imagine we overcame both the precision problems set out above. How would we decide whether a disease that makes it 20% more difficult to pursue thirty reasonable life plans has a greater or lesser impact on the normal range than a disease that makes it 30% more difficult to pursue twenty reasonable life plans? (In practice, things will probably be much more complex than this, since most diseases will not have 'flat rate' severity, e.g. they will make it 15% more difficult to pursue ten particular plans, and 25% more difficult to pursue another different ten plans, etc.). Perhaps the most straightforward thing to do is to adopt a simple arithmetic approach, where the impact a disease has on the normal range is just taken to be the number of plans it frustrates multiplied by the extent to which it frustrates those plans. But is such a simple approach acceptable? Several objections could be raised, with perhaps the most prominent being that it treats all reasonable life plans as alike in terms of their value: any twenty reasonable life plans will count as twenty 'units' for the purpose of the calculation. Many will feel that this glosses over salient differences in the value of life plans: we ought not to consider the frustration of twenty life plans marked by the pursuit of totally trivial leisure activities (counting blades of grass on lawns, say)[14] to be equal in value to the equally severe frustration of twenty life plans given over to the pursuit of worthwhile and socially useful careers.

This leads to the third problematic area. While most will object to the idea that all reasonable life plans are completely equal in value, there would still seem to be a good deal of disagreement regarding exactly how much value to accord to particular life plans and about how to rank plans as being more or less valuable. This is very reminiscent of the problem I set out in the previous section of how we rank different kinds of medical benefits as being more or less important. I hinted there that what underlay those disagreements were deeper disagreements about the relative value of the things that medical benefits allow us to do or be: when thinking about the value of a medical benefit, individuals will inevitably consider how that particular physiological restoration will fit in with the kind of life they want to lead. Here however we have gone directly to the core of the problem, bypassing medical benefits to go straight to a consideration of the value of the things these benefits allow us to do. I would press similar points here to those I set out above. The

[14]　The grass-counter example, much used in moral and political philosophy as an example of a worthless pastime, comes originally from John Rawls (1972) p. 432.

bulk of the disagreement that currently pertains over which life plans are most valuable can be considered to be reasonable, since we currently lack the kinds of reasons required to demonstrate rationally that some life plans are more or less valuable than others.[15] As such, we should consider these disagreements to be at least currently intractable, and accept that it seems very unlikely that they will be overcome in anything like an appropriate timeframe.

Given these problems, it is perhaps no surprise that Daniels himself never built on the 'basis' provided by his opportunity approach in addressing the question of which sub-optimal distribution of health care to prefer. In fact, in his more recent work on the topic, Daniels argues that 'general principles of justice' such as the principle of fair equality of opportunity are not 'determinate' enough to give us answers to this question, and 'we have no consensus on more fine-grained principles that do' (Daniels and Sabin, 2002, p. 30). So while we might *like* to answer the question set out above — exactly what sub-optimal distribution of health care is demanded by justice — Daniels is sceptical that our principles of justice as they currently stand are up to the task.

This does not mean, however, that Daniels has given up on finding *any* principled answer to the question of health care distribution. In his more recent work, frequently conducted in collaboration with James E. Sabin, Daniels has worked on developing a different kind of approach that makes use of the concept of procedural fairness. This is his so-called 'accountability for reasonableness' approach. Daniels believes we must retreat to some kind of fair procedure to solve health care allocation problems because there is simply no alternative — he claims that '[w]hen we lack consensus on principles that tell us what is fair, or even when we have general principles but are burdened by reasonable disagreements about how they apply, we may nevertheless find a process or procedure that most can accept as fair to those who are affected by such decisions' (Daniels and Sabin, 2002, p. 4). Daniels believes that individuals have certain 'regulative interests' that derive from their being participants in, and the objects of, fair procedures. He claims that the terms of participation of these procedures must be ones 'we can imagine everyone agreeing to' (Daniels, 1996, p. 329). Because no-one can 'reasonably reject' the terms of fair procedures in the light of their regulative interests, such procedures can be considered to embody a fundamental commitment to

---

[15] I say the 'bulk' of the disagreement to account for the relatively small number of cases where we do seem to be in agreement and where we do seem to possess these kinds of reasons, e.g. when we consider the relative merits of life plans given over to grass counting versus those given over to the pursuit of worthwhile and socially useful careers.

the moral equality of persons: 'This account is egalitarian because it can be justified to everyone' (Daniels, 1996, p. 329).

Daniels divides regulative interests into recognition, equitable treatment, and deliberative responsibility. His aim is not to specify a fair procedure that *optimally* or *uniquely* satisfies these interests, but rather to formulate one that cannot reasonably be rejected on the basis of any of them, and which can therefore be considered fair. Our interest in recognition stems from the interest each of us has in having a public role as a participant in fair procedures. Being denied such a role is, claims Daniels, a denial of moral status. Our interest in equitable treatment derives from our being the *subjects* of public policy. Given this, we expect fair procedures to contain safeguards to prohibit decisions that violate basic principles of justice. Finally, our interest in deliberative responsibility comes from our interest in creating public policy that is the result of debates that are adequately informed, open to a wide range of competing views, and conducted in such a way as to 'responsibly assess' these views (Daniels, 1996, p. 330).

Daniels then outlines a procedure for settling questions of health care resource allocation which has these features:

i)   a decision-making commission is either elected or appointed by appropriate authorities, and is representative of society at large;

ii)   the commission is aware of the effects of the various possible decisions on all categories of patients;

iii)   it must publicly hear arguments from the various interested parties;

iv)   it must subject preliminary decisions to public discussion;

v)   it must vote on a rationing policy within a reasonable time period.

Daniels believes that, while procedures such as this might not resolve questions of health care resource allocation 'from the point of view of moral reasoning', they do at least supply what he calls 'morally *acceptable*' outcomes in real time:

> I want to emphasise the degree to which we are relying on a democratic procedure to resolve what is an openly moral issue. We might agree it does not resolve the issue, at least from the point of view of moral reasoning, but it resolves it from the point of view of the need to formulate policy and to act on it. In thinking about our regulative interests, then, the justification will emphasise points about our reliance as moral agents on a procedure that aims at morally acceptable outcomes. (Daniels, 1996, p. 331).

Here Daniels seems to rely on a distinction between moral outcomes established by processes of moral reasoning, and something weaker he calls a 'morally acceptable outcome' established by a fair procedure of deliberation culminating in a vote. He believes that no one could reasonably reject the procedure outlined above on grounds that it fails to satisfy regulative interests. The fact the commission is representative ensures our interest in recognition. Our interest in equitable treatment is satisfied by making sure deliberations and outcomes do not offend our accepted general principles of justice: this would rule out, for example, racist outcomes that gave priority access to health care to members of a specific racial group, simply in virtue of their being a member of that group. Our interest in deliberative responsibility can only be satisfied if we feel that the procedure, which is 'designed to stand in for us as moral agents', has addressed all 'relevant considerations…as well as it is reasonable for them to be given time and other resource constraints'. This means that 'all relevant views and information' must be considered and if need be reconsidered, and that experts ought to be invited when appropriate (Daniels, 1996, p. 331). Daniels believes that after an appropriate amount of deliberation it is morally acceptable to then resolve the issue by voting. He admits this might not be the 'ideal' way to resolve a moral issue, but if due consideration has been given to moral reasoning in the pre-vote deliberation then it is at least an acceptable method:

> We may not be happy about having to resolve a moral question of policy with moral implications simply by vote, but if the deliberative process is as open as possible to moral considerations, we may have to settle for an outcome that rests on voting. The point is to try to make the process bring out the best in its participants by way of moral deliberation … Though it does not follow that the majority is right, it is not unreasonable to rely on it under the constraints I have described. (Daniels, 1996, pp. 331–2).

Daniels believes that commissions structured along the lines outlined above have to be 'accountable for the reasonableness' of the decisions they reach. Accountability for reasonableness can be attained if their decision-making is structured by these four conditions:

i) Publicity Condition: the rationing decisions and the rationales behind them must be publicly accessible. Daniels believes that meeting this condition will improve both 'formal' fairness since like issues will be treated similarly, and also 'substantive' fairness since careful evaluation of reasons means we are more likely to uncover flaws in moral reasoning which can then be rectified (thus improving the fairness of the decision).

ii) Relevance Condition: The rationales should provide a 'reasonable' construal of how the healthcare system ought to provide 'value for money' in meeting the various healthcare needs of the population under 'reasonable resource constraints' (Daniels and Sabin, 2002, p. 45). A 'reasonable' construal is one which 'appeals to evidence, reasons, and principles that are accepted as relevant by fair-minded people who are disposed to finding mutually justifiable terms of co-operation' (Daniels and Sabin, 2002, p. 45). Daniels seems to think that fair-minded people ought *actually to accept* these reasons, not just be subject to decisions drawn from reasons they could not reasonably reject (regardless of whether or not they actually accept these reasons). Such 'fair-minded people' will not accept as relevant self-interested reasons e.g. 'I want priority to be given to treatment x because this will benefit me'. Because rationing decisions will always disadvantage some patients and advantage others, merely demanding to be advantaged is not, for Daniels, a relevant reason. However, if a decision disadvantages some particular group of individuals more than another group who are identical in all relevant respects, then this must be considered a relevant consideration. By ensuring only relevant reasons feature, when the issue inevitably comes to a vote the losing minority can console themselves that they have lost to a set of reasons they can at least accept as properly applying to the issue in hand, even if they do not view such reasons as being persuasive. Daniels places 'philosophical' and 'moral' views (including full accounts about what kinds of activities and projects are of value in human life) in the category of inadmissible reasons, since '[r]easonable people differ in their religious, philosophical, and moral views, and yet we must seek terms of fair co-operation that rest on justifications acceptable to all' (Daniels and Sabin, 1997, pp. 338–39).

iii) Appeals Condition: It ought to be possible for decisions to be challenged, such as when further evidence or new arguments emerge.

iv) Enforcement Condition: A voluntary or public body ought to regulate the decision-making process to ensure that conditions i –iii are met.

The main advantage of the accountability for reasonableness approach is its willingness to tackle head-on the fact of reasonable disagreement. When thinking about how to distribute health care resources it is very natural to bring to bear views about what are the most important medical benefits, or indeed more fundamental views about what are the most important kinds of activities and projects in human life. Natural or not, these views are the subject of reasonable disagreement that does not seem to be tractable within the timescale in which we must allocate health care. The accountability for reasonableness approach is an admirable attempt to tread a fine line in response to this problem. It is not a straightforwardly subjective approach (in the sense set out in the previous section), since we do not go straight to a vote where individuals can simply express their preferences. Prior to the vote, we must have a period of deliberation where we are encouraged to debate the relative merits of various 'relevant' considerations bearing on the problem in hand. Presumably, any agreements that are struck during this phase of deliberation can be enacted. However, the approach also accepts that these deliberations are unlikely to result in agreement on all the outstanding issues, and once we hit disagreement we then resort to a voting mechanism. In this sense, the approach recognises and respects the fact of reasonable disagreement without lapsing into a purely subjective response.

However, many who think that it is considerations of justice that ground our obligations to supply health care in the first place might be left feeling rather disappointed by the accountability for reasonableness approach. While the approach is undeniably principled (drawing as it does on notions of procedural fairness), we might still think it is something of a 'second best' scenario when there is no real connection between the principles of justice that obligate us to supply health in the first instance and the process for generating and justifying particular distributions. It might be countered that the principle of procedural fairness is *itself* a principle of justice, or is at least derivable from considerations of justice. However, even if this point is conceded, the point would remain that Daniels has been forced to accept a disjunction between the *particular* principle of justice that grounds the obligation to supply health care in the first place (for Daniels, this is the principle of fair equality of opportunity), and the principles used in specifying and justifying particular distributions. Some adherents of justice based approaches to health care distribution might view such an acceptance as unduly pessimistic, and urge us to try harder to overcome the disjunction.[16]

One philosopher who might hold to something like this view is Ronald Dworkin. Like Daniels, Dworkin comes down against the usage of ideas that are currently the subject of reasonable disagreement in resolving the question of health care resource allocation. He is particularly sceptical about the usage of concepts such as benefit or goodness: he describes these as 'contested ethical concepts', and argues that the idea we should distribute health care money in order to maximise goodness or benefit 'means that it should be distributed in whatever way will make the lives of citizens better lives to have lived, and that goal cannot be restated without controversy, as the goal of making lives more pleasant, or economically more productive, or socially more beneficial' (Dworkin, 1993, p. 887). And, also like Daniels, Dworkin believes that our obligations to supply health care are obligations of justice. However, in contrast to Daniels's accountability for reasonableness method, Dworkin sets out an approach to health care distribution that avoids the kind of disjunction described above.Dworkin's essay 'Justice and the

---

[16] Daniels is explicitly pessimistic about the principle of fair equality of opportunity ever being 'determinate' enough to resolve the various disputes about which distributions of health care 'are compatible with the objective of best protecting fair equality of opportunity under resource constraints' (Daniels and Sabin, 2002, p.32).

high cost of health care' opens with a lament on the state of health care distribution in the present day USA (Dworkin, 2000). Those Americans wealthy enough to purchase the very best insurance plans receive most of the available health care, including very expensive 'cutting-edge' treatments that often confer only small benefits. Meanwhile, about one quarter of the population has very limited health insurance or none at all. Dworkin believes this distribution cannot possibly be just, since it stems directly from market transactions made from a starting point of injustice: the huge differences in wealth that drive this particular distribution of health care are, in his view, simply unjust. He claims we can get an idea about what a just distribution of health care *would* look like by thinking about the sorts of treatments that would be purchased by individuals operating in a hypothetical market who were not starting out from a position of unfairly increased or decreased purchasing power. This is the first of the working assumptions in Dworkin's so-called 'hypothetical insurance' model:

1) 'The distribution of wealth and income is as fair as it possibly can be' (Dworkin, 2000, p. 311).

The model contains two further assumptions:

2) Information about the risks, benefits, and side effects of all medical procedures are known by everyone.

3) No one has any information about the likelihood of any *particular* individual (including themselves) contracting a particular disease or suffering a particular kind of accident, though everyone does have full knowledge about the incidence rates of diseases and accidents in the general population.

Assumption two is designed to ensure that individuals are in a position to make *rational* decisions about what types of health care to purchase. As things stand at the moment, Dworkin believes some people purchase too much or too little health care coverage because they lack important information about the benefits, risks, and side-effects of various types of medical treatment. Of course, individuals operating under the conditions Dworkin sets out will not be able to make the decision that is most rational *for them*. This kind of decision would require knowledge of their personal health status and risk profile, knowledge denied by Dworkin in assumption three. This assumption is designed to ensure a measure of impartiality: while individuals can make rational purchasing decisions based on the *general* probability of various diseases and accidents occurring in the population at large, they cannot make decisions based on their *particular* likelihood of incurring specific medical conditions or falling foul of certain kinds of accidents.

Dworkin asks us to imagine the distribution of health care that would emerge as a result of decisions made in a hypothetical society structured in line with these three working assumptions. These decisions are left to individuals operating in as free a market as possible, where health care providers are free to charge whatever they like for their services. The state does not fund any health care, and there are no non-health related benefits (such as tax concessions) for those who buy expensive insurance plans. Dworkin claims we can draw two conclusions from running the hypothetical insurance model. The first is that whatever the transformed society spends on health care in total is the *just* amount for that society to spend. There can be no claim in justice, thinks Dworkin, for that society to spend any more or any less than this amount. The second conclusion is that however health care is distributed in the transformed society is the just mode of distribution for that society. Dworkin thinks that '[t]hese claims follow directly from an extremely appealing assumption: that a just distribution is one that well-informed people create for themselves by individual choices, provided that the economic system and the distribution of wealth in the community in which these choices are made are themselves just' (Dworkin, 2000, p. 313).

Dworkin believes these two conclusions can guide thinking about how health care ought to be distributed in our actual, non-ideal world. While it is difficult to say with certainty exactly what sort of health care coverage each individual in society would purchase under the ideal conditions outlined above, Dworkin believes 'we can nevertheless make some judgements with confidence that they would fit the needs and preferences of most contemporary Americans' (Dworkin, 2000, p. 313). For example, he claims it would be irrational to spend some of our just amount of resources to insure ourselves for expensive life support should we fall into a vegetative state from which there is no hope of recovery. Conversely, it *would* be rational to purchase access to decent quality nursing care for our old age (we all stand a good chance of becoming old and infirm). Using this method — thinking about what 'most prudent people' would purchase in a hypothetical situation of justice — Dworkin believes he can arrive at a set of medical treatments that justice demands *all* should have access to now. If nearly all prudent persons would buy certain forms of health care in the hypothetical market then the reason many citizens currently do not have access to such health care is 'almost certainly' because their society is not structured as justly as this (Dworkin, 2000, p. 315). It is simply because of injustice that they lack this level of health care coverage, and it is therefore (thinks Dworkin) a matter of justice that the unfairness is rectified and they do gain this amount and type of health care.

Dworkin does recognise that there will be some individuals who would prefer to purchase more specialised insurance plans, such as those with a special interest in maintaining some particular physical function, or those who are either unusually risk averse or unusually risk taking in their behaviour. Nevertheless, he thinks that 'it seems fair to construct a mandatory coverage scheme on the basis of what all but a small number of people would think appropriate', while allowing those who wish to spend extra on more specialised treatments to do so out of their own resources: provided, he admits, 'they can afford it'. Dworkin believes that including these more specialised preferences in the basic insurance package that is guaranteed to all citizens would actually constitute 'a disservice to justice' (Dworkin, 2000, pp. 314–5).

So, by using his hypothetical insurance method Dworkin believes we can arrive at a set of 'necessary and appropriate' medical interventions that ought, as a matter of justice, to be available to all members of society (Dworkin, 2000, p. 316). The method can tell us how much of its gross product a society ought to spend on health care, and which medical services ought to be provided, without making recourse to controversial ideas about the relative value of medical benefits or ideas about what kinds of activities and projects are valuable in life, since it utilises only the aggregated *preferences* of individuals. These individuals might or might not consciously link their preferences to more or less worked out conceptions of what is valuable in life, but for the purposes of Dworkin's model they *need* not. All they need claim is that, under the conditions of justice Dworkin describes, 'these are my preferences'.

Moreover, it might seem that, in contrast to Daniels's accountability for reasonableness approach, Dworkin's method provides a satisfying linkage between the considerations of justice that lead us to supply health care in the first place and the process by which we specify and justify particular distributions of such care. For Dworkin, the obligation in justice to supply health care stems from the fact that rational persons operating in a hypothetical situation of justice would take steps to ensure they had access to medical treatment. This fact allows us to say that it is usually an injustice if individuals in the real world are denied access to health care (as is the case for many individuals on low incomes in the contemporary USA). The method Dworkin uses for specifying and justifying a particular distribution of care is to think about the *particular kinds* of treatments that would be purchased by nearly all rational individuals operating in this hypothetical situation of justice.

However, while it might offer this comparative advantage, Dworkin's model is not without its problems. It could be argued, for example, that the package of care that emerges from the model is unacceptably small. In order for a treatment to be included in the package of health care that ought in justice to be made available to all citizens, Dworkin demands that it must be the kind of treatment that would be purchased by nearly all prudent persons operating in his hypothetical market. It might legitimately be wondered, however, exactly how *extensive* is the set of medical treatments for which it is reasonable to assume there would be this high level of agreement in the hypothetical market. There are, of course, likely to be some treatments that all rational people would purchase: emergency appendix removal for example, and many other relatively cheap, safe, lifesaving procedures. Given the low cost and massive benefit of these treatments, any other decision would be irrational. Similarly, there are likely to be some treatments that no rational person would purchase in this market (e.g. Dworkin gives the example of costly life support when we are in irreversible comas). The converse ratio applies here: given the very high cost and negligible benefits, a decision to purchase would be irrational.

However, there also seem to be an enormous number of treatments that, it seems very likely to assume, many rational individuals would choose to purchase, and which many other *equally rational* individuals would not. Modern chemotherapy drugs are a good example. Oncology is one of the most research-active areas of modern medicine, and as a result there is now a huge range of chemotherapy drugs. Many of these are expensive, and while they cannot cure the patient's cancer, they can usually provide extra months of good quality life (often in the 'prime of life' period, since cancer is not exclusively a disease of old age). Would 'nearly all' prudent persons choose to purchase these drugs as part of their insurance plan? Or would 'nearly all' choose not to? It is surely plausible to assume that many prudent individuals would, and many would not. Many would choose to purchase these treatments because the diseases they treat (cancers) are relatively common, and the benefits they confer are, although small, deemed not insignificant. Many others would choose not to purchase these treatments because, in their view, an extra few months of life does not justify the high cost of the drug. Neither of these decisions — either to purchase, or not to purchase — is more rational than the other. The different purchasing decisions here are to be explained not in terms of degrees of rationality, but simply in terms of differences in individual preferences.

Chemotherapy drugs are just one example of the kinds of 'middling' treatments over which it is not plausible to expect near unanimity of preference. It would seem there are many other medical treatments that are relevantly similar to chemotherapy drugs: they are fairly expensive, and they confer 'smallish' benefits the value of which can reasonably be disputed. Examples include the many costly forms of medical and surgical palliative care, forms of physiotherapy that bring small but significant gains in mobility, expensive ophthalmology procedures that can restore an element of lost eyesight, fertility treatments (reasonable people disagree about how important it is to reproduce), and drug treatments for chronic neurological conditions that can bring about some

reductions in symptoms.[17] Since equally rational individuals are likely
to disagree about the value of these treatments *none* would be included
in the package that emerges from Dworkin's hypothetical insurance
procedure.

Of course, Dworkin might well be untroubled by this outcome. In his
view, near unanimity of preference is a necessary condition on the justice of any particular distribution of health care. It would be, for him, a
'disservice to justice' to 'force' all citizens to have an insurance plan that
would be favoured by only a sub-set of their number (Dworkin, 2000,
p. 315). It might well be the case that in societies such as ours, which are
marked by the kinds of reasonable disagreements discussed above, the
requirement of near unanimity of preference means the package of
health care we guarantee to all citizens will be relatively basic in character (since it will exclude the many middling treatments I describe
above). But Dworkin might retort that this is an acceptable consequence.
Justice demands near unanimity, and under conditions of reasonable
pluralism the health care package that emerges from his procedure is the
best we can hope for. This package will reflect whatever level of agreement there is in society, reflecting the small area of intersection amongst
all the diverse preferences that abound. Where this agreement runs out
the boundaries of the basic package are drawn, and indeed *ought* to be
drawn. The hypothetical insurance method excludes all contested preferences, and it is a demand of justice that it does so. Why *should* collective
resources be used to supply medical treatments that only a sub-set of citizens would prefer to purchase in the hypothetical insurance market?
Individuals with specialised health care preferences (i.e. preferences
that are not shared nearly unanimously) can satisfy these preferences by
privately purchasing 'top-up' insurance over and above the basic insurance package guaranteed to all citizens as a matter of justice — provided
they can afford it.

However, we might wonder whether justice is in fact well served by
Dworkin's model. While there is no *particular* package of treatments
more extensive than the one that emerges from Dworkin's method that
would be purchased by nearly all individuals operating in the hypothet-

---

[17] Specifically on the latter kind of treatments, the UK's National Institute for
Clinical Excellence (discussed at length by Howard Glennerster in the next
chapter) recently decided to withhold public funding for two drug treatments for
multiple sclerosis (beta interferon and glatiramer acetate), on grounds that 'the
modest clinical benefit appears to be outweighed ... by very high cost' (the full
ruling can be found at www.nice.org.uk/pdf/betainterferonfad.pdf).
Unsurprisingly, many multiple sclerosis sufferers and their lobbying groups
disagreed and argued that the benefits, although small, were significant enough
to merit the costs. This is an example of precisely the kind of reasonable
disagreement over 'middling' treatments with which I am concerned here.

ical insurance market, it is likely that nearly all rational individuals operating in such a market would choose to purchase a package that is more extensive than Dworkin's basic package — even if the particular more extensive package purchased would differ from person to person. In other words, nearly all rational individuals operating in the hypothetical market will want more than is in the Dworkinian package, although they will disagree about what the additional components should be. There might be some individuals for whom the Dworkinian package happens to contain *all* the treatments they would purchase in the hypothetical market, but they are likely to be few in number. As I claimed above, the range of treatments over which there is likely to be reasonable disagreement — that is, disagreement between equally rational individuals caused by their different preferences — is likely to be huge. The sheer number of these treatments makes it likely that nearly all individuals will choose to purchase at least some of them in the hypothetical insurance market. Dworkin himself claims it would be a 'disservice to justice' to force all individuals to have insurance plans containing treatments that they would not have purchased in the hypothetical market. If it is a disservice to justice to force all individuals to have more extensive coverage than they would have purchased in the hypothetical market, it is presumably also a disservice to justice to force all individuals to have *less* extensive insurance than they would have purchased in this market. This latter outcome is guaranteed by the near unanimity condition.

Thus, it is not the case that Dworkin's method isolates the full extent of the agreement about health care distribution that will exist even in societies marked by a plurality of reasonable opinions about what are the most important medical treatments. If I am right about the number and kinds of treatments that would be excluded from his basic package, it is likely that nearly all rational individuals would want a more extensive package of health insurance than Dworkin's basic package. Dworkin makes it plain that the results of the hypothetical insurance method are supposed to apply to 'our own, imperfect and unjust community' (Dworkin, 2000, p. 313). Thus, even though in the workings of the hypothetical market there is an assumption of a just distribution of resources, the results of the experiment are taken to apply to real societies where resources are *not* distributed justly. This means that those individuals with an unjustly large amount of resources will have little trouble securing for themselves the extra treatments they desire, whereas those with an unjustly small amount will face significant problems, and may have to forego many treatments.

Note that this problem of insufficient provision would not necessarily arise with Daniels's accountability for reasonableness approach, since the threshold level of agreement required for public provision of a health care good on that model would appear to be less than near unanimity. After an appropriate period of deliberation, the method calls for a vote. Daniels gives no indication that this is anything other than a standard simple majoritarian procedure, so nothing as stringent as near unanimity would be required to carry the vote. This means it is certainly *possible* for treatments excluded from Dworkin's basic package to be publicly funded on the accountability for reasonableness approach. To take just one example: consider again fairly expensive chemotherapy drugs that confer modest but not insignificant benefits and which are excluded from Dworkin's basic package because enough citizens to breach the near unanimity condition would choose not to purchase them on the hypothetical market. On the accountability for reasonableness approach it is at least possible for this treatment to receive public funding if after an appropriate period of deliberation of the kind Daniels favours a simple majority of citizens vote for the treatment to be publicly funded.

So, there seem to be symmetrical benefits and drawbacks in the approaches set out by Daniels and Dworkin. Daniels's approach suffers from being disconnected from the principles of justice that he thinks ground our obligation to supply health care in the first instance (considerations of fair equality of opportunity), though the approach is capable of justifying a more extensive package of health care than emerges from Dworkin's hypothetical insurance method. For its part, Dworkin's method embodies no such disjunction between the considerations of justice that ground obligations to supply health care in the first instance and those used to specify and justify determinate distributions, though the package of care that emerges from the model would be considered insufficient by nearly everyone. Given this seeming symmetry, could we simply combine the approaches? Could we recognise that the basic package that emerges from Dworkin's procedure ought in justice to be made available to everyone, but augment this package with additional treatments that have emerged as candidates for public funding through the deliberations and voting of the accountability for reasonableness approach?

One major downside of any such combining of the approaches would be the creation of a new disjunction. Were we to combine the approaches in this way, there would be a disjunction between the considerations that lead us to supply the kinds and amounts of health care in the Dworkinian basic package (considerations about what most rational persons would purchase in a hypothetical situation of justice) and those that lead us to supply treatments over and above what is in this package (concerning the outcomes of fair procedures that satisfy relevant regulative interests). Moreover, these different considerations appear be in tension with one another. Dworkin seems to believe that near unanimity of preference under the conditions he describes is a *necessary condition* on the justice of any distribution of health care: he describes the public funding of treatments that cannot command this level of approval as constituting a 'disservice to justice'. As such, the less demanding level of approval utilised by the accountability for reasonableness approach (i.e. simple majority voting) might well allow for the provision of more treatments, but would fail the test of justice set by Dworkin's approach. The two approaches do not seem to combine happily.

Given this, are those who wish to take a justice-based perspective on health care resource allocation destined to choose between the approaches? Must they opt either for the coherence of the Dworkinian approach and the limited package of health care it justifies or the disjunction embodied in Daniels's approach and the possibility of justifying a more extensive package of health care? The choice might not be as stark as this if we reflect a little on the shared aspirations that lie behind both approaches. Both Daniels and Dworkin are sensitive to the fact that many of the ideas that might naturally feature in our thinking about how to distribute health care resources—such as ideas about the relative value of the different kinds of activities and projects that medical treatments can allow us to pursue—are currently the subject of disagreement. This disagreement is reasonable (we lack reasons to rank positions in the disagreements as being better or worse), and seemingly intractable within an appropriate timeframe. Both Daniels and Dworkin also argue that our thinking about how to distribute health care resources ought to be free of these reasonably contested ideas. Since public resources are being used to fund a package of health care that will cover all members of the community the construction of this package ought not to favour the views and opinions of particular subsets of citizens. Daniels's response is to set out a putatively fair procedure that attempts to forge agreement on a particular distribution of health care via deliberation (free of contested ideas) followed by voting. Dworkin's response is to isolate the kind of nearly unanimous agreement that would obtain if individuals were to operate in a hypothetical situation of justice.

However, if we drop the assumption that our goal is to construct a singular package of health care to be provided to all citizens it becomes possible to discern the outlines of an alternative justice-based approach to health care distribution that overcomes the problems in both Daniels's and Dworkin's approaches. What if we were to divide health care resources in such a way as to give individual citizens the means to construct their own health benefit packages, perhaps by way of a publicly funded health care voucher? This approach might seem to hold some promise. If publicly funded vouchers were sufficiently valuable they could allow all citizens to insure themselves to a level beyond that provided by Dworkin's basic package: individual citizens, irrespective of their personal income, would be able to insure themselves closer to the level they would have chosen in Dworkin's hypothetical insurance market. However, since we would not be supplying a singular package of health care to all citizens, no individual would be forced to have any particular kinds of health care that they would not have purchased in this market. And, if the method used to strike the value of the vouchers drew upon the same considerations of justice we believe ground the obligation to supply health care in the first place, we would avoid the disjunction in Daniels's approach.

It might be possible to amend Dworkin's approach to health care distribution in such a way as to achieve these goals. Although the particular recommendations Dworkin makes about which treatments should be publicly funded are based on his own speculations about the likely preferences of prudent persons operating on the hypothetical market, he argues that his method will work best in practice if these decisions are made by an 'agency … made up of representatives of different groups that might be expected to make such judgements differently' (Dworkin, 2002, p. 317). The point of constructing such a commission and making it demographically representative is, I assume, to represent accurately the full span of decisions that would be made were each individual in society to think about what they would want to purchase on the hypothetical market. I further assume that the reason for constructing a commission rather than taking a society-wide poll is one of pragmatism: it is impractical to ask all members of large societies to embark on this task. Not only will it be immensely expensive and time-consuming to collect and collate the data, there are likely to be problems of representativeness since the social skewing so often evident in electoral turnouts would almost certainly be replicated in polling of this magnitude.

Continuing the theme of pragmatism, we ought not to place too much emphasis on the idea of trying to give representation to, as Dworkin puts it, 'groups' in society likely to make distinctive purchasing decisions. While individuals of similar backgrounds are likely to converge to some degree with regard to these decisions it is unlikely that there are neatly demarcated groups in society with non-overlapping memberships made up of individuals who would make identical or nearly identical purchasing decisions on the hypothetical market. Most individuals are members of a number of social groupings each marked by its own shared understandings, and it seems likely that individuals will draw on many of these understandings when making purchasing decisions. In the broad run of cases there will be no simple correlation between membership of a particular social group (or set of groups) and the making of distinctive purchasing decisions on the hypothetical market. It might seem, then, that the best we can do when constructing such a commission is to make it large enough to ensure all or nearly all of the social groups in society are represented, and that it mirrors society's main demographic features (e.g. the relative proportions of different ethnic groups and ages on the commission should reflect the spread found in society at large).

Having constructed the commission, we would then issue instructions to its members. Assume that we can secure agreement on what counts as a just amount of resources, at least for the purposes of running the commission.[18] Assume also that we can provide full information to each commissioner about the general population-wide incidence rates of various diseases and their effects, and about the costs and benefits of various treatments. Further assume that commissioners are capable of adequately processing all this information. Each commissioner would be asked to think about the set of medical treatments they would wish to purchase when possessed of this amount of resources and information. The commissioners would also be asked to operate only with the general incidence rates, and to try to forget about their own personal health-related risk profile. It is important that they try to do so because each commissioner is effectively standing in for a large number of individuals in society at large, most of whom will not share the commissioner's own personal risk profile. It will be impossible to give representation on the commission to each of the vast range of risk profiles that abound in society. Given this it seems fair to ensure that, as far as possible, no particular risk profile is represented.

The set of treatments that would be purchased by nearly all members of the commission are the ones that would make up Dworkin's basic package. But what if we were to focus not on the set of treatments for which there happens to be near unanimity of preference, but on the complete list of treatments that would be purchased by each commissioner? The complete list for each commissioner is made up of all those treatments that would be purchased by nearly all other members of the commission, plus all the additional treatments the commissioner would choose to purchase in the hypothetical insurance market. These additional treatments are the ones I described above, i.e. the many 'middling' treatments whose value will be disputed by equally rational individuals. If my previous arguments are sound, nearly all the commissioners would choose to purchase at least some of these additional treatments in the hypothetical market. Thus, almost of all of these complete lists will be more extensive than the set of treatments in Dworkin's basic package.

With lists of medical treatments as determinate as these complete lists, I assume it will be possible to work out how much it would cost to supply any individual commissioner with all the treatments on her list. Of

---

[18] Dworkin himself believes it is possible to secure this kind of agreement (Dworkin, 2002, pp. 311–12).

course, this cost will vary from commissioner to commissioner – the additional treatments that make up the complete lists are, after all, the subject of reasonable disagreement. Some commissioners will choose to purchase only a small number of fairly inexpensive additional treatments, preferring instead to spend their just amount of resources on other goods. Other members of the commission might place a higher premium on aspects of physical health and would use their just amount of resources to purchase a significant number of fairly expensive additional treatments in the hypothetical market. However, despite the fact that the costs of the complete lists will vary, it might be possible to use costings of complete lists to justify the value of health care vouchers.

For simplicity, assume a commission made up of ten members, A to J. Let us also assume that Dworkin is right to claim that, when distributing publicly funded goods in societies marked by reasonable disagreement about the relative value of these goods, justice demands a distribution that would meet the approval of nearly all citizens. Let us further assume that the members of our ten member commission can agree about what counts as near unanimity on the commission: say they agree that the threshold of nearly unanimous agreement lies at eight out of ten (i.e. anything less than 8 out of 10 does not count as nearly unanimous agreement).With these background assumptions in place, it might be possible to justify the value of health care vouchers in the following way. Imagine we cost the total list of treatments each commissioner would purchase on the hypothetical market, and end up with the following figures: commissioner A's total list would cost 100, B's would cost 115, C's 120, D's 125, E's 130, F's 135, G's 140, H's 145, I's 150, and J's 180. We would then begin with a suggested voucher value of 100 – the cost of the cheapest package that would be purchased by any member of the commission – and ask the commissioners if vouchers should be *at least* this valuable. Presumably, all ten commissioners would agree. We would then increase the putative voucher value to 101, and ask the same question. Presumably, the agreement would go down to nine out of ten – commissioner A (who would spend only 100 on health care in the hypothetical market) would object, claiming that vouchers ought not to be this valuable. Although vouchers of this value would allow her to access all the treatments she would have purchased in the hypothetical market, she will object to what she sees as excessive amounts of public resources being devoted to health care at the expense of other valued social projects. We would continue in this incremental way until the agreement dropped to seven out of ten. Looking at the figures I have provided, we can predict this would occur when we suggest a voucher value of 121 – it is at this point that commissioner C will dissent, joining the two earlier dissenters (A and B). Given that there is prior agreement that the threshold for near unanimity on the commission is eight out of ten, the highest voucher value that can secure nearly unanimous agreement on the commission is 120.

This voucher value will in all likelihood allow individuals to access all the treatments that would be in Dworkin's basic package, plus at least some additional treatments. This is so because the value is based on the *total* lists of treatments that commission members would purchase on the hypothetical market. If my earlier arguments hold up, it is likely that nearly all the commissioners (assuming the commission is representative of society at large) will want to purchase more treatments than would be in the Dworkinian package. I tried to model this roughly in the figures listed above. Commissioner A speaks for the 10% or so of the population who would purchase only the treatments in the Dworkinian package (which would cost 100 to supply). Commissioners B to J represent the 90% of the population who would purchase more than is in this package, with the additional treatments purchased ranging from only a few fairly inexpensive ones (commissioner B) to many fairly expensive ones (commissioner J). Deriving a voucher value in the way I have described will allow all members of society to access additional treatments over and above those supplied in the Dworkinian basic package to the value of twenty (since the basic package costs 100).

Such a method for setting the value of health care vouchers is designed to satisfy Dworkin's demand that we ought to aim for near unanimity of preference. Clearly, a lot of work in securing this level of agreement on the commission I describe is done by phrasing the question asked of the commissioners in a particular way, i.e. 'Do you think health care vouchers should be *at least* this valuable?'. The 'at least' clause is a device to ensure that nearly unanimous agreement on a voucher value is at least *possible*. Were we to drop this clause and ask simply 'Do you think health care vouchers should be this valuable', there would be no hope of attaining *any* kind of agreement on the commission.

Clearly, some commissioners will be much more satisfied with the outcome of the voucher setting procedure than others. In the example I give above, commissioner C will be most satisfied — vouchers are just valuable enough to purchase all the health care she would choose to purchase on the hypothetical market, with no remainder. Members A and B will be satisfied in the sense that vouchers will be valuable enough to purchase all the health care they would have purchased in the hypothetical market, but will also be somewhat dissatisfied because what they would view as excessive public funds will be devoted to health care provision at the expense of other public services. Members D to J will also be dissatisfied, although for a different reason: vouchers will not be valuable enough for them to purchase all the treatments they would have purchased in the hypothetical market. D will be least dissatisfied in this

regard, and J will be most dissatisfied. Now, 120 is of course not the *only*
figure that would attain nearly unanimous agreement on the commission. Looking at the example I have provided, vouchers of any value
between 100 and 119 inclusive would also be met with nearly unanimous agreement when we ask the question 'Do you think vouchers
ought to be *at least* this valuable?'. However, fairness would seem to
demand that we somehow reflect decisions made at *both* ends of the purchasing spectrum — high and low. Setting the voucher value at the *highest* level that would be met with nearly unanimous agreement seems to
give the most recognition we can to the preferences of those members of
the commission at the higher end of the purchasing scale, without
thereby sacrificing near unanimity of preference. This seems fair.

The method I describe also seems to take seriously the fact of reasonable disagreement regarding what are the most important medical treatments. Since the commission is demographically representative of
society at large, the total lists of treatments constructed by the commissioners can be considered to be broadly representative of the entire span
of purchasing decisions that would be made were all individuals in the
society to operate on a Dworkinian hypothetical market. Since the
method I describe for justifying a voucher value from these total lists
does not unjustifiably privilege any particular list, the method cannot be
considered to unjustifiably privilege any particular set of ideas about the
relative value of different kinds of medical treatments.

Perhaps most importantly given the earlier discussion, this method
does not seem to involve any kind of disjunction between the considerations of justice that lead us to supply health care in the first instance and
those used in the process of specifying and justifying a particular distribution. This is unsurprising since the method is thoroughly Dworkinian
in inspiration, and coherence is, as I've argued above, one main virtue of
Dworkin's approach. We agree with Dworkin that the reason we ought
in justice to supply health care in the first instance is because nearly all
rational individuals placed in a hypothetical situation of justice would
choose to avail themselves of such care. The method used for striking the
value of health care vouchers draws heavily upon this idea. The commissioners are asked to list the treatments they would purchase when
placed within this very situation of justice. The workings of the commission are designed to secure the level of agreement Dworkin believes is a
necessary condition on the justice of any particular distribution, i.e. near
unanimity.

As well as involving no disjunction between different considerations
of justice, the approach I set out might offer another comparative advantage over Daniels's accountability for reasonableness method. I argued
earlier that Daniels's method offers the possibility of justifying a more
extensive set of treatments than is in the Dworkinian basic package,

since it seems to involve a simple majoritarian voting mechanism. Whether or not any particular treatment actually receives public funding is dependent on whether or not the relevant vote can be carried. Poorer citizens' access to particular treatments excluded from Dworkin's package is by no means guaranteed under Daniels's approach. Under a voucher system of the form I describe, where the value of the voucher is sufficient to purchase all the treatments included in Dworkin's package and some additional treatments, poorer citizens would seem to have a greater degree of control in accessing particular treatments not included in Dworkin's package. Their access to these treatments would not be subject to the contingencies of voting.

Of course, the approach I have set out here is merely one direction that those sympathetic to justice-based approaches to health care distribution might choose to take. There are many others. Some who are sympathetic to such approaches might agree there is merit in voucher-based systems when thinking about how to distribute health care resources in societies marked by reasonable disagreement about the relative value of different medical treatments, but disagree with the particular voucher system described above. They might, for example, query the idea that justice requires nearly unanimous agreement under certain kinds of conditions. This is a strong requirement, and on the system I set out above it serves to restrict the value of health care vouchers. Were we to drop the requirement, we might be able to justify health care vouchers of higher value. We could, for example, imagine arguments to the effect that it would be just to take an arithmetical average of the figures above (which would give a voucher value of 134) or to select the median figure (which would give a value of 132.5, which is midway between the figures of commissioners E and F).[19]

Others favourable to justice-based approaches to health care distribution might wish to retain the commitment to near unanimity as the appropriate level of agreement when settling important matters of justice, but express reservations about voucher systems per se. They might argue that moving away from the provision of single packages of health care accessed by large numbers of citizens towards voucher schemes will mean losing the considerable economies of scale that can be

---

[19] It might seem that the approach of selecting the median figure offers a comparative advantage over that of taking an arithmetical average since averages can be skewed by 'extreme' numbers at either end of the scale. Any member of a commission of the form I set out who constructs either an extravagantly lavish or an unusually small package of treatments would, arguably, be exerting an undue amount of influence on the overall figure extracted from the commission if this figure was derived by taking a simple average. It seems fairer for each commissioner to exert an *equal* influence on the figure arrived at, which would be the case were we to select the median figure.

wrought by using the former kind of system. As a result, there is a risk that using vouchers could result in less health care being distributed overall.[20] Another important concern is ensuring that the notorious information asymmetries in health care provision can be overcome: when using their health care vouchers, many citizens will need a source of reliable and impartial advice about what treatments are best for them to purchase.

Just as with basic benevolence approaches, then, there are a range of options open to those who would seek to develop justice-based approaches to the question of health care distribution. However, it might seem that there is *greater* scope to develop justice-based approaches than approaches grounded in considerations of basic benevolence. As I suggested above, basic benevolence approaches seem committed to the idea that there is an objective hierarchy of goods, with some goods occupying such an exalted position within the hierarchy that there are, under certain circumstances, obligations in basic benevolence to supply those goods. This commitment made it problematic for basic benevolence theorists to embrace subjective approaches to the ranking of different kinds of medical benefits as being more or less valuable. Justice based approaches can operate without any commitment to the notion that there is an objective hierarchy of goods — as I argued above, obligations in justice to supply particular goods need draw only on notions of *entitlement* to those goods, and can remain agnostic about their relative values.[21] Not having this commitment means that Daniels

---

[20] In response to this concern, there is nothing in the method I set out that would mitigate against the use of a 'mixed system' of health care provision. After running the commission, we could isolate the set of medical treatments that would be purchased by nearly all the commissioners: this would be the Dworkinian basic package of health care. It might well make good financial sense to supply this package to all citizens via a single provider capable of leveraging large economies of scale. We would then supply citizens with a voucher to purchase the particular additional treatments they prefer (in the model commission I set out above, this would be a voucher to the value of twenty). They would be free to use this voucher in procuring their favoured additional treatments from the provider of their choice, be it the provider of the basic Dworkinian package or some other organisation. Such a mixed system will ensure we preserve some of the economies of scale found in single provider systems, while providing citizens with the latitude to procure additional treatments from more specialised providers.

[21] This is of course not to say that conceptions of justice *must* avoid taking a stand on the relative value of different goods, only that respectable exemplars of such conceptions *can* do so. As I explained above, the capability approaches developed by both Sen and Nussbaum, which are concerned with the objective value of certain kinds of goods, are themselves justice-based approaches. I also explained that neither Sen nor Nussbaum develops an objective ranking of goods that is fine-grained enough to make much headway with the problem of health care

and Dworkin can develop approaches to health care distribution without the need to justify any kind of objective ranking of health care goods. In societies marked by reasonable and currently intractable disagreement about what are the most important such goods, this would seem to be a considerable advantage.

Conclusions

The problem of health care distribution — essentially, the existence of a genuine mismatch in even wealthy societies between available funds and what it is now possible to purchase in the vast and expanding medical marketplace — is a moral problem. It is so because individuals can, under certain circumstances, legitimately consider themselves to be the bearers of moral claims to receive health care. The fact that we cannot afford to do all that we can for the possessors of such claims means we are forced to think about what kinds of sub-optimal distributions of health care are morally demanded. I have suggested here a broad two-fold characterisation of the kinds of moral considerations that can be invoked to ground claims to receive health care: considerations of basic benevolence, and those of justice. This division is, of course, a heuristic device, and there may well be parallels between the two types of considerations that have not been fully drawn out above. Nevertheless, such differences as there are remain salient and instructive, and serve to illuminate the range of philosophical issues that bear upon the problem of health care distribution.

There are dimensions to the problem that I have not touched on here, but which it might seem any fully developed philosophical approach ought to address. One such issue concerns states of ill health that are caused by the behaviour of those who suffer from them. Often cited examples include: lung and cardiovascular diseases that can be causally linked to smoking; liver problems that stem from the over-consumption

---

allocation, with Nussbaum also claiming that there is reasonable pluralism with regard to the specification of the central human capabilities. In recent years there has been a lively debate within political philosophy about the extent to which theories of justice can operate without making reference to ideas about the nature of the good life for human beings: John Rawls has argued that theories of justice can operate with only a 'thin' conception of the good life (Rawls, 1972, pp. 395–452); critics have countered that such theories must draw upon much more substantive considerations about the nature of the good (Taylor, 1989, pp. 88–9). I do not wish to take a position here within this long-running debate. My point is a modest one: even if justice-based approaches to the problem of health care distribution must rely (implicitly or explicitly) on some notions about the nature of the good life, these notions can be much less substantive than those seemingly at the heart of basic benevolence approaches (i.e. those which seem to make it difficult for the proponents of such approaches to adopt subjectively-derived rankings of medical benefits).

of alcohol; and diabetes, hypertension, and musculoskeletal problems caused by obesity which in turn is linked to poor dietary habits. What, if anything, happens to a moral claim to receive health care if the treatment claimed is for a 'self-inflicted' medical condition? Some have suggested that when we are allocating health care resources we can justifiably give such claims lower priority than claims for treatments for non-self inflicted conditions (Moss and Siegler, 1991). Others have urged considerable caution in using notions of personal responsibility for disease when deciding how to distribute health care. Daniel Wikler (2002) has argued that any downgrading of the claims of those who require treatments for seemingly self-inflicted conditions depends on demonstrating a tight causal connection between the behaviour and the disease, showing that the agent made a truly free choice to engage in the relevant behaviour, and providing a clear forewarning to those who engage in such behaviour that their health care needs will be downgraded as a result. In practice, it is very difficult to satisfy all of these conditions.

I have not taken a position here regarding the absolute superiority of basic benevolence or justice-based approaches. Both broad types of approach can be developed in any number of ways, and it is difficult to make a judgement in the abstract about which is likeliest to yield a more satisfactory answer to the problem of health care distribution. Nevertheless, it should be clear from the foregoing that I perceive some comparative advantages attaching to justice-based approaches. Chief among these is the seeming ability of such approaches to function without arriving at any kind of objective ranking of the relative value of different kinds of medical treatments as being more or less valuable. When the members of modern pluralistic societies confront the problem of how they ought to allocate their health care resources, avoiding the construction of any such ranking seems like a major boon.

Whichever broad approach is chosen, and however that approach is developed, we can confidently predict that the *need* to supply morally justified answers to the problem of health care distribution is likely to remain forcefully in existence. Some have argued that the very exercise of openly and transparently attempting to justify a particular distribution of health care carries costs, such as undermining our sense of the overwhelming importance of human life (Calabresi and Bobbitt, 1978), and others have considered these costs to be so great as to mitigate in favour of a behind the scenes approach that draws on pragmatism and on the spot intuitions rather than fully worked out moral justifications (Mechanic, 1997). But if there was ever a time when 'muddling through' in private was feasible, it is over now. As I described in my general introduction to this volume, there is now intense public interest in health care resource allocation, and the timbre of public debate suggests that what is demanded from those in authority is not just any old justification, but one which appeals to recognisably moral considerations. The task of morally justifying particular distributions of health care might well be unavoidably difficult, but it is difficult to avoid.

Howard Glennerster

The UK System of Health Funding and Resource Allocation

What Ethical Foundations?

I take some of the main points from Niall Maclean's chapter as my starting point.

- Seemingly powerful arguments can be marshalled in support of the idea that there is a moral obligation, falling upon citizens generally, to supply health care to those that need it.

- There is widespread and reasonable disagreement about which set of principles should govern the distribution of resources within publicly funded health care systems.

- Given this disagreement, we should strive to find morally justifiable procedures for arriving at particular distributions of health care resources. However else these procedures are structured, they should be open and transparent, and sensitive to the relevant considerations bearing on any particular distributive question.

In this paper I discuss how far the UK system of health care funding and resource allocation reflects these ideas, first in terms of funding and then in terms of procedures for distributing health care resources. I end by urging philosophers not to wash their hands of the substantive issue. Even if procedures for settling resource allocation questions are reasoned and open, they have to be conducted using some set of ethical assumptions (whether fully explicit and agreed or not). Budget shares have to be hammered out, allocation formulae agreed, methods used to reach decisions about the cost utility of particular forms of treatment. In taking these practical procedural steps ethical principles are inevitably adopted. In what follows I try to make these principles more explicit. It is critically important that they are better understood and debated. In the long run the legitimacy of public funding depends on it.

Funding According to Medical Need not Capacity to Pay

The United Kingdom has achieved widespread and lasting agreement on the funding of health care ever since the hard fought battles of 1946–8 over the creation of a tax funded, free at the point of use, health care system. The debates at the time were highly charged and turned on deeply held views about what was 'fair' in the case of health care resource allocation (Webster 1988; Glennerster 2006). The conclusions of these debates were broadly similar to those reached by many modern liberal egalitarian philosophers. Aneurin Bevan, the politician who drove through the creation of the modern National Health Service against the official opposition of the doctors' trade union, the British Medical Association, put the moral issue thus:

> No society can call itself civilised if a sick person is denied medical aid because of lack of means (Foot, 1975, p. 103).

There are clearly many ways in which that goal can be achieved other than a centralised tax funded service of the kind Bevan bequeathed. The continental European social insurance schemes are a case in point, though these are also moving towards a greater degree of tax funding, Germany being the latest case. Nevertheless, in the UK the case for free care at the point of need funded largely from taxation won widespread acceptance in 1946–8, and has become woven into the fabric of British political and institutional life in subsequent generations.

Although a Conservative Government was able to de-nationalise the whole of the United Kingdom's basic industries in the 1980s, the state funding of health care, and free access to primary and hospital provision, remained politically untouchable. In her introduction to the white paper that introduced major changes in the way the NHS was to be organised, Mrs Thatcher said:

> The National Health Service will continue to be available to all, regardless of income, and to be financed mainly out of taxation (Cm 555, 1989, 'Forward by the Prime Minister').

The UK's way of funding health care places it at one end of an international spectrum.

- The UK funds rather more of its health services from public funds than most other nations. Little more than 1% of its GDP is spent on privately funded health care. This is half that in the European Union as a whole, about the same as Sweden, but one sixth of the share in the US. (See Table 1 below). Note that the share called 'private spending' includes charges made for services provided within the NHS, so the amount allocated by pure market forces is even smaller.

- Most of this public spending is financed through general tax revenue and not by employer / employee insurance contributions. Here the UK is similar to some other countries like the Scandinavian countries, Italy and Spain, and different to Germany and France.
- All the tax revenue in the UK is raised nationally — unlike Sweden, which relies largely on local taxation.

This set of funding attributes puts the UK central government in a potentially powerful position to determine how much of the nation's resources are devoted to health care and where and how health resources are allocated.

How Much to Spend on Health Care?

There has been relatively little explicit discussion in the UK about what proportion of the national income should be spent on health. The committee set up to consider the question soon after the NHS was created (the Guillebaud Committee of 1956) concluded that there was no rational basis on which to decide how much was 'enough', and that the issue ought to be left to the interplay of political debate. The members of the Committee did contribute to that debate by pointing out that the share of GDP devoted to health care had fallen since the NHS had been created, and that capital buildings were particularly neglected. That led to a rise in the share of resources going to the NHS; nevertheless, history remained the prime indicator of what was justifiable. In the 1970s the Department of Health and Social Security introduced a programme budgeting process which enabled the Department to make a more effective case for increases to the previous year's budget in the public spending round (Banks 1979; Glennerster 1974). The growth of the elderly population, drug prices, and the neglect of particular client groups were all used to justify more funds. But it was not until the 1990s that a serious attempt was made to answer this crucial question: how much does the state need to spend to reach defined standards of care for particular client groups and medical conditions? This task was undertaken by the Wanless Enquiry for H.M. Treasury (2002), though the real spur was a rather simpler political calculation by the Prime Minister that the UK should spend as much as 'the Europeans' on health care in order to satisfy public criticism.[1] The Treasury are currently undertaking a reappraisal of the proportion of GDP that ought to be devoted to health by revisiting the Wanless conclusions.

In short, the UK has moved towards a rather more open and quantifiable debate about 'how much is enough' in the past decade but it is still shrouded in mystery, largely decided within the Treasury and is inevitably a political decision about competing political ends. In the next

---

[1]   For an account of this somewhat off the cuff commitment, see Glennerster (2005).

decade it is clear that pensions will take a much higher priority. The principle, 'someone else's turn now', will bulk large around the Cabinet table.

Table 1
Public and Private Spending on Health Care as a Percentage of GDP in 2003 (UK figure is from 2002)

Country	Public	Private	Total	% public
USA	6.7	8.3	15	44.4
France	7.7	2.4	10.1	76.3
Germany	8.7	2.4	11.1	78.2
Italy	6.3	2.1	8.4	75.1
Spain	5.5	2.2	7.7	71.2
Sweden	7.8	1.4	9.2	85.3
UK	6.4	1.3	7.7	83.4
Source: OECD Health Data 2005				

It should be noted that since 2001 'central government' in the UK has changed its meaning. Westminster decides on the overall national funding for services devolved to Scotland and Wales, but the Scottish Parliament and Welsh Assembly decide their own priorities for spending the money. Scotland can add to the sum devolved by choosing to raise the level of income tax paid by Scots, but has so far chosen not to do so.

Allocating Health Care within a Publicly Funded Health Care System

Once the share of the GDP devoted to public health provision has been decided, the next set of decisions concerns how it is to be spent. It is here that agreement amongst philosophers breaks down, yet the need for some ethical basis for political judgements grows.

Comparative research suggests that tax funded health care systems, though perhaps 'fair' in fund raising terms, have spent less on health care than systems with social insurance funding and systems with significant private insurance components (Gerdtham and Jonsson, 2000). In tax funded systems ministries of finance hold the purse strings, and the UK Treasury is one of the most powerful of all such ministries. It has managed very tight control on the health budget until very recently.

After a period of unparalleled health spending growth in the last eight years, the Treasury's traditional tight control is being reasserted. The rate of increase after 2008 will slow significantly (H.M.Treasury, 2006).

However, despite the recent largess the gap between what the UK could spend and what it does spend has grown. The available universe of health technologies is set by budgets available in the USA. In their recent study of American and UK spending, Aaron and Schwartz (2005) compare the scale of treatment available to British citizens with that enjoyed by the average US citizen. They also compare the present situation to that of 20 years ago when they undertook their previous study (Aaron and Schwartz, 1984). They take as examples kidney dialysis and transplantation, haemophilia, hip replacement, coronary heart surgery, radiology and stem cell transplantation. They find that despite recent increases in funding the gap between USA and the UK with regard to the provision of these treatments has widened since the 1980s. In these specialties alone the UK would have to spend *one third more* on the NHS merely to provide the UK citizen with the health services that the US provides as an overall average (i.e. to its insured and uninsured population taken together). But the medical practitioners Aaron and Schwartz interviewed in the UK seemed prepared to accept the view that access according to need was more important than higher levels of provision inequitably distributed. Indeed, they show that what is considered to be good medical practice has adapted in the UK to take account of relative scarcity. Applying every test in the book and providing every heroic last stage of life treatment are not considered good medical or ethical practice in the UK. The funding regime in the UK imbues the whole profession with a different attitude to scarcity. It may not be one that a more consumerist and litigation prone public will continue to accept, but at the moment this value system seems to be holding. Yet such a system makes decisions about how to allocate public resources increasingly difficult. The whole rationale for the system is that rationing shall be according to need not capacity to pay. How we ought to do that is still a matter for dispute.

Rationing Defined

Having introduced the term 'rationing' I should attempt some definition before going further. All scarce resources are rationed in one way or another. Even simple societies evolve ways of rationing scarce resources that minimise social conflict. In this I am following Levi-Strauss (1969). He argues that the more central to human existence resources are — land and sexual relationships in simple societies — the more socially embedded the rationing process has to be. This end is achieved in simple societies, he argues, by taboo, stigma, tradition, and status. In more complex societies markets evolved to cope with the complexity of the rules involved in many transactions.

However, in times of danger and extreme scarcity, for example in war time, societies revert to collective forms of rationing for basic necessities such as food and shelter. Other resources are so central to human existence that most societies have evolved some kind of collective responsibility for ensuring they are not denied to the wider population. Health care is one of them, and even in the USA Medicare and Medicaid exist to do this. Political institutions would lose political legitimacy if they did not reflect that moral imperative.

Calabresi and Bobbitt (1978) distinguished four kinds of rationing:

- the market;
- political allocations that are accountable to public discussion;
- pure lotteries;
- unaccountable customs and practices of professionals and bureaucrats.

Economists tend to confine themselves to using the term 'rationing' to refer only to decisions made about allocations that take place outside a market. This is unhelpful in my view since almost no one can have access to medical resources regardless of their price. Many will not be able to afford private medical insurance. Few will be able to afford private insurance for all possible conditions for unlimited time periods, even if such cover is available. Hence private insurance companies decide what treatment they will pay for and how much they will pay. Private insurance companies thus ration every bit as much as public health care systems, though in very different ways.

A Reasonable and Accountable Process?

Having reminded ourselves that all health care systems ration in some form we set out a schematic map for the rationing mechanisms at work in the UK. See Figure 1 below.

In the top two boxes we give examples of rationing decisions that could be described as 'explicit and reasoned'. These are explicit decisions taken by democratic agencies, operating according to some open and reputable process e.g. Daniels's notion of 'accountability for reasonableness' (see Niall Maclean's chapter in this volume). In the second row of boxes we have 'inexplicit and unreasoned', often unrecognised, un-debated decisions about resource allocation taken perhaps as a by-product of political decisions that have little to do with health care, or by professionals in their day to day lives agreeing to see one patient and putting off another just as part of the daily round.

Figure 1: Types of Health Care Rationing in the UK

	NATIONAL	LOCAL
EXPLICIT and REASONED	Cabinet NICE guidance ACRA formulae National Service Frameworks Scottish Executive	Strategic Health Authorities Primary Care Trusts Service agreements/ contracts
INEXPLICIT and UNREASONED	National media campaigns	Local media campaigns against cuts Management/clinician deals Clinical decisions

The columns distinguish the location of the agents who influence or take the decisions. At the national level there is the United Kingdom Westminster Cabinet deciding how public spending is to be allocated within the UK and deciding between competing public purposes. The results of these behind-closed-doors negotiations do eventually see the light of day in published documents which are the focus of much public debate: namely, the Comprehensive Spending Reviews.[2] The shares of overall public spending devoted to the range of services that has been devolved to Scotland and Wales are then transmitted to the devolved Parliament in Scotland and the Welsh Assembly. These shares depend on a judgement based on what we may call 'modified historical precedent', to put it kindly (McLean and McMillan, 2005)![3] In each constituent country of the UK different formulae are then used to allocate resources to local health agencies who decide how it shall be spent in their areas. In England these local agencies are called Primary Care Trusts (PCTs). At the bottom are the front line decisions made by professionals. Slightly higher in this hierarchy are political compromises made between hospital managers and the leading clinicians.

If we go back thirty years it would be true to say that the great bulk of decisions were made in the bottom right hand box. They were decisions made about who would get what share of the hospital budget that had been set by historical precedent and by individual clinicians. The princi-

---

[2]   See for example H.M.Treasury (2004a and 2007).

[3]   For an analysis of diverging policies followed in spending those sums see Alvarez-Rosete et al (2005).

ples involved were largely unexamined. If a hospital had received £ *x*000 the year before it would get £ *x*000 plus a small increment next year. Since the number of hospitals and beds in that area was largely a function of history and to a limited degree recent population increase, the resultant allocation of resources reflected the way resources were spread historically before the NHS ever existed. Those areas that had been able to afford to pay for new buildings in the early part of the last century got most. More prosperous expanding regions were able to justify more new hospitals on grounds of population growth. There had been attempts to even up the spread of clinicians and GPs after the NHS came into existence but resources were not related to differential need. If anything there was an inverse care law: the greater the need, the less the resources. To some extent this reflected the professional power balance within the system. High profile specialties gained resources to the neglect of those that were concerned with groups like the elderly and mentally ill.

Moves to a More Accountable and Open Process of Resource Allocation?

1976 marked the beginning of a series of changes to the way resources were allocated in the NHS, and the ramifications of these changes are still underway. The changes can be summarised as an attempt to push the locus of rationing upwards and to the left hand box in Figure 1. There were four steps in this general move. We describe each in turn and then discuss the ethical and political issues each raises in the following section.

Move One: An attempt to set spending priorities through a more centralised, explicit and publicly accountable process rather than leaving them to be set by inertia and professional politics at a local level.

This move can in its turn be seen to comprise distinct steps. A series of budgetary, managerial and organisational changes have been taken which can be seen as attempts to ensure that political rationing priorities are actually carried through to reach front line services.

- The first step came in 1976 with the publication by the Department of Health and Social Security of the programme budget I discussed above. This set out target spending for a series of neglected groups that had become priorities because of a series of damaging political scandals in facilities supposed to cater for the elderly, the mentally ill and what were then called the mentally handicapped. In practice, it proved difficult to ensure that money won from the Treasury on these grounds actually ended up being spent on those groups because of the power of local professional politics to siphon off the funds.[4] Though originally designed as a way to negotiate funds with the Treasury, the thinking was that these spending priorities, along with a programme budget, should be driven down the NHS so that local health agencies could be held accountable for spending the sums won for particular purposes. This is still far from the case.

- General managers were introduced in the 1980s as another attempt to wrest some power over resource allocation away from clinicians. This was only marginally successful.

- The separation of 'purchasing' from day to day management in the early 1990s endowed health authorities with the duty to decide on an area's health priorities. They were to decide what priority to give to what services and how much of what activity to buy for the local community. Local providers were to compete to get these 'contracts' or 'commissions'. In practice, such 'purchaser' bodies were weakly resourced and did not (and still do not) carry the professional clout or have the information base to do that task properly. Scotland has abolished the purchaser provider split, bringing the management of local providers back within a stronger chain of command.

- 'Payment by results' in England is intended to reward hospitals who respond well to the priorities set by health authorities and to patient choices regarding which hospital or service to use. How this more demand-led system is going to be effectively rationed is less clear. Scotland has declined to adopt this policy.

Each change has been intended to enable agencies responsible to the public for setting health priorities to ration more effectively and to hold service providers to account for the provision of particular kinds of services. It is still not clear that any such devices have been very effective. The probable shortfall in spending intended for the mentally ill is a case in point (Sainsbury Centre for Mental Health, 2003). The powerful specialties and acute hospitals, by virtue of their attracting relatively larger amounts of public sympathy, have been able to exercise a great deal of leverage over elected officials. The elderly and mentally ill come off badly as a result. But at least the decisions have become a little more open and debatable. We can now discuss how far the government has fallen short of its claims to spend more on the mentally ill. We used not to know how much was spent on this or other client groups, either nationally or locally. No explicit decisions were taken to determine such overall priorities.

---

[4] See Glennerster et al (1983).

Move Two: An attempt to ensure equal chances of access to health care for those in equal need where ever they live.

As we have seen, until the mid 1970s there was no attempt to allocate health resources between different parts of the country according to any concept of need. Budget allocations from the centre were made on the basis of historical precedent. The major break though came in 1976 with the publication of the report of the Resource Allocation Working Party (RAWP) (Department of Health and Social Security, 1976b). Civil servants and ministers were persuaded that a more scientific basis could be established for allocating health cash on the basis of need. RAWP set the NHS's objective as 'being to secure, through resource allocation, that there would eventually be equal opportunity of access to health care for people at equal risk' (Department of Health and Social Security, 1976b, para 1.30). That has remained the stated objective of this whole process through successive changes in the actual mathematics of the formula over the past thirty years.

Despite being framed in this way, the resulting budgets were specifically not designed to tell those in local areas, then regions, how much should be spent on what. It was agreed that this would have conflicted with professional and local freedoms. In so far as government wanted to set national standards, these were to be set and enforced by a separate procedure. The aim was to give local agents an overall budget that reflected local health risks. That would give them an opportunity to respond to those risks in the same way as other areas, though they were free not to do so if they wished. If they had twice as many old people as the average area their budget allocation would reflect the demands that an older population might be expected to put on services. Yet if they chose to spend less per old person and more on children or the mentally ill they would be free to do so.

The political strategy was, moreover, not to reduce the resources available to some areas and give to others but to set an 'ideal' target and then allocate the *increments* in each year's budget in such a way as to 'move local health authorities towards target' year on year. There would be no *absolute* losers in any one year. That was to prove a shrewd political move.

The RAWP report recommended that recurrent (i.e. not capital annual spending cash) should be allocated to regions on the basis of their share of a weighted national population. The population should be weighted on the basis of the likely risk of people in a given population making demands on the health care system. The most important difference compared to the previous practice was that resources reflected the size of the population! The next most important was weighting that population by age. People in their eighties have something like eight times as much spent on them as people in middle age; women of child bearing age being one exception.

The final stage in the calculation was a weighting that gave more to areas with higher standardised mortality rates — an indicator of likely higher demand and need for care. Despite criticisms of the latter measure, the formula attracted enough support to form the basis of allocations for several years. It was then revised, and revised again, and is now under regular review by a committee called the Advisory Committee on Resource Allocation for England (ACRA) on which I sit.[5] The formula was originally used to allocate resources to large regions (ten or so) in England and Wales. The formula now allocates down to much smaller units — Primary Care Trusts with populations of 350,000 or so. However, from 2005 the Department of Health is also producing a recommended formula for setting shadow budgets for individual general practices so that they can undertake 'practice based commissioning' for services they want for their patients. Comparable though different formulae are used in Scotland, Wales and Northern Ireland, though they do not go down to the level of practices.

Since 1976 each of these separate formulae in the UK have been concerned with cash for hospital and community services. Allocations for primary care (general practice) have been treated quite differently. Each general practitioner attracted a separate sum, and more was added to cover the costs of running a practice with large numbers of patients. Extra was added for other services provided, and for practices operating in deprived areas. Following an agreement with the BMA in June 2003 primary care in England has been financed on the basis of a formula too. Its logic has been to give more money to practices serving poorer and less healthy populations. Practices also get paid for providing particular services and meeting targets for such things as immunisation, chronic care and screening at risk groups. Scotland remained with the old pattern of GP payments.

In 1999 ACRA was asked by the new Labour Government to adapt the formula to help achieve the goal of reducing inequalities in health outcomes. This proved technically very difficult to do. Most of the drivers of health inequality lay outside the health care system. To go some way to meet the Government's aim ACRA did agree to include an attempt to tackle the issue of unmet need. Some groups fail to demand care even though they need it. The English formula had been criticised on the ground that it responded to differential demands for services by varied

---

[5] For those interested in the history of the formulae and why they have been changed see Glennerster, Hills and Travers (2000). For an account of the present formula for England see *Resource Allocation: Weighted Capitation Formula* (Department of Health, [2005a])

social and ethnic groups but not to medical needs in the population that were never expressed by poorer or less educated people who might not go to their doctor at all. In the last round of changes ACRA tried to meet this criticism. Studies had shown that demand for some services from some social groups did not fully match the known prevalence of the condition amongst those groups. Hence the figures for demands on the service were 'enhanced' in these cases. Quite separate measures were taken by government to try to raise the actual use of some services by these groups.

A very similar set of debates has taken place in Scotland. The methods used in the two countries have interacted, with one learning lessons from the other. A key report to the new Scottish Executive (2000) created the formula which took the name of the committee chairman: Professor Sir John Arbuthnott. It faced the same criticism that it reflected differential demands from different populations but not the unexpressed or unmet needs of some groups.[6] In the end the Scottish Executive set up some pilot projects to see how far groups who failed to access available services could be encouraged to do so.

The Welsh Assembly (2005) tried a completely different approach. They rejected the use of differential *demands* on services as a proxy for differential *needs*. In its place they have put something they call a 'direct' method of measuring need. This is based on a survey of individuals in Wales who are asked to record their self assessed health status. Seventeen conditions were listed. They were asked if they suffered from any of these conditions. These included back pain, arthritis, respiratory disease, hearing failure, diabetes and stroke. The conditions had to be broad and simple enough for lay people to understand. Twelve conditions were used in the eventual allocation. The percentage of the population suffering from each condition in each area was scaled up to produce the population at risk. For each condition the average national spend per person on that condition was then applied to the local population at risk. The range of risks taken into account is much less detailed than that in Scotland or England because the conditions covered in the questionnaire have to be understood by ordinary people. Even so, the same kinds of poor areas come out as being most needy under both approaches.

In brief:

- There have been genuine attempts to allocate resources differentially depending on the needs of particular areas. The methods employed to do so have differed in different parts of the UK, but the processes have been open and reflective. Good scientific methods have been employed and changed in the light of criticism.

[6]   For an excellent review of the issues see McConnachie and Sutton (2004).

- Actual resource redistribution to the least advantaged areas has been quite considerable. A deprived area of Manchester, for example, has a target need allocation which is roughly half as high again as a prosperous suburb of London. Thirty years ago that Manchester ward would have had less resources than a more prosperous and healthy area of London.
- However, the final outcomes on *health* have been disappointing.
  - Between 1976 and 1996 health inequality widened on various measures (Acheson Report, 1998).
  - From 1997 to the present there has been a slight narrowing on some measures of inequality in England and a worsening on others (Department of Health, 2005b).

The main driver of these outcomes is not the scale of health care resources but other inequalities in the social structure. This does not, however, render invalid the aim of giving those who do become ill an equal chance of access to health care regardless of income or location.

Move Three: The attempt to secure more common standards of treatment across the NHS.

Clinicians adopt different treatment strategies, which might be equally good but just different. Some strategies might be outdated, some just plain odd, and some can even be dangerous. Clinical audit and more careful monitoring of individual clinician's safety and success rates have been one response. But with many chronic conditions like asthma or diabetes the quality of care depends on many service partners and their collaboration. This may work well if there is a charismatic clinician or a local pressure group, but there is little to *make* it happen. After 1997 there has been an attempt to agree on best practice in some priority areas of treatment—a process called 'setting National Service Frameworks (NSFs)'. Once again 'national' does not mean 'UK wide'. There are variants in the process in the constituent parts of the UK. Protocols worked out by the Royal Colleges (professional bodies representing different areas of medicine) that summarise their view of best practice have existed for a long time, but NSFs were an attempt by government to draw together best practice for a whole *condition* (the treatment of which will involve different specialties and professions). This was then recommended to practitioners and service providers. In theory this framework would be backed by appropriate resources. The first conditions chosen were cancer, coronary heart disease and mental health. These have been relatively uncontroversial in professional terms though whether enough money has been allocated to make the recommended treatment patterns possible would be disputed by those in the services concerned.

Move Four: The technologies and drugs used by the NHS should be cost effective. Implicitly this means that some may be considered too expensive for use under the NHS. Money would be better spent elsewhere.

This is the most controversial of the moves I will discuss, and it raises the most serious ethical issues. It is relatively easy to argue that medical 'wants' like cosmetic surgery should not be provided on the NHS if there are other competing needs. Even here, though, someone disfigured by a car accident may well need such treatment to be able to appear in public again without losing self respect which may lead onto more generally recognised medical needs such as depression. In the 1990s individual health authorities did begin to make rules that excluded such 'wants' (Klein et al 1996). Then in the mid 1990s the Conservative Government began an experiment providing national guidance. It set up an Advisory Committee on Health Technology Assessment to give advice to health authorities on the cost effectiveness of new health treatments and technologies. It was a body on which I served. The Labour Government of 1997 gave its successor body full statutory powers.

Cost Effective Treatments and NICE

The National Institute for Clinical Excellence (NICE) was proposed in the 1997 white paper (Cm 3807) *The New NHS: Modern, dependable*. The new body came into existence in March 1999. It had three functions:

- It published appraisals of new and existing health technologies to provide guidance to health professionals on their use in England and Wales.
- It developed clinical guidelines to advise professionals on care programmes for particular conditions in England and Wales.
- It gave guidance on whether interventional procedures used for diagnosis or treatment were safe enough and worked well enough to be used routinely in England, Scotland and Wales. (Note the different geographical cover. Scotland has its equivalent but separate body for the first two functions.)

While continuing to perform these functions, in 2005 NICE also took over the functions of the Health Development Agency and now goes under the title the National Institute for Health and Clinical Excellence. It is responsible not just for advice on clinical matters but for advice on good practice about promoting health (National Institute for Health and Clinical Excellence website; 'About Us' section).

The controversial heart of NICE's work is that on appraisals of 'health technology'. This term covers new and existing treatments and medicines. To put this in context, NICE had undertaken just over 100 such appraisals at the time of writing in May 2006. There are thousands of existing treatments and medicines and hundreds of new ones available or developed each year. Thus NICE is only touching the surface. However, from January 2002 the NHS has been legally obliged to provide funding and resources in England and Wales for treatments and medicines recommended by NICE. A Primary Care Trust is not obliged to provide funding for a technology NICE has not approved. It seems possible that a PCT spending money regularly on a technology not approved as cost effective by NICE might be taken to court by the Audit Commission or by an individual taxpayer for acting without due 'economy, efficiency and effectiveness' (Local Government Finance Act 1982, section 26). By the same token an individual clinician is not forced to abide by the guidelines. But if she did not follow the guidelines she would know that there would be less resources for other patients.

'Technology' as defined by NICE covers medicines, medical devices such as hearing aids, diagnostic techniques, surgical procedures, and health promotion activities. NICE states: 'We base our recommendations on a review of clinical and economic evidence. Clinical evidence measures how well the medicine or treatments works. Economic evidence measures how well the medicine or treatment works in relation to how much it costs the NHS—does it represent value for money?' (National Institute for Clinical Excellence website; What do we do, about technology appraisals, section). In explaining this to the public it says: 'NICE may not recommend a particular treatment. This is usually because there is not enough reliable evidence that the particular technology is a more effective treatment than others for the same condition. This means that for the time being it should not be prescribed routinely on the NHS, and your doctor should talk to you about other treatment options available to you.' (National Institute for Health and Clinical Excellence website, 'What do we do', NICE guidance section).

This is an important statement of principle. It implies that someone can and should be denied treatment that is available and is of proven worth if it can be shown that that money could be better used on other treatments. The economic case is clear, as is the 'close at hand' utilitarian reasoning, as Maclean puts it (see page 59, n.11) that underlies it. Given a budget constraint, if treatment A is not undertaken and the cash that would have been spent on it is used to treat more patients with the same disease using less costly treatments B and C more individuals will find their health improved. There may be objections to any kind of budget constraint being applied to health care but in practice all societies have to apply one. The simple logic underlying NICE's position expressed in these terms is difficult to reject. It is when we come to think more deeply about how to do it that the problem arises, as we shall see in the discussion at the end of this chapter.

Each NICE appraisal is accompanied by the disclaimer: 'This guidance does not however, override the individual responsibility of health care professionals to make decisions appropriate to the circumstances of the individual patient, in consultation with the patient and/or the guardian or carer.' (see for example NICE Technology Appraisal 94, 2006, p.2). This puts the individual professional in an unenviable situation.

I describe below how an appraisal is done and how the cost utility judgement is made. However, first it is important to be clear about the *process*.

NICE Process

NICE produces clinical and cost effectiveness guidance on health technologies for the NHS in England and Wales. Guidance on whether intervention procedures are *safe* cover England, Scotland and Wales. The Secretary of State in England, in consultation with the Welsh Assembly, has to refer a technology or medicine to NICE.

Scotland has then, in theory, chosen independence on the cost effectiveness issue. From devolution it created a body called 'The Health Technology Board for Scotland'. It 'worked to improve Scotland's health by providing evidence based advice to NHS Scotland on the clinical effectiveness of new and existing health technologies' (NHS Quality Improvement Scotland website, 'Glossary' section). From January 2003 it became part of 'NHS Quality Improvement Scotland'. In fact, this body takes NICE's work on technology as its starting point. It reviews NICE guidance published since 1 May 2001 and considers whether each is right for Scotland. If so, the same guidance goes out. If not it can be adapted or 'developed' to suit Scotland.

The Department of Health in England develops a brief known as a 'scope' that sets out what the appraisal should cover and what questions it needs to answer. NICE then identifies which organisations should be consulted — the manufacturers, health professionals, carers and patient groups. A draft 'scope' is discussed at a workshop and a final specification produced. Under the NICE procedure 'Consultees' are named to give evidence. Again, these are the manufacturers, academic specialists and user groups. 'Commentator organisations' include manufacturers of rival products.

An academic centre is then commissioned to review the published evidence and prepare an assessment report. This is then sent for comment to the parties mentioned. Their comments are taken into account and a final evaluation report written. An independent Appraisal Committee examines the report and takes verbal evidence. It produces an 'appraisal consultation document' which is sent round for comment. After comments have been considered a 'final appraisal determination' is written and sent to the NICE Board for approval. Consultee organisations can then appeal. These are considered by a NICE Appeal Committee. They can recommend changes. If not the Appraisal is published.

It is a long process and one heavily embedded in due process. On the whole NICE has built up considerable respect for its difficult work and the 'reflective equilibrium' implied in the process is, I think, exemplary.

An Example: The use of statins for the prevention of cardiovascular events

Published in January 2006, the NICE guidance (NICE Technology Appraisal 94, 2006) begins with a description of cardiovascular disease (CVD) and its importance as the most common cause of death in the UK. Incidence varies by socio-economic group, being experienced more often by those in manual occupations. The impact of the disease also varies considerably by area. The paper then discusses the range of treatments and preventive measures commonly used and for which there are proven effects. It goes on to discuss the use of statins, with descriptions of what they do in general and of the five that currently have UK marketing authorisation in particular. It describes each in turn and the commercial form they take.

The nub of the paper, 'Evidence and Interpretation', falls into two parts. The first summarises the clinical effectiveness of the drugs as measured in placebo-controlled trials. It compares the effect of the different statins and any side effects. It also looks at compliance — whether people actually take the tablets. The second part of the paper summarises the comparative cost effectiveness of the drugs by using five published studies, evidence submitted by the manufacturers, and a model developed by the Assessment Group itself. Two common measures of effectiveness were used. One is the cost per life year gained (LYG). The other is the cost per quality-adjusted life year gained (QALY). The first assumes that any year of life gained by treatment is equal to any other, whether the life is one of a bedridden patient in pain or a healthy active life. The second is methodologically more complex. Economists in the UK (Rosser and Kind, 1978; Williams and Kind, 1992) argued that people would generally agree that they were more prepared to pay for a treatment that led to a healthy year of life than a bedridden one. Samples of UK (and later European) populations were asked to compare and rank healthy and less healthy states. Illness states were categorised, for example, in terms of mobility, capacity for self care, capacity to work or care or be active at home, social relationships, pain and mental health. Responses enabled a ranking to be calculated that ranged from a full healthy year of life (given the value 1), to death (given the value 0). A negative number indicated states in which people were signifying they

would rather be dead. Any condition could in theory be assessed for the
state of health to which it gave rise. Hence it was possible to count how
many 'quality weighted lives' a given treatment might save.

Clearly, ethical issues arise here about the derivation of such weights.
Some argue that no such judgements can be made. Other critics will
argue that such weights cannot be derived from anyone other than the
patient concerned. Economists tend to respond that that would be reasonable if the patient were paying for the care herself but such trade offs
should be made by the wider community who are paying. Hence, the
community, or its representatives, have a legitimate voice in calibrating
the comparable utility gained from each pound spent. In practice there
are also many difficult ethical and technical problems wrapped up in
these calculations and we discuss them further at the end of the chapter.

To return to the example, the review group produced a model that
combined all the available economic evidence and concluded that for
secondary coronary heart disease prevention the incremental cost per
QALY ranged from £10,000 to £16,000 for the age group 45 to 85 years for
men and women similarly. For those with a history of diabetes the cost
per life gained was below £9,000. These results were sensitive to the cost
of the statin used, and these costs varied a lot. Cost effectiveness varied
over the age range of those treated, with the cost being highest for younger age groups where the drug was less likely to have an effect. The
group concluded that statin therapy was cost effective for all people
with a history of coronary heart disease. Compared to the costs per life
saved of other treatments for other conditions this was a good use of
money. However, such comparative figures are not actually set out for
comparison in the paper and that is common practice.

The paper then goes on to discuss the use of statins for preventive purposes where there are clear risk factors involved, like high cholesterol
being present. Here the conclusions were less certain. The advice in brief
was that:

- 'Statin therapy is recommended for adults with clinical evidence of
  CVD' (para. 1.10)
- 'Statin therapy is recommended as part of the management strategy
  for the primary prevention of CVD for adults who have a 20% or
  greater 10 year risk of developing CVD' (para. 1.2). NICE goes onto
  say how this risk should be calculated.
- Where the decision is made to prescribe a statin the therapy should
  'usually be initiated with a drug with a low acquisition cost' (para.
  1.4).

I think this gives a good indication both of the thoroughness of the
assessment and its openness, but also of the substantial ethical assump-

tions that underlie the work. Next, I describe a controversial case that shows what happens before NICE can get involved.

Another Example: Herceptin

This drug is used for late stage breast cancer, but the manufacturers claimed from clinical trials published in the autumn of 2005 that it was more effective than existing therapies for treating early stage breast cancer. Roche of Switzerland applied for approval from the Australian regulatory body in October 2005. In February 2006 the American subsidiary applied to the US Food and Drug Administration and the company said it would do so in Europe later. This left health authorities in Europe in a difficult position. In the past no reference to NICE has been made until a treatment has been approved as safe. The NICE processes then can begin if the Secretary of State so triggers them.

In this case, however, women began to press for the right to be prescribed the drug before approval of any kind had been given and threatened to take their health authority to court. Several authorities backed down in the face of such a challenge. The Secretary of State said she thought money should not stand in the way of health authorities approving its use but it was up to them to decide. However, she promised to speed the NICE process by agreeing to refer the case to NICE at the same time as the regulatory body was considering its safety. That could not happen until the drug company sought approval.

In one case the local PCT stood firm. It was not prepared to approve the drug's use until it had been approved as safe. The woman concerned, Mrs Rogers, took her case to the High Court. The High Court judged that the PCT in Swindon was within its rights to refuse to pay for the treatment. It had not acted irrationally or arbitrarily or without due process. However, Mrs Rogers was given the right to appeal and meanwhile she should be able to have the drug. The Court of Appeal found that the PCT was 'irrational' in the sense that it had not produced a clearly reasoned case for not approving the use of the drug (*The Times*, 2006, April 27). The case not only illustrated the political power and sensitivity of these issues. It also illustrated the clash of moral positions and the importance *in law* of such decisions being rationally grounded. (In June 2007 NICE ruled that Herceptin should be offered as an option for those women with early stage breast cancer after they had taken radiation or or chemo therapy.)

Does Anyone Take Any Notice of NICE?

It is one thing to worry about the grounding of NICE decisions but another practical issue is this: how far do clinicians and Trusts actually *follow* these guidelines? The answer is that they often do, especially when they are clear and the evidence strong, particularly so in the case of pharmaceuticals. Nevertheless, compliance is varied. Sheldon and colleagues (Sheldon et al, 2004) took twelve pieces of early guidance from NICE as 'tracers'. They followed up the impact on prescribing from the national prescribing returns and the use of procedures and devices using a range of statistical sources and interviews. They concluded that clinical practice had changed in line with NICE guidance especially where prescribing was involved but it was less influential for surgical procedures. Compliance by Trusts varied considerably. Sheldon's paper provoked considerable correspondence and some responses that were critical of its methodology but it remains the only serious independent academic attempt to test what impact NICE has had. NICE has now commissioned its own tracking of compliance.

Discussion

The preceding description of the way health resources are distributed in the UK raises a series of moral and political issues.

Overall Priorities

Despite the considerable technical expertise devoted to rationing resources geographically and in deciding on the cost effectiveness of a small number of new technologies and drugs the really big issues are rarely debated or even reasoned about at all in the public arena. For me, these issues include: How much money should we devote to areas of continuing care like mental health, disability and dementia, compared to extending life for a few years or even months through expensive and aggressive acute medicine? How much effort should we devote to speed and convenience of care and treatment compared to adopting the newest methods of cure? How much effort should we devote to extending healthy life rather than intervening after people are ill? How much attention should we pay to the older members of our community compared to the younger?

Decisions on these issues are already being taken by default. They are hidden by the implied political and professional claim that we can do everything. Above all they are hidden by incessant debates about health service structures and not what goes on within them. Perhaps the biggest question of all – How much can we afford for health care compared to education and pensions in the next few years? – has already been taken behind closed doors. The answer (the NHS is not going to get more as a share of the GDP, and a slower growth rate than recently) lends these kinds of debates even greater importance.

Territorial Justice

There has been surprising consensus in the UK around the moral goal 'equal access to health care for people at equal risk'. Yet there are a number of very surprising features to the way this goal is interpreted.

- It has never applied to citizens of the whole of the UK despite the fact that, as its very name implies, the National Health Service is a nationwide service funded from Westminster. In fact, the NHS has become a separate set of services: one each for Scotland, Wales, Northern Ireland and England. Despite the fact that the NHS is nationally funded, citizens of each of these 'sub-nations' get very different sums spent on them unrelated to any measure of comparative need.

- There is an unresolved conflict between the idea that everyone in the country (however that is understood) should be treated in the same way regardless of where they live, and ideas of local accountability, the right to take priority decisions locally, and professional freedom from political interference.

- National Service Frameworks and NICE Guidance imply agreement that governments should set common standards. Yet they include caveats about professionals having a duty to decide in patients' best interests. Popular opinion seems to want both. It is about time this was debated more openly.

The same conflict between the desire to achieve common standards of treatment and the need to permit professional and local freedom arises in the allocation of funds to local agents — either the old health authorities or the new PCTs in England. Both kinds of bodies have discretion as to how they actually spend the carefully calculated funds within their area. They have the opportunity to set quite different priorities from those assumed by the national formula. They may decide, implicitly, to give those with mental health less chance of access for that condition compared to breast cancer than the national formula implies. The most we can say is that the sums allocated would *enable* those making the decisions locally to spend as much as in a comparable authority. As RAWP said 'We have not regarded it as part of our remit as being concerned with how resources are deployed' (Department of Health and Social Security, 1976b, para.1.5).

Deciding on the comparative effectiveness of new treatments

At some point citizens of the UK will have to recognise that unless they are prepared to pay much higher taxes or private health insurance contributions they will never be able to enjoy the same access to new health technologies as is found in the USA. We have gone further in the UK than in many other countries in trying to work through the practical consequences of this unpleasant reality. That is what NICE does. Given that resources will have to be rationed, it is better to have this done by some publicly agreed procedure than for it to be done merely as a response by professionals and politicians to pharmaceutical industry advertising or front page stories in the *Daily Mail*.

The process of spending most on those in greatest need is something we have left to professionals to decide, and we have tried to ensure that those who practise in areas likely to have more needy patients have more resources. NICE's job is to decide what tools the public are prepared to buy for the clinician to do her job. Gold plated scalpels, for example, are not on the clinician's table. Some drugs are so expensive in relation to the job they are aiming to do that that they are equivalent to a gold plated scalpel. So far, I think, there is some agreement that NICE has a job to do, though when it comes down to well publicised cases the press and the public and the clinicians involved tend to fall back on the argument that life is so important that if there is any chance at all that a gold scalpel might be better it must be used. It is also the case that NICE has adopted a remarkably open and rigorous procedural approach. It is so rigorous that it has been time consuming and covered very few new technologies and drugs.

It is when we come to the detail of the methodology used that I suspect there is, or would be if it were understood, more disagreement. That disagreement centres upon the economic not the clinical assessment. The economic assessment has to use some method to compare the cost effectiveness of new and old treatments and between existing treatments too. It assumes that at some point the opportunity cost of a treatment can become so high that tax funds would be better spent elsewhere. That is a position some may object to. But even if we accept it, which I do, it begs the question of what method we adopt to measure the cost utility of procedures and drugs and then how we judge that some are too costly.

The very use of cost utility methods are subject to a series of 'in principle' questions, as the American expert on health care ethics Dan Brock (2004) has pointed out. Some of these and others are discussed below.

- Sample members of the public have been asked to compare states of health and disability against one another in order to draw up QALY measures. They have not all experienced disability. We know that when people have done so they come to see a disabled life quite differently. Brock (2004) makes this point strongly. The public as tax payers are perhaps the only legitimate deciders of any trade off. However, ignorance of the whole methodology, let alone ignorance of the life of a disabled person, is not a good basis for such decisions. We need a much more open discussion about the information base used here.

- If we accept that some rationing on this kind of basis is valid, the most logical way to decide on priorities would be to rank all procedures according to, say, the cost of a life saved. The government would set the overall health budget and then NICE would decide which procedures to permit doctors to use by going down the list until it ran out of money. When it reached that point government might decide it wanted to go further down the list and make more money available. The trouble is that NICE has only studied a hundred and thirty treatments. That leaves several thousand more to do—decades of work even if drug companies and manufacturers were immediately to stop inventing new ways to do things.

- NICE is very cagey about how it does set a threshold figure regarding what counts as being too costly. In practice it works on a rough yard stick. According to the Chairman, reported in *The Economist* (2006), 'NICE rarely accepts that drugs are cost effective if they cost more than £25,000—35,000 per QALY.' Where did that number come from and where has it been widely debated? Apart from a handful of health economists (Devlin and Parkin, 2004) few would know or understand what is going on here.

- The notion of cost effectiveness and the utilitarian logic that underpins it does imply that curing a large number of pain relieving situations can in the end sum to outweigh an expensive attempt to save one life or help one serious condition where suffering is great. If we were not to regularly use a drug that extended a cancerous life by a month but were able to save millions from a year's worth of hip pain many would vote for such a choice, I think. Many others would not agree. As Brock (2004) points out, there is no ready way of resolving such conflicts.

- All kinds of other implicit moral judgements are made that are not obvious. A colleague at the London School of Economics (Alex Morton; personal communication) has pointed out to me that quality of life adjusted years are usually presented as being indifferent to age of the life involved. Perhaps they should not be. Thus, five more years of life for an eighty year old is counted as better than four for a twenty year old. Yet an old person has 'had a fair innings' already.[7] It would be a small extension of life for the old person but an extension of a quarter of a life span for a twenty year old. So perhaps young people should be given preference, and perhaps treatments for old people should count for less. Certainly that is what clinicians do in their day to day practice, as Aaron and Schwartz (1984) showed in their first edition. Clinicians also tend to give preference to someone on their waiting list supporting a family. That reasoning would not be shared

---

[7] See Williams (1997) for a discussion of the 'fair innings' principle.

by the elderly lobby, or perhaps by the courts under the UK's Human Rights Act.

- The NICE calculus implicitly accepts the idea that each individual counts equally. One might argue that a given improvement in the quality of life of a paraplegic, was worth *more* than the same improvement for a less disabled person just because life's experience is so much more constrained for someone with that high degree of disability.

If rationing is going to be more intense the public are going to have to get involved in some difficult choices, if openness and accountability are the aims. Perhaps the public would rather not know or be involved.

Conclusions

All in all, it is possible to say that resource allocation decisions in the UK's health care system are now characterised by a higher degree of open reasoned debate than they were three decades ago. Nevertheless, most resource allocation decisions are still in the unrecognised and unabated quadrant of Figure 1. Furthermore, those that are in the more centralised and explicit quadrant are little known and understood by the wider public.

There is a marked difference in approach to the different kinds of allocation principles used. The geographical allocations within each part of the UK are driven by considerations of need. NICE is driven by utilitarian notions. These are not necessarily at odds. Any efficiency savings generated can be used to help the least advantaged and this situation can be justified by some notion of distinct 'spheres' of justice — some principles are right for some situations and others for other situations. But it is a situation that needs clarification and care.

It is also true that formal philosophy is better at criticising existing methods than advancing largely agreed bases for rational discussion of priorities. One option is for philosophers to agree that there can be no rationally grounded decisions on the relative deservingness of different kinds of health spending. Professional indifference or some degree of neutrality is the most justifiable response. On the other hand political indifference is clearly not an option, and will be less of an option when the funds begin to dry up after 1998. It would be good to think that philosophers could be more help than that. Certainly they should help in laying bare hidden ethical assumptions made by technocrats whether they are economists or clinicians.

John Appleby & Anthony Harrison

Better Ways to Allocate Health Resources in the UK?

Introduction

In most areas of our economic life rationing is the unexceptional process carried out by markets; private rationing decisions — choosing what we want but constrained by what we can afford — is the norm. We may not be entirely happy with the resultant inequalities in resource allocation or consumption that inequalities in income inevitably produce, but by and large we live with the fact. Yet around the world health care is treated differently. Even in that most free of free market economies, the USA, state funding of health care is substantial — in excess of 10% of GDP — and goes some way towards evening out the inevitable inequalities in consumption. The consequence of collective funding for health care means that the private rationing/allocation decisions of markets become public rationing /allocation decisions.

But if — for good reasons of fairness — consumption of health care is no longer rationed by price and the size of an individual's income, how are scarce health resources to be allocated? The answer is not straightforward. Once, as with the UK NHS, the decision is made to take the allocation of most health resources out of the market arena to be funded instead (in the main) from taxation, the fundamental issue of how much to spend in total on health care has to be settled in a different way. Whatever the precise mechanisms allocating resources, and wherever exactly decisions are taken (whether at national, country or local level), that fundamental issue remains.[1] And, once the total spend is set, there follows a need to determine how resources then flow through the health care sys-

---

[1] In some degree the total health spend in the UK is not fixed precisely. For example, some elements of the English NHS budget — e.g. prescribing by GPs — are not cash-limited, but demand-led. However, detailed modelling by the Department of Health essentially provides a national budget for demand-led

tem to, ultimately, determine the pattern of consumption at the level of individual patients. What has traditionally determined these flows in the UK are the myriad bottom-up, clinician-level professional health care decisions concerning individual patients – but constrained and to an extent directed by the top-down determination of budgets and national priorities and targets. The principal allocation guide for the former is clinical need, and for the latter a balance between equity, efficiency and health outcome objectives.

A helicopter view of the whole UK health care system reveals a mishmash of allocation principles and mechanisms which has arisen from a need to compromise on the balance between competing health care objectives (equity versus efficiency for example), the pragmatic (and perhaps ethical) limitations of a fully planned, top-down system for determining individual levels of health care consumption, and the balance between professional autonomy and patient choice (see Box 1).

Improving on this collection of allocation 'systems' is not merely a technical issue to be resolved, for example, by amassing better data to carry out more sophisticated analysis to better inform the determination of which factors to include in the weighted capitation formulae (cf Gravelle et al, 2003) used to determine how the total budget is divided between different areas. Neither does the rejection of inequitable market methods of allocation then provide an obvious and easily operationalised alternative. While equity is currently the guiding principle for sharing out the budget, even here, as the original Resource Allocation Working Party (RAWP) found, some pragmatic compromise is required over the definition of this objective, with equal access to health care (rather than, say, equal outcome) for those at equal risk being chosen as the working definition of equity (DHSS, 1976b). And, as we have just noted, other trade-offs need to be made. Equity is not a free good – its attainment will involve sacrifices – and the degree to which it should dominate other health care objectives such as efficiency requires the making of evaluative judgements: crudely, what is society willing to sacrifice to ensure equal access to health care for those in equal need?

In the first part of this paper we describe how the primary allocation decision – the setting of the overall health budget – has been made in England in recent years. We suggest an alternative based on estimating the returns – health benefits – to be achieved by extra spending. In the second part we consider how far the process for allocating the total budget to different areas has succeeded in securing the NHS's equity objective of equal access for those in equal need, and we conclude that it has

spending (and hence the ability to plan other public spending) if not a globally capped budget as applies to other NHS services.

fallen short. In the final part, we set out ways in which determining both total spend and its allocation to different areas could be improved.

Box 1
Resource Allocation 'Systems' in the English NHS (2006)

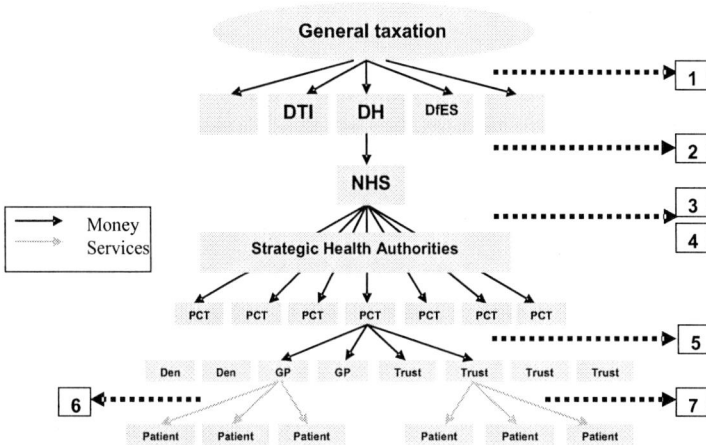

The flow of resources from the general pool of taxation to the ultimate consumption of treatments and services by patients comes as a result of many different allocation processes and decisions taken at different points in the health care system by different organisations and individuals guided by a variety of criteria and principles.

The diagram above captures some of this complexity and highlights key allocation decision points (numbers in boxes).

Decisions about the Department of Health's (DH) budget (**level 1** on the diagram) broadly arise from political trade-offs between spending departments (e.g. the Department of Trade and Industry [DTI], the Department of Education and Skills [DfES], etc.) and involve macroeconomic considerations as well as a degree of negotiation between the Treasury and the DH. Some of the DH budget (**level 2**) is retained centrally to fund a variety of services and initiatives, with the bulk of the budget allocated to the NHS.

The DH also makes allocations to Strategic Health Authorities (**level 3**) to fund regionally administered services and budgets such as clinical and other forms of training. But the bulk of the global NHS budget is allocated to primary care trusts (PCTs) by the DH (**level 4**), with the size of individual budgets informed (but not wholly determined) by a set of needs-based population weighted capitation formulae constructed on the original RAWP equity principle of promoting equal access for those at equal risk.

PCTs make further allocation decisions involving resource flows to primary and secondary care services, such as GPs, dentists ('den' on the diagram), and hospital trusts (**level 5**). At this point in the system the top-down approach to resource allocation starts to meet (and has to be reconciled with) bottom-up decisions (by clinicians and patients) which will in part determine the ultimate pattern of health care consumption by patients and hence the allocation of resources. Allocations to GPs and trusts are driven largely by patient demand, clinical decisions, and nationally-determined priorities expressed in part through the GP contract with the NHS, local PCT-determined priorities and national guidelines issued, for example, by the National Institute for Clinical Excellence (NICE).

While the equity principle remains important at **level 5**, the reality of trade-offs with other system objectives (e.g. efficiency, professional autonomy, national priorities etc) becomes more significant. At **levels 6 and 7**, patient-professional relationships tend to dominate.

It is worth emphasising that this chapter only deals with resource allocation in the English NHS. While there are clearly similarities across the UK countries in the way resources are allocated within each health care system (for example, all countries operate a needs-based weighted capitation system to allocate budgets from the centre to the periphery), there are (increasing) differences.

Nevertheless, all UK health care systems have a central concern with equity, and many of the arguments and ideas put forward here in relation to England can apply equally to the rest of the UK.

Determining the Total Public Spend on Health

The best way of describing the way in which the global NHS budget has traditionally been determined is 'incremental': the debate has essentially been about how much more should be spent than the previous year and — when five year plans were in vogue — how much more in the years which followed. How large the increment should be was generally informed by views about the impact of changes in demography, new technology and changes in demand, such as estimated changes in the number of hospital admissions.

That all changed in 2000 when the UK Government decided that the health budget should be substantially increased. This increase reflected a political judgement about the kind and quality of health care we should have. This judgement was later supported by reports prepared by Derek Wanless and his team within the Treasury (H.M. Treasury, 2002). The approach taken by Wanless in suggesting a new spending path for health care was to start with a 'vision' of what a world class health care system would look like — very short waiting times, defined pathways of care such as those set out in the National Service Frameworks — and then, broadly, to estimate the costs of achieving these goals. While such an approach had the merit of defining the scale of what had to be done, it suffered from three significant weaknesses.

- First, it did not explicitly demonstrate what health benefits the additional resources proposed by the review would produce, nor whether those resources could produce greater health benefits by being used differently.

- Second, it did not consider in detail whether there were other means of producing improved health outcomes other than through the proposed extra spending. One of the options developed, termed the 'fully engaged' scenario, did suggest that a rebalancing towards public health measures would be more effective in cost and health outcome terms, but this was not investigated in depth at the time. A subsequent report (H.M Treasury, 2004b) reaffirmed the potential of public health measures, but lack of evidence ruled out development of the scenario into a plan of action.

- Third, it did not consider what would follow *after* the target performance levels had been achieved. Implicitly, meeting these targets would mean the NHS was 'good enough'. However, by the time this was forecast to be achieved the forces making for increased spending — principally, improvements in medical technology — will have created new 'spending opportunities'.

The Wanless review's answer to the precise course of future spending was to assume a period (2003/4 to 2007/8) over which health spending in the UK would 'catch up' with other European Union states, and then later periods up to 2022 over which spending increases would reduce in order to 'keep up' with 'rising standards across all countries' (H.M. Treasury, 2002, p.78). But although this approach provided a pragmatic solution to the issue of deciding spending levels, it begs the underlying question of what the appropriate level of funding for the NHS should be. Keeping up with the Sarkozys or the Merkels assumes that France, Germany and others have broadly got the macro resource allocation decision 'right'. But, of course, there is no prima facie reason to assume this is the case.

An alternative viewpoint to take on the question of what we ought to spend on health care in total is essentially an economic one. On this view, spending on health, as on any other good, is worthwhile as long as the benefits it brings exceed those which could be obtained by other forms of spending. In other words, it is worth spending more on health as long as the benefits achieved outweigh the *opportunity costs*. Implicit in the rise in spending recommended by Wanless is the judgement that despite the increases that have already occurred in health spending, the benefits continue to be greater in health care than in other possible uses. The usual assumption, however, is that as spending in a particular area rises, there will inevitably come a point where the benefits at the margin will tend to fall, and, very possibly, for the absolute benefits to fall as spending increases still further — see Box 2.

Determining the point at which allocative efficiency is maximised (and hence the optimal level of health care spending identified) would require the Herculean task of quantifying (in commensurate units) *all* the total returns curves for *all* possible uses of the nation's scarce resources across *all* levels of spending and then allocating resources (in effect setting budgets) for *every* possible type of spending in a way which maximised returns at every level of spending until all resources are consumed. This exercise would need to be undertaken continuously to accommodate technological changes. The fact that every individual would place different values on the returns from different types of spending adds an almost infinitely complicating twist to an already near-impossible task. It is perhaps no surprise, therefore, that economists' traditionally preferred allocative/rationing mechanism is the market.

Box 2: Total Returns to Health Spending

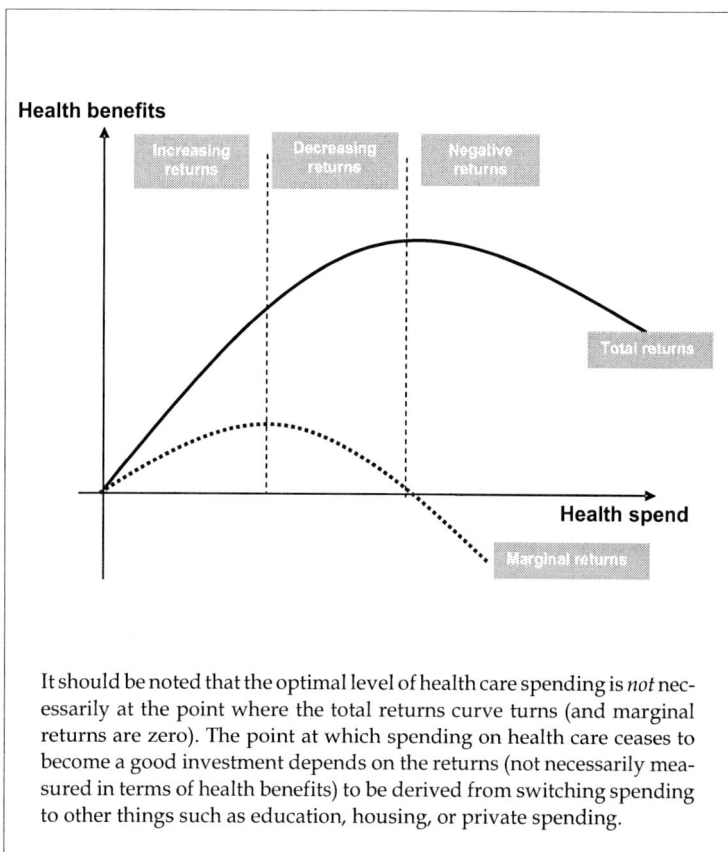

It should be noted that the optimal level of health care spending is *not* necessarily at the point where the total returns curve turns (and marginal returns are zero). The point at which spending on health care ceases to become a good investment depends on the returns (not necessarily measured in terms of health benefits) to be derived from switching spending to other things such as education, housing, or private spending.

However, given the previously described rejection of market allocation systems in the case of health care and the prohibitive nature of the alternative allocative task outlined above, a focus on the returns to health care investment alone would, within a cost-benefit framework, represent an improvement on current UK approaches to determining the global health budget, as these do not involve *any* test of the value of additional spending. The question remains however, of how to take account of the fact that different people may place different values on additional health benefits (and, indeed, value different aspects of the benefits—waiting time, clinical quality, etc.) differently. In the end, any ranking of these values must be a matter for political choice, but we believe such choices should be informed by whatever measures of value can be derived from appropriately designed research—as we go on to discuss below.

A cost-benefit approach to constructing the global budget implies that at low levels of spending, the most productive activities (in terms of 'healthiness'), such as immunisation and vaccination, along with basic primary care and the most cost-effective drugs, should be financed. As spending rises, resources will then tend to be devoted to activities and treatments which, while beneficial, yield less in terms of direct health benefits as conventionally measured by, for example, reductions in mortality or increases in life expectancy –though they may produce more in other terms (for example, convenience of access, a more pleasant care process, and so on).

It is not possible to estimate with confidence where on the curve the NHS is at the moment and what precisely the benefits are that extra spending may produce. The massive commitment of extra resources for the NHS since 2000 was not accompanied by an assessment of what those resources were expected to achieve, a gap which has not been filled by subsequent reports on specific programmes such as the Cancer Plan or the Coronary Heart Disease National Service Framework. These provide only limited insight into currently achieved health returns. Other programmes such as walk-in centres, have been designed to improve convenience rather than health. If a more explicit cost-benefit approach is to be used as a guide to spending levels, then there must be substantial investment in the data collection and research required to demonstrate what benefits extra spending is producing. Given the utilitarian nature of the cost-benefit approach –maximising health returns per pound spent[2] – what is also required is a way of dealing with the fact that constructing the budget on this basis also implies a certain *distribution* of benefits across the population.[3] This distribution might not maximise achievement of the NHS's equity principle of equal access for equal need at the level of individual patients.

This problem is of course not new (cf Broome, 1988; Wagstaff, 1991), and various suggestions have been made to resolve the conflict (cf

---

[2]   Essentially, '*QALY utilitarianism*' where the generic measure of health benefit – the quality adjusted life years – is the maximand. 'QALYs' combine the two main dimensions of health benefit – length of life (life years) and the quality of those years. Different health care interventions will affect these dimensions differently. Weighting life years for the quality of each life year provides a commensurate measure of outcome–a common benefit 'currency' –which enables comparisons between the benfits produced by diffeent interventions/ services – maternity and elderly care, for example, to be compared. On the cost side of the cost benefit equation, the common currency is, of course, money.

[3]   'Population' can be defined in any way which reflects dimensions of potential equity concern – age, sex, ethnic group, social class, disease group etc. Or, it can refer to individuals, with the implication that (some of) those in equal need may not have (completely) equal access as a result of the use of the efficiency criterion in determining the global allocation.

Dolan, 1998; Williams and Cookson, 2000; Bleichrodt et al, 2004). It is theoretically possible to construct a set of 'equity weights' to be used to adjust the *value* of the benefits of health care spending to reflect society's view of what constitutes a fair distribution of those benefits. For example, the benefits from interventions to deal with cancer may be deemed to be worth more than similar benefits from some other service. Similar equity arguments may apply to the benefits from interventions for rare diseases, or for particular population groups (e.g. the elderly) whose capacity to benefit is low (or the costs of achieving a unit of health improvement—a Quality Adjusted Life Year, say—is high), but for whom society deems it worthwhile funding on grounds of fairness. The use of such equity weights will entail a certain loss of efficiency (i.e. a reduction in total benefits), but by implication would also reveal society's willingness to pay to achieve a certain level of equity. It is very likely that there will be societal disagreement regarding what precise weightings to give to specific outcomes. Moreover, this is likely to be an example of the kind of 'reasonable disagreement' Niall Maclean described in his chapter. In order to minimise disagreement, it might be necessary to derive some kind of 'average' equity weightings. There will inevitably be a spread of views around this average; indeed, the average might not match with the set of weightings favoured by any particular individual.

An alternative approach—more pragmatic, but perhaps less satisfactory on other grounds—which we adopt here is to *ignore* the implied distributional consequences of the cost-benefit approach when used for determining the global health care spend. Equity considerations should be the focus only when *distributing* the global spend within the NHS. These considerations are of course also promoted by the fact that the NHS, with some exceptions, is free at the point of use and hence in theory available to all regardless of income. How the cost-benefit approach to global budget setting might be carried out—the data requirements, and the technical and ethical issues involved—is outlined below. First, it is worth outlining some evidence concerning the current pattern of spending and utilisation resulting from the interplay of existing allocation 'systems'.

Dividing the Total

As Howard Glennerster has shown in the previous chapter, for the past thirty years or so successive UK governments have made geographical, population-based allocations of a significant proportion of the global NHS budget on the basis of explicit needs-based formulae. The 152 or so primary care trusts (PCTs) in England now receive a unified budget made up of formula-derived elements for hospital and community health services, prescribing, HIV/AIDS, and both the cash limited and non-cash limited elements of general medical services (Department of Health, 2003a). Although the formulae and the precise channels through which funds flow have, over time, changed (in some cases substantially), the broad objective — to create the potential of equal access for equal need — has remained more or less the same.

Despite the longevity of this policy, large variations in geographical spending patterns persist. For example, using data from the Department of Health's National Programme Budget Project,[4] Table 1 shows variations in the needs-weighted spend by English PCTs per 100,000 population for 23 disease-based spending 'programmes'. The variations in spend are considerable for some disease areas, although minimum and maximum spends may give an exaggerated impression of variation due to data quality issues. Nevertheless, as Figures 1 — 5 show, taking the entire range of spending for the top five spending areas still suggests substantial variation. Why such differences exist is only partially explained by variations in need — the data standardises populations using the same methodology applied in the weighted capitation formula used to allocate resources to PCTs. Such needs weighting for the national weighted capitation formula applies to much broader service categories than the disease areas used by the National Programme Budget Project, but will, to a degree, take account of variations in need.

Despite the imperfect needs standardisation, it is hard to see what justifies the broadly two-fold variation in spending revealed in figures 1 to 5 below. Across all PCTs, only around 30% of the variation in spending can be accounted for by variation in health care needs, PCT population age structure and variations in the costs of providing services in different PCTs — all factors used in allocating PCT budgets (see Figure 6). This leaves around two thirds of the variation attributable — presumably — to a combination of different local priorities, variations in the efficiency of local providers and other, more random factors.

---

[4] This project collects, collates and publishes retrospective PCT spending on 23 largely disease-based 'programmes' of care. The aim is to reveal spending priorities across the NHS and eventually to link spending with health benefits.

Table 1: Variations in English PCT Spending per 100,000 Needs-Weighted Population: Proportion of Total Programme Spend[5]

Spending programme	Maxi-mum %	Mini-mum %	Median %	Variation Max/min
Hearing Problems	2.6	0.1	0.5	20.0
Poisoning	2.1	0.4	1.1	5.3
Dental Problems	7.2	0.0	1.1	2793.3
Neonate Conditions	4.0	0.0	1.1	155.3
Blood Disorders	4.0	0.4	1.4	11.1
Infectious Diseases	9.4	0.8	1.6	11.1
Healthy Individuals	6.6	0.3	1.8	19.8
Skin Problems	4.6	1.0	2.1	4.8
Social Care Needs	12.7	-6.7	2.1	-1.9
Eye/Vision Problems	4.3	0.4	2.4	11.2
Endocrine, Nutritional and Metabolic Problems	4.2	1.0	2.7	4.4
Neurological System Problems	6.3	1.5	3.0	4.2
Learning Disability Problems	17.9	0.5	3.6	38.6
Maternity and Reproductive Health	11.7	1.7	4.5	6.9
Genito Urinary System Disorders (except fertility)	11.8	3.0	5.2	3.9
Respiratory System Problems	9.9	3.1	5.3	3.2
Trauma and Injuries (includes burns)	15.3	3.1	6.1	4.9
Musculo Skeletal System Problems (excludes trauma)	10.6	1.6	6.1	6.8
Gastro Intestinal System Problems	9.5	3.5	6.3	2.7
Cancers & Tumours	10.7	3.2	6.4	3.3
Circulation Problems (CHD)	14.4	6.1	10.4	2.4
Mental Health Problems	22.7	5.6	12.0	4.0
Other Areas of Spend/ Conditions:	47.5	8.5	13.3	5.6

[5] Source: Adapted from National Programme Budget Project (Department of Health, 2006) data. NB: some figures reported as '0.0' due to rounding.

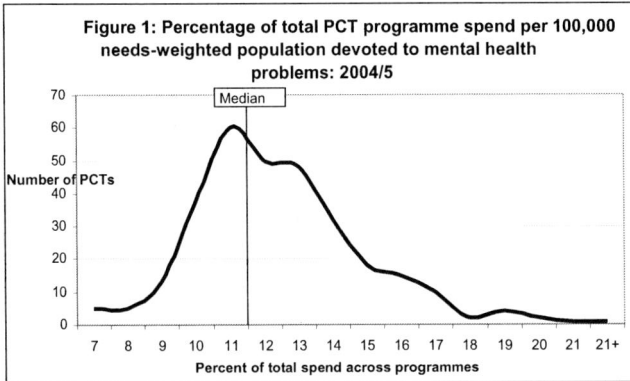

Figure 1: Percentage of total PCT programme spend per 100,000 needs-weighted population devoted to mental health problems: 2004/5

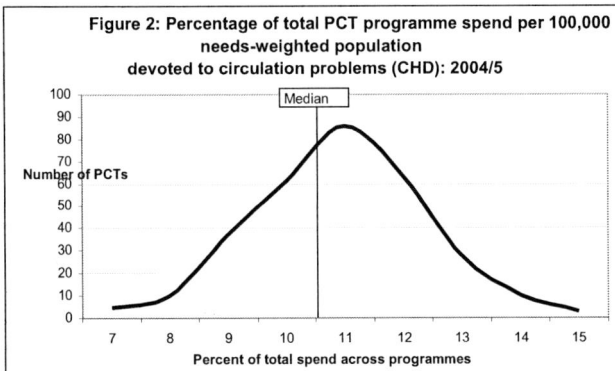

Figure 2: Percentage of total PCT programme spend per 100,000 needs-weighted population devoted to circulation problems (CHD): 2004/5

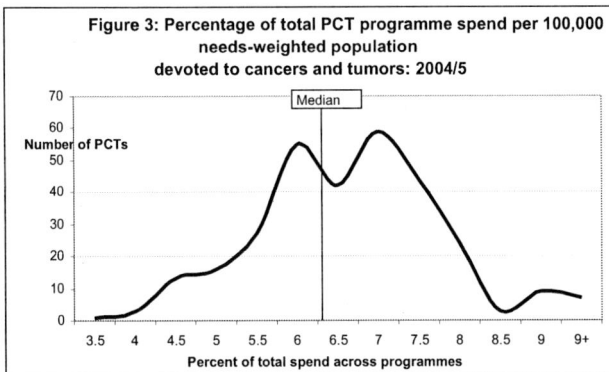

Figure 3: Percentage of total PCT programme spend per 100,000 needs-weighted population devoted to cancers and tumors: 2004/5

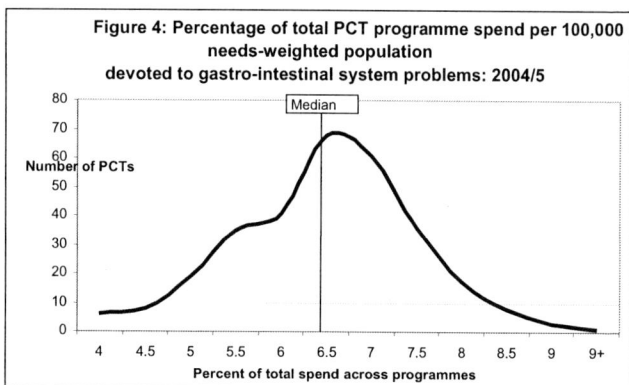

Figure 4: Percentage of total PCT programme spend per 100,000 needs-weighted population devoted to gastro-intestinal system problems: 2004/5

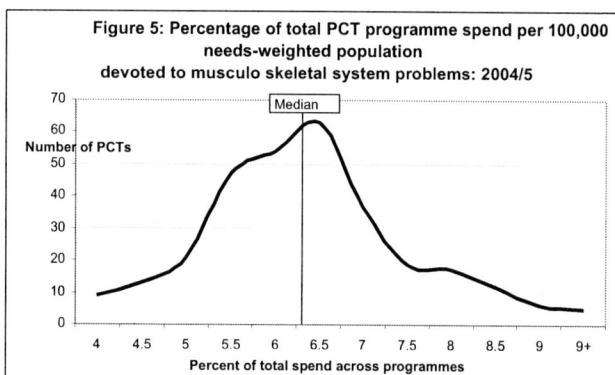

Figure 5: Percentage of total PCT programme spend per 100,000 needs-weighted population devoted to musculo skeletal system problems: 2004/5

Geographical variations in spending by disease area is one dimension of concern regarding equity, and one which is likely to reflect variations in access and utilisation at the level of individual patients. More direct evidence that individuals with similar health care needs do not have similar opportunities to access care, despite the equity-driven thrust of resource allocation processes at macro (i.e. national) and meso (i.e. PCT) levels, has been well demonstrated by investigating a proxy for access: utilisation. For example, using data from the Health Survey for England and after controlling for needs variables and supply side factors, Morris et al (2003)) revealed horizontal inequalities[6] in the utilisation of various health care services (e.g. general medical services, outpatients, inpatients and day cases) related to non-health care need factors such as income, ethnicity, employment status and education. In particular,

---

[6]   That is, those in equal need do not use health care services equally.

Figure 6: Variation in PCT spend on mental health services per 100,000 raw population explained by variations in need for health care, age structure of PCT populations and variations in costs of provision

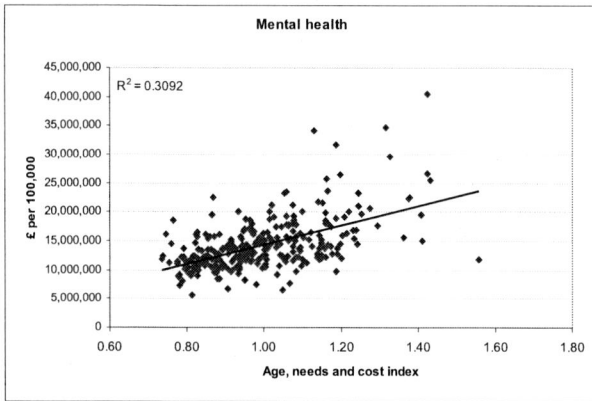

NB: A needs index value > 1 indicates greater need for health care than average for England.

Source: Authors' own calculations based on data published by the National Programme Budget Project (Department of Health, 2006)

Consider another example, that of cancers and tumours: spending here per 100,000 raw population varies at the extremes by over three fold, yet virtually none of this can be explained by variations in need, age and cost (see Figure 7.)

Figure 7: Variation in PCT spend on cancers and tumours per 100,000 raw population explained by variations in need for health care, age structure of PCT populations and variations in costs of provision

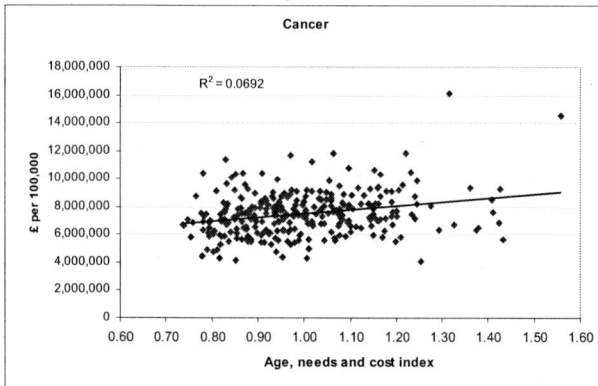

NB: A needs index value > 1 indicates greater need for health care than average for England.

Source: Authors' own calculations based on data published by the National Programme Budget Project (Department of Health, 2006)

those on low incomes, those with low levels of formal educational qualifications, and ethnic minorities, while more likely to consult their GP, were less likely to receive all forms of secondary care. As the authors note, to a large extent this confirms evidence from other utilisation studies and other types of study (e.g. Benzeval and Judge, 1994; Smaje and Le Grand 1997; Alexander, 1999; Adamson et al, 2003).

There are some difficulties and problems in arriving at a definitively clear cut view as to the extent of the inequities in utilisation revealed by these and other studies (see for example, Dixon et al, 2003). For example, even where there are apparently objective measures of 'need' (usually bio-medical, such as blood pressure or visual acuity), variations across individuals in, for example, tolerance of pain or disability hugely complicate the quantification of the extent to which inequalities in utilisation should be automatically considered to be inequities. Nevertheless, the broad conclusion most investigators have reached is that there is prima facie evidence that certain population groups, defined along different equity dimensions such as income, socio-economic group and ethnicity, fail to utilise health care services in proportion to their health care needs.

Do These Variations Matter?

It is clear from the response of the UK public to 'postcode rationing' (the phenomenon of treatments and services being available in some geographical areas and not others) that there are strong pressures for uniformity across England[7] with regard to the availability of specific treatments. These pressures have been greatest in relation to specific cancer drugs, in part because of the nature of the disease and in part because drug companies have found ways of ensuring that differences between PCTs are reported in the national media. On the latter, some of the somewhat ethically dubious hard and soft marketing tactics of pharmaceutical companies has most recently been investigated and reported by Consumers International (Consumers International, 2006). In principle, albeit with a time-lag, the establishment of the National Institute for Clinical Excellence (NICE) and the subsequent decision that its recommendations should be binding on PCTs solves the 'postcode rationing' problem. But, as the data presented above indicate, variations in other areas are substantial. Given the small proportion of total spending covered by NICE decisions, they are likely to remain so in the medium to long term. But do these variations matter?

For several reasons, it may be argued that they do not. First, they could be regarded as the expression of local choice by the organisations — PCTs — created precisely to decide on behalf of the populations they serve how resources are to be used. Second, they may be seen as the

---

[7]   The variations emerging between the four countries in the UK with regard to, for example, charges for prescription drugs and long-term social care may lead to similar calls for standardisation across the UK — but such calls are not strongly apparent yet.

necessary consequence of the discretionary nature of medical practice. Generally speaking there are no clear cut guidelines for determining when and how quickly treatment is required. Third, they also may reflect variations in the needs of each local population which no national formula can take account of fully. Fourth, they may reflect individual choices on whether to be treated or not, and what form treatment should take.

If these arguments are accepted as decisive then it could be argued that the present system of allocation is broadly appropriate. But as we have noted, when differences in the available services between areas come to light, they are invariably regarded as unacceptable in a national health service — especially given its key founding principle of providing access to health care based on need, and not on income or any other non-health factor. Moreover, in many cases the differences that arise because of the choices people make whether or not to seek treatment may be regarded not so much as the consequence of exercising autonomous choice but of poor information provided to the patient and of the poor quality of the services available to them. Furthermore, within the framework which we set out above for the macro decision about how much to spend on health, the variations identified above could be seen as evidence that the resources allocated to health are not being used to best effect. Either too much is being allocated to some services in some areas — with consequent low returns at the margin — or the reverse (returns high at the margin where spending is low). The latest report from the Chief Medical Office (Donaldson 2006) made exactly this point in relation to the large differences in the rates at which a number of common operations are carried out. On this view the financial system should be used — along with other measures — to shift resources away from low and toward high value uses.

So, for any one or for all three of these reasons, there is a case for measures which reduce the scale of variations in spending on specific services and which promote greater equality of service use for a given level or type of need. In what follows we consider what part changes to the financial system might play in reducing variations in spending on service/disease programmes.

What Should be Done?

We consider first how the total spend should be determined and then the how that total should be allocated.

Total Spend

We suggested above that the total level of spending on health should be determined by the benefits that extra spending brings: where precisely

Type of benefit	Programmes							BENEFIT (£)
	Cancer	Heart disease	Mental health	Maximum waiting times	Emergency care	Chronic care	Etc.	
Access Waiting time Travel time Booking Etc.								
Process Respect Friendliness Length of stay Etc.								
Outcome Lives Life years Etc.								
COST (£)								

Diagram 1: Cost-benefit spending/policy matrix

on the spending /returns curve the budget should be set remains, of course, a political matter. But if the political decision is to be made on the basis of information as to its implications, ways must be found of estimating where on the curve the NHS is now and where it will be if the budget is increased sufficiently to allow expansion of the services available.

The first requirement, however, is to form a view on what range of benefits should be taken into account. Most benefit evaluations — including in particular those carried out by NICE — focus on health benefits. But many recent initiatives are primarily designed to make services easier to access (e.g. walk-in centres) or quicker to access (e.g. waiting time targets). These convenience benefits may be valued for their own sake, because people dislike waiting, but they may also create economic or employment benefits if people have a shorter period of ill-health or disability. Diagram 1 sets out a matrix within which all the benefits of additional spending on different 'programmes' could be set out and compared. How the programmes are defined could be flexible. One obvious categorisation would be types of disease. Broadly, the programmes would minimise overlaps in terms of resource use. In principle this provides the framework for determining both where additional resources should be allocated and whether overall returns are sufficient to justify extra spending.

A matrix on these lines could provide a framework for the allocation of resources at national level between major illnesses such as cancer and heart disease, where national targets have been set, or be used by primary care trusts to guide the allocation of resources at local level. Provided that each of the cells can be filled in, the matrix allows the net benefits of alternative allocations of resources to be compared and the 'best' overall allocation chosen. In this way it follows through the logic of the cost benefit approach proposed for the allocation process of the overall health budget.

Attaching monetary values to the costs is usually straightforward. However, benefits present a more difficult problem as the sort of benefits noted in diagram 1 — waiting times, 'respect', QALYs etc — are rarely traded (or indeed tradeable) and hence no 'off the peg' market-derived monetary values are available. Nevertheless, it is possible through survey methods to estimate 'willingness to pay' and hence derive monetary values, for example, for a month's reduction in waiting time — or any other non-marketed health benefit, such as a QALY. Given that different individuals will place different valuations on the same benefit, some compromise in the value eventually attached to a benefit must be made. This may mean taking the average value, for example. Having said that, it is not impossible to imagine that an individual's own valuations could in fact be accommodated (up to a point) further down the system through, for example, the exercise of patient choice. So, a hospital could offer a variety of options on waiting times, with patients valuing short waits being offered these, but without a definite date, and others being offered a definite date, but a longer wait.

Obvious though the need for such evaluations may be, they are comparatively rare, and rarely, if ever, carried out in the context described here. As we have noted, most of those which are carried out focus on health benefits for which the QALY measure has come into general use (e.g. in the work of NICE and similar bodies). But there has been very little research conducted to establish the value which people place on other benefits such as convenience or, indeed, on the value of a QALY or other benefit enjoyed by different individuals.[8] Most of the additional spending in the UK since 2000 has been approved without any form of evaluation at all.

Accordingly, if the cost-benefit matrix is to be useful, a substantial technical effort is required including:

- New policy initiatives such as walk-in centres or chronic disease management programmes should routinely be subject to an initial test of whether or not they are likely to yield net benefits of the sort noted in diagram 1.

- These evaluations would require quantification of the public's *valuation* of health benefits and associated benefits of health care.

- Because the impact of new policies is hard to predict, there should be more extensive use of pilots or experiments, before new ideas are put into effect. The present government has initiated pilots in some areas but has often pressed on with national programmes before the results of the pilots have been available. And in many areas it has introduced policies without any ex ante evaluation.

- More use should be made of ex post evaluations to check whether policies in fact produce benefits initially estimated. In the case of drugs for example, there can be significant differences between trial conditions and those which obtain in practice.

These recommendations are in line with those put forward by the Cabinet Office for public policymaking (Cabinet Office 2005) and have long been the recommendation of the Treasury via its 'Green Book' (Her Majesty's Treasury, 2003). Some progress has been made: for example, impact assessments of new policies, albeit on a broad brush basis, are now routine. But it remains true that the resources devoted to testing whether or not new policies or interventions are beneficial remain modest.

---

[8] In general, economic evaluations such as those used by NICE treat all QALYs the same, whomever they accrue to.

If such work was successful then the resulting global spend derived from this process would be the sum of indicative spends for each programme, where limits on the latter are guided by the marginal returns in each spending relative to returns in the 'next best' programme (see figure 8 below). Clearly, the aggregated sum only provides a guide for what should be the actual total spend as this approach cannot define what is affordable (out of national wealth) or what may be practically realistic. However, it provides essential information on which to make the decision about what benefits are to be gained and what benefits are to be forgone given any decision about the total allocation.

Figure 8: Calculating the Global NHS Allocation

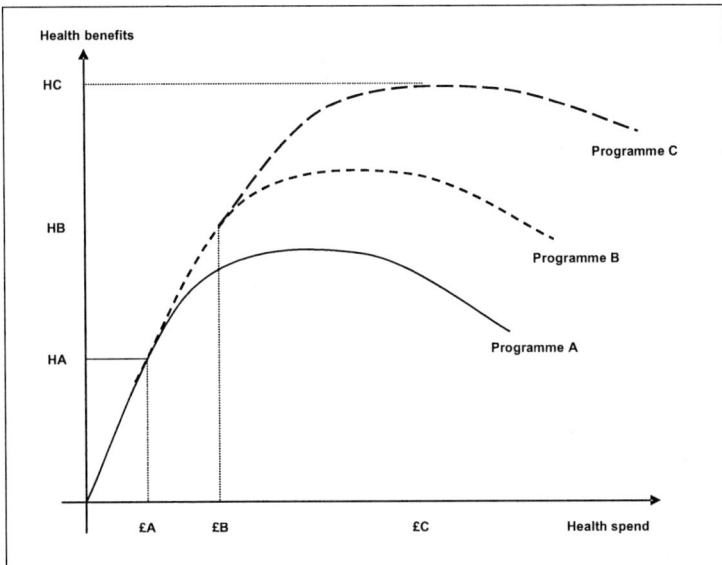

The global budget (£C) in a health care system with three programmes of care (A, B and C) could be determined by the health benefits each programme produces at various levels of spending. In the diagram above, spending limits for each programme are reached when the marginal benefits of an extra pound's spend would produce more benefits if spent on an alternative programme. On this basis, the global budget (£C) maximises the total benefit (HC) that can be produced from this level of spend. In doing so, it also sets the relative size of the budgets for each programme—in this case, roughly equal priority to programmes A and B, and roughly twice the priority to programme C.

As noted earlier, and as illustrated by the example in figure 8 above, a cost-benefit approach to deciding the global allocation for the NHS will not only indicate where maximum health benefits lie, but will also imply a particular *distribution* of those benefits — primarily between programmes and hence between disease groups and population sub-groups. When it comes to deciding on how the global allocation should distributed — and in particular, when thinking about whether local areas should be free to set health care distribution priorities that might be at odds with the priorities implied by the global calculation — we confront head-on the issue of whether the distribution implied by the latter can be considered equitable. The extent to which this implied distribution deviates from our ideals of equity is impossible to know without specifying precisely those ideals and without knowing how the implied distribution would play out in practice.[9]

However, even in the absence of this information, it remains possible to use equity considerations when we allocate the total NHS budget to local areas. We might for example use the principle of equal access for equal need to ensure equity of access to benefits *within* programmes across localities. It is also worth noting that while utilitarian approaches to setting the global allocation are essentially unconcerned about their distributional consequences, such approaches can nevertheless provide a case for redistribution. For example, given diminishing marginal returns, the goal of maximising benefits means that resources should be shifted between programmes in order to achieve most good. So again, as Figure 8 suggested, this will imply different levels of allocation to different programmes (and by implication different levels of consumption by different population groups[10]). This could mean, for example, that a service such as mental health might gain at the expense of access improvements to elective care.

Dividing the Total

Currently, PCTs receive most of their funding in the form of a general or unified allocation, which may be spent on any health care service. The pattern of spending which emerges is, as noted above, the result of the interplay of a large number of factors: patient demands, professional judgements, the efficiency of local providers, and a reflection of patterns established many years ago. Following the allocation model set out

---

[9]   It is worth noting in passing that, as Table 1 makes clear, there is currently a particular distribution of actual spending across programmes of care which has virtually no planned or rational basis; no overt decision has ever been made to, for example, devote 12% of PCT budgets to mental health services.

[10]   Although, it should be noted, only to the extent that different groups in the population will have varying needs for different programmes of care.

above for setting the level of total spend, the local allocation process could be constrained by introducing programme-specific allocations out the national total for the relevant programme. That would mean, in the case of cancer for example, that a national budget for the cancer plan was determined by a process similar to that described above and that national total would then be allocated to local purchasers to be spent only on cancer services. The allocation formula would be based on cancer-specific need indicators.

In this way, the allocation system would reach down to levels 6 and 7 in Box 1 — further than the current allocation methodology. Such a method would help to ensure that funding matched need for each programme area and across localities. In the case of cancer, as we noted earlier, there appears to be little or no connection with the present allocation methodology for PCT budgets and the needs index used to guide that allocation. And so a cancer-specific needs weighting — assuming for the moment that the data could be obtained on which to base one — would go some way to ensuring a better match between allocation and need.

Although the current UK Government has so far not considered revising allocations in this way, a process along these lines does fit the approach it has adopted to improve the way cancer and other services (such as those covered by National Service Frameworks) are delivered. In all these areas, the Government has set targets and standards which it uses to hold PCTs to account — the fact that variations in service spending on the scale reported above continue to exist years after the frameworks came into effect suggests that they are not in themselves sufficient to ensure broadly equal standards of service across the whole of the NHS.

These targets have been set without a process of the kind described above; that is, they have not been costed or evaluated. A specific grant approach would require the government to specify what the cost of providing the nationally specified services should be. This would be welcomed by local purchasers who are currently faced with what often seem to them to be incompatible demands levied by centrally determined targets (i.e. the cost of meeting all these demands simultaneously would exceed their budget). Such an approach is not far removed from that adopted in the UK for the distribution of finance to local government authorities to provide services other than health care, which involves estimating the cost of providing specific services (such as education or social care).

As an alternative to the formula approach, allocation to PCTs could, in principle, be based on the returns earned in each area — thereby mirroring the national allocation process between diseases. Such an approach could be justified in two ways. First, the returns, if measurable, might provide a better guide than needs indicators to where resources could be used most effectively. Second, it would provide an incentive to both purchasers and providers to keep costs down and seek out the most cost- and clinically-effective use of funds.

Both approaches put the Department of Health in the role of investor seeking the best portfolio of 'disease' investments/programme. Within each programme it must decide how to allocate resources to local areas. It might use a formula to do so, or it might make judgements based on how well each area used the resources at its disposal. Currently cancer services in England are managed through thirty four networks which involve a number of PCTs working together with their local providers to serve local populations of up to two million people. Each could be regarded as a subsidiary company to which the Department allocated resources on the basis of evidence of good performance in finding and treating cancer and alleviating suffering. In other words, the efficiency of local purchasers and providers could also influence the allocation. Those achieving higher returns would get more and vice versa. If this were done then the micro allocation would be linked to the macro total budget allocation: the returns being achieved at local level would pro- vide the evidence needed to determine the total allocation.

Such an approach might seem like an economist's fantasy—and, pushed to the limit, it is. But the current UK Government has already gone part way down this path with its recent revisions to the GP con- tract. These allocate resources to general practitioners (UK family doc- tors) in relation to specific actions they take—such as checks for diabetes, hypertension, immunisation and vaccination rates (Depart- ment of Health, 2003b). These activities by their nature can to a large extent be systematised—like social security programmes—with rules of eligibility, frequency of contact, etc. That is, they could be seen as entitle- ment programmes, for which all with the relevant characteristics (age or disease state) qualify. They allow personal discretion on the part of the patient—whether to participate or not—but not local, PCT or practice discretion.

Similarly, the current UK Government has, through its waiting times guarantee, effectively created a right to treatment within a given timescale, which local areas must honour. If they do not, then recent case law has established patients have a right to seek treatment abroad and the NHS is legally obliged to meet the cost (European Court of Justice, 2006). Variations may still arise because clinicians do not use uniform national criteria to determine when to treat. But as we have argued else- where (Harrison and Appleby, 2005), such thresholds are required if national policy is to be put on a rational basis—and work is going on in some areas to define them.

National Service Frameworks can be viewed in the same way. Although they do not create rights conferred on individual patients, they are intended to move the allocation of resources in the direction which the relevant government ministers and the Department of Health considers most beneficial. As we suggested above it makes sense to purchasers for there to be a link between the resources they receive and the service improvements they are required to make.

However, other areas of care cannot be systematised in this way. In some areas, demand is not predictable enough, or it cannot be so easily managed (such as 'demand' for preventive measures), or there may be genuine local differences in specific needs which would make standardisation difficult. Furthermore, from around 2002 onwards, in the face of criticism that the NHS was too centralised, the Government began to develop an alternative 'management model' which — in principle — is intended to allow greater local discretion. Under this model, patients are allowed a greater say through the exercise of various choices about the services they receive, and they thereby come to exert a broader influence as citizens. The specific programme allocation model suggested here does not fit this philosophy. The existing allocation framework embodying general grants is more appropriate in that it does not in itself constrain local choice whether by users or purchasers.

How the allocation system should work depends, therefore, on a number of prior issues:

- the extent to which care can be systematised and national rules defined to determine what should be provided;
- the extent to which equity should be defined in terms specific to particular conditions, such as cancer, or broad services such as elective (waiting list) care;
- the extent to which professional discretion can be limited by guidelines, such as those provided by NICE, that define when treatment should be offered;
- the desired or tolerable scope for local variation arising from the use of discretion by PCTs, professionals and individual users.

There are also practical considerations. As with the information needed to pursue the cost-benefit approach for determining the global allocation, allocation to localities along the lines suggested here would also require significant investment: not only in the collection of new forms of data, but in the construction of programme-specific needs-based allocation models which, with the exception of mental health, do not currently exist.

Conclusion

We have argued that the level of total spending on the NHS ought to be determined by an explicit assessment of the benefits which would accrue if the budget were increased — and the converse if cuts were being considered. While this may seem like an obvious way forward, it will prove very hard to implement in practice: the programme of work we have set out above will be hard to undertake, requiring as it does substantial technical developments and a significant commitment of resources to collect and analyse the required data.

We have also argued that the allocation system could be used to reduce unjustified variation between similar services in different parts of the country. Such a system could also reflect more closely than the present allocation system does exactly how decisions to use resources are actually made: that is, the strong central influence exerted over services such as those covered by national service frameworks or targets such as elective care. The greater that influence, the stronger the case for an allocation system which reflects the fact that it is the centre which is currently determining how much is spent on those services.

But such an allocation system would require new distribution formulae for determining what the appropriate budget for each disease programme in each PCT area should be. Composing such a formulae would require much more information about the incidence of different diseases at local level than is currently readily available.

In addition to these practical difficulties, there are issues of principle as well. The cost-benefit approach if implemented would almost certainly pose awkward equity issues around, in particular, the distribution of NHS funds between programmes. Furthermore, any cost-benefit approach may 'threaten' small user groups for which the costs of achieving specific benefits such as a week of extra life may be very high. However, many of these problems are already latent within the existing allocation system. For example, any additional funding for specific areas already comes at the expense of funding for other areas — however, we do not within the current system know a great deal about what the benefits and costs of these funding shifts are. Because of the muddle of central and local influences bearing on PCTs, and the lack of useful information of the benefits of increasing spending in different areas, explicit choices between different groups of beneficiaries are rarely made. The primary virtue of the model we set out here is *transparency* — it allows for explicitness regarding the costs and benefits of various allocation options, and thereby for more explicit choices between these options.

Our model also poses political (in the broad sense) questions about who should make allocation decisions. In principle, PCTs exist to make decisions as to the use of the resources they are allocated through the 'cascade' of finance shown in Box 1 above. In practice, PCTs represent a kind of buffer zone where top-down pressures imposed by national targets or clinical standards collide with demand pressures from individual residents of the geographical area served by the PCT, and by various health care professionals. The result, as we have shown above, is substantial variations in service provision. These variations are hard to explain and to justify, in either equity or efficiency terms.

To sum up: there are significant weaknesses in the way resources are allocated to and within the NHS. To remove or (perhaps more realistically) to reduce them will require a substantial investment in new data, research and analysis. Even so, improvement will be slow. But if that investment is not made, then we will be no clearer in five years time than we are now as to whether the total budget is 'enough' and whether it is being allocated to best effect in terms of both efficiency and equity.

Leonard Fleck

Just Caring

The Ethical Challenges of Health Care Reform in the USA

Introduction

Angel Diaz is sixty-nine years old and in the very advanced stages of Alzheimer's disease. He had been a machine operator in Philadelphia. The first signs of the disease came in the early 1990s. His brother cared for him until May of 2002 when Angel choked on some food and required emergency hospitalisation. He became dependent on a ventilator and a feeding tube, and was discharged to a nursing home. In February of 2003 Angel developed pneumonia and intestinal bleeding. He spent 140 days in the hospital at a cost of $280 000, less than half of which was covered by insurance. This represented a very large drain on the charity care resources of the hospital (Anand, 2003).

State Senator Robert Emerson from Flint, Michigan has told the story of his son's roommate from college, 'Bud' (pseudonym).[1] 'Bud' did not have health insurance. He was diagnosed with pneumonia, and given a prescription. In total, this episode of care cost him $200. His physician told him to return in ten days if still ill. After ten days he was feeling worse than before, but he did not have another $200. He decided to tough it out. Three days later Senator Emerson's son found him dead. This was clearly a preventable death.

How should we, citizens of a society that wants to be (and be seen) as being just and caring, think of these two cases? We might be tempted to dismiss the latter as a tragic and unfortunate mistake. Young people die in automobile accidents daily. We do not see that as a societal moral flaw. However, that analogy is misleading. It yields comforting moral self-deception. For the most part deaths in auto accidents are not the product of any societal policy choices. That is not true, however, with

---

[1] This story was mediated in a personal communication.

regard to our uninsured. In late 2006 there were 46 million Americans without health insurance (Henry J. Kaiser Family Foundation, 2006) without assured access to needed health care. Those are not 46 million 'accidents'. Those individuals are uninsured as a result of deliberate social policy choices. How should we assess morally those policy choices? That is the central question of this essay.

What do we find most puzzling and troubling about our two cases? Bodenheimer and Grumbach (2005, p. 3), following Enthoven and Kronick (1989), describe the US health care system as a 'paradox of excess and deprivation.' How could we possibly spend so much money on Mr Diaz, who has lived a full life and whose disease process is both irreversible and totally debilitating, while at the same time allowing a young man to die from an easily treatable medical problem? This is both puzzling and morally troubling. But how can it be 'morally troubling' to try to save Mr Diaz's life? After all, one survey showed that both American and British physicians would be willing to spend $270,000 on an accident victim even if they knew when that individual was brought into the emergency room there was less than a 1% chance of saving his life (Aaron and Schwartz, 2006, p. 109). Of course, if this were the 'whole story', this would not be morally troubling. It is only when this story is juxtaposed to the stories of millions of Americans who are denied access to needed and effective health care because they are unable to pay for that care that we see this as morally troubling. Again, if it were literally impossible to control health care resources so that they were allocated to meeting the health needs of the uninsured rather than the health needs of Mr Diaz, then we could describe that outcome as tragic and unfortunate (for the uninsured), but not as unjust or morally troubling. However, Canada and most European nations provide universal access to needed health care, which means that the paradoxes of excess and deprivation are not a necessary feature of our health care system. Other choices are possible, which means we are open to legitimate moral criticism.

In this essay I argue that American health care policy is open to moral criticism for being unjust. This is not a utopian or idealistic claim. From that perspective all health policies and health systems are unjust. This is not a morally useful outcome if the goal of moral criticism is reform. Why trade one unjust health care system for another? What we need is a practical non-ideal conception of health care justice (as explained below), sufficiently complex that it can be responsive to the technological and organisational intricacies characteristic of advanced health care systems today. One goal of this essay will be to spell that out. This conception will be internally morally pluralistic and complex, very much reflecting the diversity of reasonable comprehensive views of justice characteristic of our political life.[2] Such a conception will evolve over time in response to concrete social problems generated by innovations in medical technology or changing political, economic, cultural, or organisational circumstances. Such a conception will be complex and pluralistic to its core. No one dominant value, such as liberty or equality or utility, will be *the* defining feature of that conception of justice. Instead, in concrete circumstances multiple justice-relevant considerations will have to be noted and balanced against one another to yield a considered judgment of health care justice. Such judgments will need to be justified in two different ways (for reasons explained below): firstly, by a process of 'wide reflective equilibrium', as described by Rawls (1971) and Daniels (1996, chs. 1, 2, 8, 16); and second, through rational democratic deliberation (Fleck, 1992, 1994, 1999, 2002; Gutmann and Thompson, 2004). Wide reflective equilibrium will yield adequate (not perfect) coherence and consistency across the field of our judgments of health care justice sufficient to permit critical reflection, *and* define deliberative boundaries constraining enough to yield 'just enough' concrete judgments of health care justice to be practically useful and morally reliable (not infallible).

What is the problem of health care justice today? It is the 'just caring' problem: What does it mean to be a 'just' and 'caring' society when we have only limited resources to meet virtually limitless health care needs?[3] Or, if we do not have enough money to pay for all the health care

---

[2]   Here I draw on the work of John Rawls in *Political Liberalism* (Rawls, 1993), who in turn drew on the pragmatic perspective of John Dewey. See especially chapter one of *Political Liberalism*, where Rawls writes 'Under the political and social conditions secured by the basic rights and liberties of free institutions, a diversity of conflicting and irreconcilable — and what's more, reasonable — comprehensive doctrines will come about and persist if such diversity does not already obtain.' (p.36). Some readers will find Walzerian (1983) allusions in the view I describe here because of my commitment to 'complex justice' that might be seen as a version of Walzer's 'complex equality'. However, I would want to avoid the excessively relativistic aspects of Walzer that have troubled Dworkin (1985, pp. 214-20) without being quite as 'principled' as Dworkin. Rawls's language of reasonable pluralism captures best (to my mind) what health care justice must be about.

[3]   Two deep moral obligations (justice and benevolence) seem threatened when we are faced with health care rationing challenges that reflect *fiscal* scarcity rather than *absolute* scarcity (only one heart to transplant and five people who need it). This question captures the point: How can we think of ourselves as a kind or caring or benevolent society when we have the capacity to save or prolong an individual's life but we refuse to do so for monetary reasons? The slogan invoked by those who see this as a rhetorical question with an obvious answer is that 'human life is priceless'. But I (Fleck, 1990) and others (Ubel, 2000) deny that slogan captures a morally defensible commitment. My point in invoking the language of '*just* caring' is that our obligations to care for others by commanding

that individuals in our society might need, then which health needs can be justly met and which justly ignored? Were Mr Diaz and 'Bud' equally entitled to all the health care resources they might need, no matter what the cost, no matter how little the benefit? Does our commitment to 'equal respect for all persons' require equal effort to meet the health needs of both individuals? But, we reply, we simply do not have the resources to do that. However, we can always take the money from 'elsewhere', which we have been doing for the past forty years in the US. In 1960 in the US we spent 5.2% ($26 billion) of our GDP on health care. In 2006 we spent 16.5 % ($2.16 trillion) of our GDP on health care (Borger et al., 2006, p. 67).[4] We have tripled the fraction of our GDP that we spend on health care. Were we morally obligated to do this? If so, we can hardly lavish moral praise upon ourselves, given that the number of uninsured persons (like 'Bud') increased steadily to the present forty six million. Again, our paradox of excess and deprivation: How can we be spending so much more on health care today and have such an increase in deprivation? Section one of this essay will answer that question through a survey of US health care policy.

The short version of my entire argument is as follows. The US sought after World War II to provide health insurance to most citizens. Both moral and non-moral considerations motivated specific policy choices. But the deepest value shaping the policy process was respect for individual and corporate economic liberty, and non-interference by government in making health care financing decisions. This meant that the mechanisms for financing health care would be extremely fragmented and extremely differentiated (thousands of health insurance companies and thousands of different policies), and the delivery system would be equally fragmented and differentiated. Two major practical consequences of this would be extreme economic inefficiency (including minimal ability to control escalating health care costs) and increasing inequalities of access to needed health care. I shall emphasise that these economic inefficiencies generated inexcusable injustices.

The second part of this essay will explore the problem of escalating health care costs, driven primarily by costly innovative medical technologies disseminated in a liberty-based, competition-oriented system for financing and delivering health services. These medical innovations dramatically expanded socially recognized health needs (see Callahan, 1990, ch. 2). There were only 2500 urgent annual needs for a heart transplant when we transplanted only natural hearts at $200,000 each. But once the artificial heart was invented and any number could be pro-

---

social resources to save or prolong their lives is limited by considerations of health care justice (the details of which are specified below).

[4]	Their projections to 2015 put that figure at 20% of GDP (roughly $4.03 trillion).

duced annually, then we suddenly have hundreds of thousands of new (socially recognized) very costly health needs. Most European countries spend only 8–10% of GDP on health care compared to the US figure of more than 16% in 2006 (Anderson et al., 2006).

If all these medical innovations were equally effective in meeting substantial (morally significant) health needs, then a just and caring moderately egalitarian society would have a prima facie moral obligation to make certain that patients with the relevant needs had access to these technologies. But this is contrary to fact. Many of these specific innovations yield only very marginal, uncertain, costly benefits. No society can afford to fund an indefinite expansion of those sorts of benefits. Hence, choices must be made and priorities must be established. This is health care rationing. The key conclusion of this second part of the essay will be that health care rationing is unavoidable and that we must devise policies that can accomplish rationing justly. However, it is virtually impossible to achieve that objective in a very fragmented health care system built upon an ideological commitment to individual liberty and the virtues of economic competition.

In the third part, I shall briefly examine different conceptions of health care justice. We shall see that respect for individual liberty is a necessary and respectable strand of an inclusive pluralistic conception of health care justice, but it cannot be the dominant value in such a conception. There are multiple legitimate components within the pluralistic conception of justice I will defend. No one component can be dominant, as we shall argue, especially if our ultimate practical political goal is to have a conception of health care justice that can be understood and endorsed by reflective citizens in our liberal pluralistic society, and that can be used by those citizens to assess proposed health policy reforms. This will yield only non-ideally just or 'just enough' outcomes. Trade-offs will typically be necessary among relevant legitimate considerations of health care justice in most concrete circumstances. These trade-offs ought to be articulated and legitimated through a process of rational democratic deliberation that is open to all who might be affected by a particular policy choice. The general idea (clearly for rationing decisions) is that a fair and rational deliberative process will result in rationing protocols that all members of the conversation are willing to impose upon their future possible sick selves (because the decisions will be democratically legitimate). Such decisions would be autonomous in a morally compelling sense (unlike current rationing decisions that the economically powerful impose upon the economically powerless). Such deliberative conversations would occur in 'moral and political space' delimited by certain elements of our comprehensive conception of health care justice, what we refer to as 'constitutional principles of health care justice', so named because their role would be to invalidate conversational outcomes that violated these principles as adjusted and configured in reflective equilibrium with one another (Fleck, 1992, 1994b, 2002).

In the final section, I will apply this comprehensive conception of health care justice to some current health reform proposals in the US. This will necessarily be sketchy since it cannot replace actual democratic deliberations.

(1) Health Care Distribution in the US: An Ethical Critique

Let us go back to the year 1900. Vigorously asserting a right to health care then would have earned many individuals a right to an early grave. Medicine was empirical in the worst sense: risky, dangerous, non-scientific. But the push for scientific medicine had started. Medicine quickly became increasingly effective in preventing premature death and restoring health. Medicine also became more expensive. This was the beginning of the problem of health care justice. If effective medical care had remained inexpensive, universal access to all effective treatments in unlimited amounts would have been easily achieved, and the problem of justice obviated. But this is contrary to fact.

In the early twentieth century in the US, efforts were made to introduce a social form of health insurance by Progressives, who called attention to similar programs in England and Germany.[5] However, the compulsory nature of social insurance (contrary to the individualistic commitments of our political culture) evoked opposition from business, labour, and the medical profession (Starr, 1982, pp. 235–66).

The beginning of private health insurance in the United States is usually traced to 1929 when Baylor University Hospital offered insurance for hospital treatment for up to twenty-one days to Dallas schoolteachers, for a flat premium of six dollars per person per year. Too many people at the time could not afford hospital care, which meant unpaid hospital bills. An insurance mechanism spread the risk and the cost across a group of generally healthy individuals. This assured both access to needed hospital care for the sick and payment to the hospital for its services. Little by way of moral argument was given at the time for why arrangements should take the form of *private* insurance.

---

[5] The Progressives represented a social reform movement from the 1890s into the 1920s with goals of improving social justice, general equality, and the quality of government. They successfully pushed through constitutional amendments that earned women the right to vote, put in place the progressive income tax, established direct voting for US senators, and created Prohibition. They believed that science was the key to solving all social problems rationally. The American philosopher, John Dewey, would be a prime example of a Progressive intellectual.

Health insurance caught on quickly. Blue Cross and Blue Shield plans rapidly emerged in individual states in the US. These plans had two virtues. First, they allowed individuals to choose whatever hospital they (or their physicians) wanted; individuals were not contractually tied to one hospital, as with the Baylor Hospital scheme. Second, these were 'non-profit' plans that could offer 'community rating' to their members. 'Non-profit' meant that these plans were not accountable to stockholders with expectations of high returns. 'Community rating' meant that the health status of members did not affect what members paid as an insurance premium. Individuals with heart disease or cancer paid the same for their health insurance as individuals who were currently in perfect health. However, this changed dramatically after World War II. While employers in the US during this period were subject to wage and price controls, they were allowed to increase the benefit packages offered to their employees. Health insurance quickly became a cheap and desirable benefit. This is how, as a pure historical accident, health insurance came to be tied to employment in America.[6] An additional side-effect was the drawing of for-profit health insurance companies into the market. Collectively, workers would be well above average in health status, and hence more profitable to insure. For-profit insurance companies relied upon 'experience rating' to choose their customers. This meant they could either reject outright known chronically ill individuals, or they could charge far higher rates to compensate for the additional financial risk. An obvious (and morally troubling) consequence of this system was that those who had the greatest health needs were least likely to have the financial means (through health insurance) to access needed expensive health care.

When this moral criticism was directed toward private insurance companies, their response was that it was not 'actuarially fair' to charge the same price for health insurance to both the sick and the well. They would invoke analogies with either auto or life insurance. They would argue that safe drivers ought to be rewarded with lower premiums than drivers involved in multiple accidents. Likewise, it would clearly be unfair for an individual diagnosed with a terminal illness to be able to buy a million-dollar life insurance policy for a few dollars that would allow them to leave a nice inheritance at the expense of other insured members. These analogies, however, are both flawed and, in part, disingenuous. The analogy with drivers is flawed. Bad drivers are *capable* of

[6]   The Roosevelt Administration had briefly considered in 1935 building into its Social Security program some form of national health insurance. The Great Depression had certainly created a political climate conducive to that effort: access to medical care was reduced by 50% for working class America. However, intense opposition from the American Medical Association quickly killed that initiative (Starr, 1982, pp. 266–75).

being better drivers. In general, illness befalls individuals for reasons that are largely outside their control, and they personally can in most instances do little to alter the course of their illness. Charging higher premiums to the ill and likely ill (or denying them health insurance altogether) can do nothing to 'correct their behaviour', nor would preventive efforts have been generally successful (despite contrary views by many who, in my judgment, have been too quick in assigning blame for illness). If individuals are subsequently denied access to needed health care because they cannot pay, and if they die prematurely as a result of that, then this certainly looks unjust.[7]

The life insurance argument has more persuasive power. Imagine an individual being given a cancer diagnosis, then running out to buy a health insurance policy for a few dollars to pay for $100,000 worth of cancer care (not having paid for health insurance for the preceding thirty years). That does seem unjust to other members of the insurance pool who have paid premiums while healthy for those thirty years. However, what is disingenuous about this argument is that insurance companies fail to mention their practice of dumping individuals from an insurance pool who have paid premiums for thirty years who are *now* diagnosed with cancer, or some other expensive chronic illness. This is possible in the US since private health insurance needs to be renewed annually. Individuals attached to large employer groups are protected from such treatment by insurance companies, unless they are laid off or change jobs or the company goes out of business. Insurance companies will defend this practice by saying that they are only selling insurance for a year at a time, that past history with the company is (morally) irrelevant. But then this looks a lot like the sort of exploitation by the newly sick that insurance companies were so quick to decry, except the exploitation now is of the newly sick.

American political culture places an extraordinarily high value on liberty for both individuals and corporations to form political and economic and social associations as they wish. This is what gives a presumptive legitimacy to the behaviour of insurance companies. Health insurance was viewed by many as just another product provided in the market in accord with the rules of the market. Maximizing effi-

---

[7]   The reader should regard this sentence as no more than a moral observation for now aimed at countering the appeal to actuarial fairness. There seems to me to be something morally troubling about denying individuals access to needed and effective medical care simply because an individual cannot afford to pay for that care. We (in our society) are reluctant to regard health care as 'just another consumer good.' We are more inclined to see it as being 'morally special' (see Daniels, 1985, for a full discussion of why health care has special status; see also Daniels, 1995, chapter four, for a concise critical assessment from the perspective of health care justice of the appeal to 'actuarial fairness' as a moral construct).

ciency was the key to success. Hence, health insurance companies dropped unprofitable people, expensive sick people in this case. This will strike most morally sensitive individuals as being at least unkind. Insurance executives might feel the same way. But they will justify their conduct by pointing out that they are not charitable organizations. Other organizations in society need to take on that responsibility, such as government or churches or other private charitable groups.

One solution to the 'charity care burden' problem would be to spread out equally this burden among all insurance companies. None would be competitively disadvantaged. But that would require the coercive powers of government to achieve the necessary coordination and stable equity (fair sharing of the economic burden). Political conservatives see this as a violation of basic economic and political liberties. Insurance companies would argue that they had no obligation to be charitable enterprises. They were not denying the sick needed health care. They were not in the business of providing *health* care. This was the responsibility of physicians and hospitals; they should be the focal point of a coordinated social charitable response.

This, however, is only the beginning of our story. Insurers offered thousands of different insurance packages to employers. Which of these was supposed to be made available to the rejected ill by all insurance companies for purposes of fairly sharing this economic burden? Some employers provided only relatively minimal health insurance; others provided more comprehensive coverage. Government could dictate that insurers provide an average package of health benefits to the rejected ill. But the very *seriously ill* would find their health needs unmet, i.e., not paid for by an average plan. That would still leave a large charity care burden for someone.

Government could assume responsibility for meeting the expensive health needs of the otherwise uninsurable. However, this yields another morally awkward outcome. Such a program would be paid for with tax revenues. Many millions of those liable to pay these taxes would themselves have only fairly minimal health insurance. They would in a sense be financially liable for excess health costs incurred beyond the coverage limits of their own employer's policy. They will argue (not unreasonably) that it is unjust that they would be responsible for these costs (or be denied care because they were unable to pay for it) while having to pay taxes for others who had expansive access to needed care (because government was absorbing those costs). Why, they will argue, should government intervene (in effect) to protect the profit margins of insurance companies by paying for health care for the uninsurable (as defined by insurance companies) while failing to provide equal protection to the basic income of equally sick (but underinsured) and needy working

Americans? The force of this argument is felt keenly in the US, and helps to explain why no such program exists there.

Nevertheless, the logic here is instructive for understanding the problem of assessing US health policy morally. Governments must treat their citizens fairly, and one aspect of this is to provide equal treatment in relevantly similar circumstances. Thus, Medicare provides the very same package of health benefits for *all* the elderly *no matter what their prior state of health has been*. Similar expectations do not govern the behaviour of corporate America. Consequently, health insurance companies can treat in radically different ways the likely healthy and likely sick, including in some cases denying health insurance to those with the greatest health needs. Such behaviour creates irresolvable moral problems in other social sectors, such as government. The inequities in access to needed health care generated by health insurance companies are often impossible to resolve by government without creating more such inequities, as illustrated above with our example of various degrees of underinsurance created by exclusions built into insurance contracts. The same thing happened in 1971 when Congress created the End-Stage Renal Disease [ESRD] program to pay the extremely high annual costs of dialysis or kidney transplantation because private insurers generally refused to insure such patients. These patients were facing death in two weeks without dialysis. A society that saw itself as being just and caring could hardly allow these patients to die prematurely when we had the technology that could prolong their lives for years. However, when our capacity to do major organ transplants was perfected, then government found itself paying for kidney transplants as part of this program. Insurers were dumping patients needing heart and liver transplants, but Congress refused to include these patients in the ESRD program because this would create an open-ended entitlement to all costly life-sustaining or life-saving medical technologies (and dozens of such technologies were in the pipeline at that time). Government was then open to genuine moral criticism for violating the minimal requirements for equal treatment of its citizens: why kidney transplants but not heart transplants or AIDS drugs etc.? This is not a flaw in government. Rather, the problem is that government must operate in a sea of competing for-profit health care corporations that write thousands of individualized benefit contracts constructed without any norms regarding fair access to needed health care.

Note also the language we use to characterize health insurance in the US. It is a 'benefit' (historically) of employment, freely given by employers, equally freely taken away or redefined by employers in accord with their judgment of corporate interests. This also implies that government does not have the legitimate political authority to require employers to provide this 'benefit.' Nevertheless, this benefit is very socially desirable and must be stable for both moral and medical reasons.[8] This stability can be *freely* achieved if government provides 'incentives' to the relevant political actors, i.e., tax deductions. Corporations may deduct from profits the cost of employee health insurance. Likewise, employees have a 'tax free' benefit. Economists call this a 'tax expenditure.' This represents revenue the government could have collected as taxes. In 2004 in the US this tax expenditure amounted to $113 billion for the federal government (Employee Benefits Research Institute, 2006) and an additional $35 billion for state governments.

Here we need to draw attention to another fairness issue. Two streams of economic incentives converge with disastrous consequences for social justice, one for health insurance companies, the other attached to the 'tax free' status of health benefits for employers and employees. Ironically, both sets of incentives aimed at morally praiseworthy outcomes at their inception. Health insurance companies designed health benefit contracts with no economic incentives for their interfering in medical practice. Doctors alone should practice medicine in accord with their best medical judgment, totally divorced from concerns about the interests of insurers. But this meant insurance companies had no incentive to control costs. The more medical care patients demanded, the more physicians provided, the more health costs increased. Employers received a generous deduction for absorbing these costs. The more costs increased, the more dollars passed through the hands of insurers, the greater the net profit for insurers. The tax incentives provided by the federal government represented a 40–45% subsidy on the price of health insurance to employees, now strongly motivated as rational economic actors to 'buy' more health insurance in contract negotiations rather than higher wages subject to full taxation. To be sure, the primary generator of escalating health costs since 1960 was the rapid development and deployment of innovative medical technologies. But that deployment would have been substantially slower without the vast economic resources made available to medicine through the insurance mechanism as shaped by tax incentives. In the mid-1970s, for complex reasons, manufacturing jobs in the US were shipped to low wage countries, which resulted in the creation of low wage service sector jobs in the US without health insurance. That began the gradual expansion of a pool of uninsured workers. This is where a fairness problem appears in connection with the tax incentives.

Many employers who do provide health insurance have costs in excess of $8000 per worker, which are not affordable by low-wage employers. That means workers for low-wage firms must enter the

[8] Imagine withdrawing funding for dialysis ($55,000 per person per year in 2006) with 400,000 patients in the US medically dependent upon it for life itself.

insurance market as (healthy) individuals (not with large group discounts, not as a tax-free benefit). The unfairness seems obvious. Those
who are financially well off (high-paying jobs) receive a very substantial
government subsidy in the form of tax-free health insurance while those
who are substantially less well off are effectively denied that benefit
(because they cannot afford to purchase the insurance). As noted, that
subsidy exceeds $140 billion annually (and is growing). That subsidy
encourages the well insured to demand more and more costly advanced
medical care, which further drives up health costs, which drives up the
average cost to employers of providing a reasonably comprehensive
health care package, which drives out of the insurance market marginal
employers, which results in annual increases of two million uninsured.
How can government perpetrate this sort of unfairness upon its (already
disadvantaged) citizens?

One answer is that government is not denying the tax subsidy to anyone. Rather, employers freely choose not to take advantage of the subsidy
for reasons reflecting corporate self-interest. Likewise, workers 'freely
choose' not to purchase health insurance for themselves for their own reasons of economic self-interest (practical unaffordability). Such free
choices, the argument goes, may result in inequalities, but inequalities are
not necessarily inequities. However, this appeal to 'free choice' has a morally disingenuous quality to it because it ignores the morally troubling
fact that a large portion of the American health care system is publicly
subsidized through taxes. Half the costs of medical education are paid for
publicly. The federal government spent $28 billion for funding basic med-
ical and scientific research at the National Institutes of Health [NIH] in
2005. Most private hospitals in the US have tax-exempt status. These public expenditures are morally and politically justified because they aim to
improve the quality of health care *for all*. This is a public interest that individuals as individuals could never adequately advance because of the classic 'free rider' problem. No one will pay for basic medical research if they
know they will enjoy the benefits without having to pay the cost. But if both
the insured and the uninsured have paid taxes to support these public
expenditures, then all ought to have an *effective opportunity* to enjoy the benefits of these investments, not just those who have excellent health insurance benefits. The uninsured have no effective opportunity to choose to
access the fruits of the taxes they paid.

The uninsured have access to needed health care in the US, but not
assured access. For at least fifty years after World War II American
non-profit hospitals systematically 'overcharged' their well-insured
patients in order to generate 'excess revenue' used to cover the hospital-

ization costs of the uninsured.[9] Insurance companies tolerated this practice so long as they continued to make a profit on the volume of dollars that flowed through their hands (and excess charges increased that volume). In theory, this sort of 'compensating practice' could yield a 'just enough' outcome. In practice, this never happens, especially in larger urban areas where the uninsured might be concentrated in relatively poorer neighborhoods. Hospitals serving those neighbourhoods will not have enough insured middle class patients to offset their disproportionate 'charity care burden.' The result is not so much 'rough justice' (where that means reasonably just outcomes, evenly spread) as 'random justice' (where that means reasonably just outcomes, unevenly spread). Clearly, the latter has a quite different moral quality.

The Medicare and Medicaid programs were put in place in 1965. Medicare may be thought of as national health insurance for the elderly (those over age sixty-five). A payroll tax, some general federal tax revenue, and some contributions from beneficiaries (premiums and co-payments) finance it. In contrast, the Medicaid program is intended to meet the health care needs of the poor. Unlike Medicare, Medicaid is comprised of fifty different state programs. The federal government defines a core set of benefits, which each state must provide to program beneficiaries. States have the right to enrich that benefit package, if they wish. The federal government pays at least half the cost of Medicaid and as much as 75%, all depending upon the relative wealth of each state. Each state is free to determine who is poor enough to deserve access to health care under the Medicaid program. Consequently, some states may provide Medicaid coverage only to those who are at or below 20% of the federal poverty level. Only one state (Oregon) provides coverage for 100% of those below the poverty level. Some states have special programs that provide coverage to children whose family income is below 150% of the poverty level.[10]

Medicare came into existence largely as a consequence of our creating health insurance programs tied to employment. As older individuals

---

[9] For a contemporary assessment of this cost-shifting phenomenon, see Dobson et al. (2006).

[10] Though Medicaid is spoken of in this collective sense, it is really three distinct programs. The first of these programs provides what might be called access to traditional health services for the non-elderly poor. About 35% of Medicaid dollars go to this program. A second program covers health care costs for the impoverished elderly who are unable to pay for prescription drugs or other individual costs required by Medicare. But the bulk of this program pays for long term care for the impoverished elderly, who otherwise would be entirely responsible for these costs. About 45% of Medicaid dollars support this program. Finally, 20% of Medicaid dollars support a collection of programs for persons with serious disabilities.

retired they found that private insurance companies would not sell them affordable insurance. Very substantial health care costs were tied to being older. To be precise, the 13% of the population in the US over age sixty-five in 2005 consumed about 35% of all the health dollars spent in that year (roughly $670 billion). A mix of moral and non-moral motives precipitated the creation of the Medicare program. How could a society as wealthy as ours simply allow the elderly who had worked so hard to create this wealth to suffer and die for lack of access to needed and effective health care? The implicit appeal in this rhetorical question is to considerations of kindness and desert. But Medicare was not to be thought of as a 'welfare' program. Instead, roughly 3% of the earnings of the employed funded this program to a large extent, which meant that the elderly were entitled to this social benefit for which they had already (in part) paid. On the non-moral motivational side, roughly 40% of hospital income is tied to providing health care for the elderly. If the elderly had only a marginal capacity to pay for needed health care, hospitals would be faced with an insuperable social and economic crisis. They could hardly refuse admission to the very ill elderly, but they could hardly afford to provide any care if they did admit them. Medicare prevented that potential crisis and a comparable one with regard to physicians as well. A mix of social interests and self interests generated Medicare.

Note two other moral oddities regarding Medicare. First, the value of the Medicare benefit package increased every year with advancing medical technology. Medicare was an 'open-ended' entitlement package. Medicare did not operate with a fixed budget; it simply paid the bills from hospitals and physicians. Predictably, costs of the Medicare program escalated rapidly to its 2006 cost of more than $420 billion (compared to $82 billion in 1987 and $210 billion in 1997 [Borger et al., 2006]). Second, though Medicare has been described as national health insurance for the elderly (with the implication that all the elderly received roughly equal access to needed health care), the elderly actually have considerably differentiated access to needed health care depending upon their overall economic status. This is because prescription drugs were not covered in the original Medicare legislation. At the time (1965) prescription drugs were relatively inexpensive, and the belief was that these should be paid for out-of-pocket. However, the past twenty years have seen dramatic increases in the costs of prescription drugs and in the length of time that individuals are recommended to be on these drugs (especially for chronic illness). Consequently, the healthy middle class could afford to buy Medi-Gap insurance policies that would cover most of these costs while working class elderly would have to do without drugs they could not afford (often enough with deadly consequences). What should be emphasised here is that the elderly who were least well off health-wise would be least likely to be able to access some forms of expensive pharmaceutical care they needed, which would seem to violate widely shared moderately egalitarian moral intuitions.

In 2004 the US Congress passed legislation creating Part 'D' Medicare coverage aimed at improving access to prescription drugs for all the elderly. That legislation took effect in January of 2006. As always, a multiplicity of diverse goals and values shaped the actual program. The political goal was to improve access to prescription drugs for the relatively poor elderly. But the projected ten-year costs of prescription drugs for the elderly were staggering, roughly $2.4 trillion for the period 2006–2015. So the program was crafted with stringent cost control goals, though most of the burden of these controls fell upon the chronically ill elderly. The best estimate now is that the federal government will have to cover about $780 billion in costs over ten years. Seniors who did not meet poverty criteria would have to pay $450 per year in premiums, an initial $250 deductible each year, then 25% of the costs of their drugs up to $2250, then 100% of the costs for the next $2850, what has been referred to (infamously) as the 'doughnut hole.' After that the federal government would pick up virtually all the costs. Roughly 10% of all seniors have prescription drug needs that will force them into that doughnut hole. This will have very uneven (inequitable) effects so far as access to needed prescription drugs is concerned, depending upon the financial resources individuals have available to them. Many who are less well off medically and financially will have to forgo needed medications. How should we assess such an outcome, morally speaking? How should we assess the Medicare Part 'D' benefit, morally speaking? As we shall see again, our capacity to make clear moral judgments will be badly muddied by features of the program itself.

If we ask, from the perspective of non-ideal justice, whether the elderly are better off so far as secure access to prescription drugs is concerned through Part 'D', the answer would have to be affirmative, most especially the elderly with greater health needs and less financial resources. However, that global utilitarian judgment disguises some very troubling distributional consequences and quality of care consequences that were avoidable (and hence regrettable) features of the Part 'D' benefit as actually enacted. The 'doughnut hole' is a perfect illustration of what we have in mind. It was intended to compel individual Medicare recipients to make more cost-effective choices with regard to their prescription drugs (which permits bureaucrats and policymakers to say that they are not interfering in the practice of medicine or making rationing decisions). So we imagine a typical cardiac patient (with some degree of heart failure) who is on several cardiac medications, including a drug to reduce cholesterol, and an anti-depressant. If he were prescribed Prozac and Lipitor (branded drugs under patent protection), these two drugs alone would have annual costs of $2500, the edge of the doughnut hole. The four other medications would send him deep into that hole. He would have to pay 100% of their cost. In some cases patients will simply not purchase a drug their physician strongly recommends, such as an anti-hypertensive. Some will suffer no medically significant consequences as a result of that choice while others will suffer a stroke or heart attack or kidney failure. But it will be impossible as a practical matter to make the judgment with medical confidence that this individual would not have suffered these consequences if only he had taken his anti-hypertensive medication, which means that these consequences cannot be judged (politically) to be morally problematic and attached with sufficient certitude to the way in which the Part 'D' benefit was structured.[11] Responsibility for bad outcomes is both diluted and diffused, or more easily attached to 'choices' that individuals made. Concerns about injustice are effectively dissipated as well (this is a descriptive, not a normative point: it becomes more difficult to *make* claims in justice under these circumstances).

We should emphasize that controlling the cost of the prescription drug benefit is a morally reasonable goal (given other costly unmet health needs of the elderly, and given the marginal effectiveness of many costly medications). However, the mechanism used here does not yield a 'just enough' outcome since, as a practical matter, the outcome is mostly determined by the ability to pay of individuals rather than urgency of need, or magnitude of risk of harm, or other justice-relevant factors.[12] With regard to this point, we must note that the legislation that created Part 'D' deliberately outlawed Medicare itself bargaining with pharmaceutical companies to extract very large discounts on drug costs.

---

[11] We (researchers) would know with high statistical confidence that some proportion of these adverse medical outcomes were linked to individuals not being able to afford the needed medications. However, that abstract knowledge will not motivate political reform in the way that identifiable patients dying from lack of dialysis motivated creation of the End-Stage Renal Disease program. The experiential clarity and certainty of those connections made ignoring them politically impossible.

[12] There are times when individual ability to pay will be a morally permissible (not unjust) basis for allocating health care. Speaking broadly and as a moderate egalitarian (such as Daniels), I will contend that no one has a just claim to health care interventions that are very costly and only marginal beneficial, e.g. a cancer drug for $50,000 that yields three extra months of low quality life. Hence, a poor elderly individual denied that drug has not been treated unjustly. However, what the part D doughnut hole allows is a middle class individual to pay $2500 for that drug to cross the doughnut hole so that taxpayers then pay the next $45,000. From a moderate egalitarian perspective it is unfair that the well off middle class should have this benefit paid for in part by the Medicare taxes that the working poor would have paid (since all workers pay the same flat Medicare tax). What a moderate egalitarian would require for fairness is that the middle class person pays the full cost of this drug from their personal resources.

With 39 million lives Medicare could easily extract discounts of 50% and more on most of the drugs needed by the elderly (done by many European nations). The prime motive for this limitation was to protect the profit margins of these pharmaceutical companies (Kuttner, 2005).[13]

Much of the burden of cost control fell then to those elderly who were less well off health-wise and wealth-wise, which will strike most as prima facie unjust. What Medicare required instead was that hundreds of private insurance companies had to provide this benefit. Such companies could only obtain discounts on these drugs of 10–15%, which still required restricted formularies. If the elderly wanted this benefit, they would have to sign up with one or another of these insurance companies. But the elderly had to examine dozens of them to see which company's covered drugs and specific discount pattern best matched their own specific prescription drug needs. Further, these insurance companies had the right to alter their formulary every month while the elderly were allowed to switch from one company to another for this benefit only once a year. Predictably, this has generated considerable confusion as well as huge and unnecessary administrative expenses.[14]

Medicare has had administrative costs of around 4% while private insurers have administrative costs in the 10–20% range or more. These excess administrative costs purchase no health care at all; they meet no health care needs. They make less money available to meet health care needs. If these excess administrative costs were necessary to yield a more just and more efficient meeting of health needs, then they would have some moral justification. But the exact opposite has been the result of putting into place these hundreds of private prescription drug plans under the guise of giving Medicare patients 'more choices.' That language clearly has a libertarian patina to it. But, what is the point of providing the elderly with multiple choices if the elderly would reject all of these choices for an option that provided more continuous care for all at lower cost (which is what a government negotiated plan would do)?

---

[13] Ironically, the US Department of Veteran Affairs [VA] will pay $253 for a year's supply of Protonix (ulcer drug) per beneficiary while this same drug will cost Medicare beneficiaries under the Bush program $1080. Likewise, the VA will pay $251 for a year's supply of Zocor (lowers cholesterol) per beneficiary while seniors will have to pay $1323 (Kuttner, 2005).

[14] In the early part of 2006, US newspapers have been filled with horror stories regarding the implementation of this Medicare Part 'D' benefit. Those most likely to be adversely affected by administrative errors and denials were the mentally ill (Pear, 2006), nursing home patients, and the poorest Medicare recipients, some 6.4 million low income seniors. The confusion has been so massive and so pervasive that at the time of writing twenty-nine states have intervened and created special programs to pay for prescription drugs for these low income seniors until the confusion generated by having all these hundreds of private options is sorted out.

We should return briefly to Medicaid. Again, are the poor better off (in some utilitarian sense) with Medicaid? The short answer is affirmative and misleading. *Some of the poor* have more in the way of assured access to needed health care than they would have had if Medicaid had never been created and they were entirely dependent upon private (and unreliable) charitable responses. But this outcome is hardly 'just enough' simply because it is an improvement for some in access to needed health care. To see the point, imagine a society with abundant food stocks that allowed millions to starve to death because they could not pay for the food. Then society institutes a lottery so that 100,000 poor starving individuals are now provided a reasonable supply of food. Some of the poor (those 100,000) are better off, but this latter state of affairs hardly deserves legitimation as being 'just enough' when millions of others suffer needlessly in the midst of abundance. That, in essence, is the situation with Medicaid.

The fifty states set widely differing eligibility levels. That means Medicaid covers different fractions of the poor in each state. These judgments reflect local political expediency, nothing more morally significant than that. States do have the capacity to provide the Medicaid benefit package to all below the federal poverty level, which is why this state of affairs cannot be described as just in any sense. Individuals should not be allowed to starve to death or die prematurely or suffer serious medical harm needlessly for lack of access to health care when we have food and medical resources in abundance. That last statement is intended to capture a moral obligation, which for now may be thought of as either a matter of beneficence or justice. The point is that it is a *social* obligation, which cannot be effectively or fairly addressed (or even recognized as a problem) as long as we have the highly fragmented system for financing health care we have now. In the current US system for financing access to health care patients are put into financing silos (or in the case of the uninsured they are outside all the financing silos), and the understanding is that no insurer (or anyone else) has responsibility for meeting health needs outside the silo for which they have responsibility. The silos effectively block the making of moral comparisons across silos. That means our social capacity for recognizing health care injustices is stymied. The 'owners' of any silo will deny the relevance of any comparison to what others might have in the way of access to health care in another silo.

A summary of the foregoing might be helpful at this point. Our central question is this: What appears to be morally troubling about the US health care system? First, we spend more per capita on health care than any other country in the world, yet we have forty-six million individuals without health insurance (without assured access to needed health care). There is lacking any close connection between having a serious (morally significant) health need and a social commitment to meeting that need. Second, those who have health insurance through their employers or Medicare or Medicaid have little assurance that their health needs will be met because of the enormous variation in coverage decisions which are largely left to the whims and worries of employers or insurers or legislators. Third, those individuals with the most substantial and costly health needs are generally least likely to have their health needs met, most often because insurers will not want to accept the economic losses these individuals represent. Fourth, public subsidies for health insurance largely go to individuals who are already well off health-wise and wealth-wise, as opposed to those who have significant health problems and are likely to be struggling economically as well. Fifth, a very strong emphasis on choice and market liberty has led to the creation of a health care system and financing for the system that is extremely fragmented (the silos), economically inefficient, and ethically arbitrary. Woolhandler et al (2003) have shown that roughly 10% of total health care dollars spent in the US (around $200 billion) represents excess administrative costs that other countries in the world (generally with universal health care) do not tolerate. The morally troubling feature of these costs is that they fail to provide a dime's worth of needed health care for the forty-six million uninsured in the US.

The major premise behind these summary moral criticisms is that it is morally imperative that health needs be met. Perhaps surprisingly, this premise is so ambiguous that both libertarians and egalitarians can endorse it. In endorsing this premise libertarians will not concede that any of the moral criticisms listed above have force. They will argue that thousands of health care institutions and programs as well as millions of well-motivated health professionals have freely provided charitable energy and resources to address health needs not covered through normal insurance mechanisms. They will concede that some serious health needs go unmet, but they regard such failures as unfortunate and regrettable side effects of a system of liberty, not injustices that would warrant the coercive interventions of government. More diligent efforts aimed at moral persuasion in the private sector would be a reasonable remedy for those shortcomings, nothing more than that. They deny the health system needs reform. If egalitarians wish to reject this conclusion, then a strong case must be made for the claim that persistent and systemic injustices are endemic to our health care system as presently structured, and that only major systemic reform can be expected to remedy those injustices. One major practical problem represents both an obstacle to and an opportunity for major health reform. That is the problem of escalating health care costs, which we address in Part Two.

(2) The Problem of Escalating Health Costs

Escalating health costs represent an obstacle to major health reform because, as the costs of health insurance increase (causing an increase in the number of uninsured), the cost of covering the uninsured with an adequate health insurance package increases as well. That makes it more politically challenging to 'sell' health reform. Either taxes would have to be raised or else redistribution within the health care system would be necessary, i.e., a thinning of the health package enjoyed by the currently insured. Neither option is politically attractive. But escalating health costs also generate opportunities for reform. Predictions are that the US may have 55–60 million uninsured by the year 2012. A large portion of that figure will be middle class individuals who are politically active, and who appreciate the fact that roughly half of all personal bankruptcies are attributable to health care costs. Still, what ultimately defeated the Clinton Administration health reform effort in 1993 (despite broad middle class anxieties about secure access to health care) was that the sacrifices required to achieve reform were sacrifices that each politically active health constituency expected others to shoulder while they themselves would be exempted. There was no shared sense of what would be a 'fair' or 'just' sharing of this burden (Fleck, 1994b).

What precisely is that 'burden'? We have unlimited health care needs and only limited resources for meeting those needs. The burden is that of inescapable health care rationing. The practical moral question is whether that rationing should be accomplished through libertarian or roughly egalitarian social policies. I will argue that predominantly libertarian health care policies will consistently fail both to bring health care costs under reasonable control and to yield distributions of health services reasonably judged to be even marginally fair. But we need to add that any simple egalitarian theories will fail as well, in part because of the complexity and heterogeneity of the health needs that must be fairly prioritized, and in part because of the complexity of our current health care system.

Health care rationing means denying individuals who have genuine health needs what we (societal policymakers and health professionals) would judge to be marginally beneficial health care that costs too much relative to the size or probability of achieving the desired health outcomes (Ubel, 2000, chs. 2–3). We have a rough sense of what should count as a health need, to which we attach some degree of moral significance, as opposed to a health want, to which we attach no moral significance. All individuals who are facing death in the foreseeable future as a result of a progressive disease process have health needs in a paradigmatic sense. If no interventions can slow or reverse these disease processes (generally true prior to 1960), then we have a situation that is tragic and unfortunate, but not one that is unjust. However, when we have an intervention that can effectively forestall death, such as kidney dialysis, and when that intervention is very costly relative to the economic means of an average individual ($55,000 per person per year in the case of dialysis), and when those costs alone are a barrier to individuals accessing that technology, then we have a morally troubling situation because we have a predictable death that is preventable and premature. Under such circumstances we have a very strong social consensus that allowing such a person to die is morally wrong, since it is both unjust (Daniels, 1985) and unkind (Buchanan, 1983).[15]

These intuitions of unkindness and injustice are essentially what motivated the passage of the End-Stage Renal Disease (ESRD) 1972 amendments to the Medicare program which pays for renal dialysis (or kidney transplantation) for every US citizen in kidney failure, no matter what the work status or health status or insurance status of that person (Rettig, 2002). This program has been effective, yielding average gains of life expectancy of seven years, with tens of thousands of individuals gaining fifteen to twenty extra years of life. Program analysts in 1972 predicted that the program would reach its peak cost of about $500 million per year, and then level off thereafter. That proved incorrect. In 2005 the ESRD program cost about $20 billion and sustained about 390,000 individuals (Xue et al, 2001).

Such a program could not be stably sustained through voluntary charitable giving over a thirty-five year period. It would be very vulnerable to economic swings and charitable whims, with potentially deadly consequences for tens of thousands. Note also that virtually none of these 390,000 individuals would be able to purchase health insurance that would cover dialysis or renal transplantation in the private market since an insurance company would have to charge each of them about $60,000 per year for the coverage. It takes the coordinating and coercive powers

---

[15] Buchanan will argue that a 'reasonable libertarian' will accept obligations of beneficence. We can think of this as a matter of 'easy rescue' where we have effective medical interventions that can save someone from death or serious medical harm. However, it is not an 'easy rescue' for any individual as an individual. For that we need the coordinating power of government to give effect to the obligation of beneficence we each have but that as individuals we could not effectively carry out. Buchanan is trying to provide a moral argument for a 'minimally decent package of health benefits' that both libertarians (for reasons of effective beneficence) and egalitarians (for reasons of justice) could endorse as morally acceptable. As for myself, the language of 'just caring' is meant to suggest that we need both moral concepts for effective health reform. The language of justice really does two things: it provides criteria for identifying a range of health services we are morally obligated to provide to all in specific health circumstances, *and* it helps identify other health services that are *outside the scope of justice*, i.e., services that can legitimately be the focus of rationing decisions.

of government (via taxation) to make such a program possible, which is to say that a fundamentally libertarian approach to financing health care and meeting health needs would have been completely inadequate for meeting the needs of these patients. A global libertarian approach to health care financing in this case yields an outcome that appears neither kind nor just.

The US experience with the ESRD program was intended to affirm a seemingly widespread reluctance to embrace health care rationing when human life was at risk. Policymakers (often reflecting public sentiment) expressed the view that human life was priceless. In 1972 this might have been an affordable and morally defensible moral judgment. That is no longer true today. Callahan (1990, ch. 2) has correctly diagnosed the core problem. First, prima facie morally significant health care needs are endless, primarily because our understanding of health needs is very intimately attached to advancing medical technology.[16] Second, no bright lines mark off the point at which what we all regard as health needs shades off into something closer to health wants. This is what Callahan refers to as the 'ragged edge' problem. Third, the costs associated with attempting to meet these (expansive) needs are socially unsustainable; and consequently, the need for health care rationing is inescapable.

Callahan's first point can be readily illustrated. In 1965 in the US there was no need for bypass surgery. Bypass surgery had not been invented as yet, so there could not be an 'actual need' for it.[17] But in 2004 in the US

---

[16] Callahan's use of the concept of need might have more of a sociologically descriptive than a morally prescriptive dimension to it. This represents a sociological fact that we cannot ignore if our ultimate goal is actual health reform, i.e. a more just health care system. Any health care intervention that promises to prolong life (for however short a period of time) or reduce the risk of death (no matter how small or uncertain that risk might be) or prevent serious medical harm (no matter how remote the likelihood of effectively preventing that harm) will be seen by most Americans as something that a sick individual 'needs.' That is, Americans would resist saying that these are 'just wants.' My own view is that the language of needs in health care is too expansive and too unregulated to yield reliable moral guidance as to what our obligations are as a society to meet these needs. The role of our conception of justice in conjunction with a process of rational democratic deliberation is to identify those needs that we would have a social obligation to meet.

[17] Coronary arteries no doubt have been clogging up for thousands of years. That, however, is a bare biological fact that generates no specific medical need by itself. To generate a 'need' in some practical sense we must have a well-founded theory about coronary artery disease and effective interventions for managing or ameliorating that disease process. What we have today are dozens of drugs, devices and surgical interventions related to managing coronary artery disease with a very large range of effectiveness and cost. Should a physician's judgment that a patient *needs* (might be better off with) one or another of these interventions

there was a need for more than a half million cardiac bypass surgeries at a cost of about $65,000 each, 1.2 million coronary angioplasties at a cost of about $30,000 each, and 200,000 implantable cardiac defibrillators (ICDs) at a cost of $40,000 each. About 13 million Americans were taking cholesterol-lowering statins in 2004 at a cost of $1100 per patient per year. We have recently seen the introduction of the left ventricular assist device (LVAD) for patients in end-stage heart failure. About 200,000 Americans annually are potential candidates for that device at a cost of $180,000 each. In addition clinical trials are in progress for a totally implantable artificial heart (TIAH), the cost of which will be about $200,000 each with the surgery and related follow-up care. Computer models suggest that as many as 350,000 Americans annually would be candidates for that device.

The above items yield total costs per year above $150 billion (which does not include dozens of other cardiac procedures, drugs or diagnostic options). Projected cardiac deaths in the US have been reduced by about 50% since 1975 (not all of which is attributable to these technological interventions since there has also been a steep reduction in smoking). But none of these life-prolonging interventions confers immortality. Instead, prolonged life expectancy with heart disease means an increase in the total social burden of chronic illness, various cancers or strokes or Alzheimer's or arthritis and any number of other chronic degenerative conditions, most of which have long trajectories with the need for increasingly costly medical interventions to manage symptoms and complications. Virtually every area of medicine has seen costly technological advances. Callahan's description of 'endless needs' is no hyperbole. This propels health care costs inexorably upwards.

Next question: Are all of the health needs above correctly thought of as generating a roughly equal degree of moral weight? Should the degree of benefit or likelihood of benefit or the kind of benefit or the overall clinical circumstances of a patient have any relevance in determining how morally weighty any of these needs might be? Callahan's notion of the 'ragged edge' has saliency at this point, but there is also the issue of heterogeneity of need and incomparability of need. Is a just and caring society morally obligated to assure access for all to medical technologies that can address life-threatening needs, no matter how high the costs of those technologies, and no matter how marginal or how uncertain the benefits of those technologies might be for individual patients? What follows is a representative series of questions aimed at concretising our general question. We should ask ourselves how we might answer these questions from a moderately egalitarian perspective

be sufficient to generate a *just claim* to that intervention? My own view is that such a judgment is necessary but not sufficient.

or a libertarian perspective or a utilitarian perspective. Also, can any one of these perspectives yield consistently reasonable ('just enough' answers that we could accept so that it would be most rational and most just to think through all our health care rationing problems from that perspective?

We may begin with this question: If anyone has a just claim to renal dialysis to forestall death from renal failure, then do all with renal failure have an equal just claim? Are all justly entitled to the same treatment? Think of the patient in renal failure with end-stage Alzheimer's disease who might be able to live an additional two years with the help of dialysis at a cost of about $105,000 per year (nursing home and dialysis costs)? That is, should this patient and a forty-five year old in renal failure otherwise in reasonable health with a potential life expectancy of twenty years have an equal just claim to societal resources? Again, there is no shortage of dialysis machines; the issue of making just rationing decisions is about fiscal scarcity.

We noted earlier that if we took as a societal moral obligation the prevention of 'premature' death from cardiac failure (when we have the technological capacity to achieve that result), then in the US we would be obligated to implant about 350,000 artificial hearts (TIAH) per year at a cost (in current dollars) of about $200,000 each, or aggregate additional annual health costs of $70 billion. On average, recipients would gain five extra years of life expectancy (with varying degrees of quality of life). That would yield a cost per life-year saved of $40,000, which is substantially less than the cost of a saved life-year on dialysis. However, if we have a patient in end-stage heart failure who will almost certainly die within three months if he does not receive a TIAH, and if that patient also has metastatic colorectal cancer with a predicted life expectancy of two years, then should such a patient have an equal just claim to that TIAH as a patient who had a predicted life expectancy of at least five years? Should it matter, morally speaking, that the patient with the cancer is age 55, or 75, or 85? This is a perfect illustration of Callahan's 'ragged edge' problem. Hundreds of variations can be done on this scenario. There are no 'bright lines', morally speaking, that inform us (citizens/policymakers in a just and caring society) who ought to be included or excluded from receiving a TIAH at public expense. Should we then accept the very demanding implications of a strict egalitarianism in addressing this problem (either do everything for all or do nothing for all)? Or should utilitarian considerations dictate a fair and reasonable allocation? Or should libertarian considerations (individual ability to pay) determine entirely who would or would not have access to this technology? Should the absolute first commitment of a just and caring society be to saving and prolonging lives, no matter what the cost?

We mentioned the implantable cardiac defibrillator earlier (ICD), intended to prevent sudden death from an arrhythmia. We implanted 200,000 ICDs in the US in 2004 at a cost of $40,000 each. We could be implanting 600,000 per year by 2010 (Goldberger and Lampert, 2006). What justice-relevant considerations should determine how many of these we implant per year? Pauker et al (2005) argue that if cost-effectiveness matters then we ought to be implanting only 50,000 of these devices annually in the US at a cost of about $2 billion rather than 600,000 at a cost of $24 billion. Is it the case that those other 550,000 devices per year do no medical good at all? No. All the patients who have these devices implanted have some chance in any given year of having a fatal arrhythmia. However, as we get beyond that first 50,000 that chance gets progressively smaller and more remote, but it does not drop to zero.[18] For 81% of these patients this device will not fire for five years or longer. No doubt this device provides psychological comfort, but with costs as high as $4 million per life-year saved at those higher rates of implantation. Still, at the 600,000 level some very tiny, very remote chance of saving a life remains. And, if our prime moral directive were to spend anything to avoid any medically preventable death, then we would have a moral obligation to buy that 600,000th ICD (at least as strict egalitarians who had no capacity within this framework to justly limit this variation of the ragged edge problem).

Thirteen million Americans are on statins, which levies an annual bill of $15 billion. A recent report suggests that 64 million Americans ought to be on these drugs, which would take the annual cost to $70 billion. This is supposed to reduce the annual incidence of heart attacks and strokes. If savings of $70 billion were achieved (and those savings could be captured in the health system and used to meet other high priority health needs), this would be a good moral and economic argument for supporting that investment. But that argument cannot be made. Again, *if* saving and prolonging human life is the prime moral directive in medicine (no matter how marginal the benefit or how small the probability of prolonged life or what other non-life-threatening health needs go unmet), and if we have no way of morally managing the ragged edge problem, then we would be morally obligated to spend $70 billion on statins.[19]

---

[18] Even in the case of Dick Cheney, who would certainly be a candidate for one of the first 50,000 of these devices because he has had four heart attacks, the device has not been triggered for more than four years.

[19] Recently, the UK's National Institute for Clinical Excellence (NICE) approved expanded access to statins for funding by the National Health Service. Currently 1.8 million Britons are on statins, roughly 3% of their population, resulting in a saving of 7000 lives per year. NICE approved tripling the fraction of the

These same issues are now emerging with regard to a very large number of advanced cancer drugs. All these drugs are extraordinarily expensive, and they provide some very marginal gain in life expectancy. Avastin is a colon cancer drug with costs of $4400 to $8800 per month; it may increase life expectancy an additional fifteen months (Editorial, Post-Dispatch, 2006). Gleevec is used to treat chronic myeloid leukemia. Recent reports show that 92% of patients are alive 4.5 years after starting treatment. The cost of this drug is $2200 per month, and it may need to be taken indefinitely. Gleevec has also been used against gastrointestinal cancers, though drug resistance occurs after eighteen months. At that point, patients can be put on sunitinib ($38,000 annually), which slows disease progression for an additional six months. This same drug represents the last line of defense for patients with advanced kidney cancer (32,000 new cases annually). This drug yields a time-to-tumour progression of 27 weeks. Sorafenib is also used against advanced kidney cancer with a cost of about $52,000 per year (Mano, 2006).

Herceptin is a drug for breast cancer, especially for women who test positive for HER-2 receptors (25–30% of all breast cancers). Women in this circumstance have a cancer that will progress much more rapidly. Herceptin blocks these receptors and slows disease progression. This drug costs $70,000 for a course of treatment, yielding an average gain in life expectancy of 6.5 months. This drug is now being given to women in earlier stages of this cancer with results that are being touted as dramatic, e.g. a 50% increase in survival at three years.[20] One male patient with breast cancer, Wayne Townsend, has been struggling with the dis-

---

population to be covered, which is projected to yield 10,000 more lives per year saved (*The Guardian*, January 25, 2006, at p.8, reported by Sarah Hall). If the US were to make a comparable change with a population five times greater than that of Great Britain, we could in theory save 85,000 lives per year at a cost of about $45 billion for those statins. That is about $500,000 per life saved. Virtually all of these patients will have the opportunity again to have their lives 'saved' by medicine from a cancer or advanced heart disease or renal failure or several of these disorders. An important moral question then becomes, 'How often must a just and caring society save such lives, and at what cost?' This is yet another aspect of the ragged edge problem.

[20] For a layperson this language sounds exaggerated. For the control group the three-year survival was about 80% while in the experimental Herceptin group the three-year survival (both groups are early cancers) was 90%. That ten-percentage point difference (absolute risk reduction) is what is being referred to by the 50% figure (relative risk reduction) (Moss, 2006). In order to appreciate what this means in economic terms, all the women in the Herceptin group would have to be given that drug in order to achieve that gain of ten extra percentage points, which means that the real cost of achieving that gain is the cost of giving all those women that drug, as opposed to just the last 10%. That looks more like a marginal gain from an economist's perspective as opposed to a 'dramatic' gain. The use of the relative risk number exaggerates the gain.

ease for nine years. He is presently on a combination of drugs (Herceptin, Avastin, and Abraxane) with monthly costs of $25,000. A combination of Erbitux and Irinitocan for metastatic colon and liver cancer can have costs of $140,000 for a year's treatment. Iressa can yield an extra year of life for the 10% of lung cancer patients who have a genotype responsive to this drug. Iressa costs $31,000 per year. More generally, evidence is growing of very aggressive (and very costly) cancer care up to within two weeks of death or less (Murillo and Koeller, 2006).

This is only a short list of these very expensive cancer drugs. None are curative; they increase disease-free survival, a not inconsequential but a very costly marginal gain. Are we morally obligated, as a just and caring society, to provide access to all these very expensive cancer drugs for all patients who could benefit? There are 700,000 US cancer deaths annually. For the vast majority of these patients now, one or another of these drugs is a last chance option. At $50,000 per case, that adds $35 billion to annual health costs ($70 billion at $100,000 per case). Again, these costs would be manageable and morally obligatory if cancer was the only issue, but these technological advances are emerging in every area of medicine.

In 1996 protease inhibitors were introduced for advanced HIV patients (700,000 in the US) at a cost of about $20,000 per patient per year for triple therapy. These are relatively young patients who would otherwise die premature deaths from opportunistic infections. It would be difficult to mount a compelling moral argument for not funding these drugs, especially when we spend $55,000 per life-year saved for dialysis patients. (This judgment reflects both egalitarian and utilitarian moral perspectives.) But aggregate numbers matter. There are twice as many HIV patients on these drugs as there are patients on dialysis; and hence, aggregate spending for the two groups has been nearly equal. However, the HIV virus has recently mutated around this triple drug combination; and consequently, a fourth drug needs to be added, fusion inhibitors that raise the annual per patient cost to $35,000. This generates aggregate costs far above aggregate costs for dialysis. The fusion inhibitors are likely to be defeated as well by future mutations of the HIV virus, but other costly drugs are in the pipeline that may address that problem and permit additional life-years of reasonable quality for HIV-positive patients. Do HIV-positive patients have equally strong just claims to all these successor drugs (assuming comparable effectiveness), no matter what their cost? What if those drugs are only 50% as effective but three times as expensive?

Further, prior to the protease inhibitors HIV-positive patients could expect to survive 7–10 years, the last two of which would involve struggling with multiple opportunistic infections. Such patients had last-year-of-life costs of about $127,000. If these various HIV-controlling drugs are successful in giving these individuals an additional 24 years of reasonable quality life for $600,000 or more (Schackman et al., 2006), then do these individuals continue to have an equally strong just claim to any costly interventions that might help stave off death from these opportunistic infections for that extra year at a cost of $127,000 (just like the cancer patients above)?

Roughly half the haemophiliacs in the US have the most severe form of that disease. They need Factor VIII to stem debilitating or potentially deadly bleeding episodes. For such patients Factor VIII will have annual costs of $100,000. In 1970 these patients would have been fortunate to reach age twenty. With Factor 8 these patients can reasonably expect to reach age 50. Is a just and caring society morally obligated to assure access to this drug for all these haemophiliacs?

One of the morally significant practical considerations we must note with respect to dialysis patients, most cancer patients, most cardiac patients, HIV-positive patients, and haemophiliacs is that the life-prolonging interventions we have mentioned are not one-time costly interventions, such as a heart or liver transplant. Rather, these interventions (and related costs) accumulate on an annual basis for the rest of their lives. This means that the size and cost of each patient cohort is increasing annually (because of the success of the intervention in prolonging life). Patients in the ESRD program will increase in number to 600,000 by 2012 (and are likely to continue to increase far beyond that due to the epidemic of diabetes in the US, which is linked to renal failure and heart disease). The haemophiliac population will increase for fifty years due to the effectiveness of Factor VIII. Here again we run up against a very painful ragged edge. Roughly 15% of the haemophiliacs with the most serious form of the disease are Factor VIII resistant. They will have much shorter lives of very diminished quality. But now there is an intervention that has a 70% chance of overcoming that resistance by 'challenging' the immune systems of these children with massive doses of Factor VIII over an eight-month period. This intervention requires hospitalization in an ICU for that entire period of time, thereby generating a cost of $2–3 million per case. Is a just and caring society with limited resources and unlimited health needs morally obligated to provide this intervention?

At any point in time in the US there are 280,000 patients with spinal cord injuries. Spinal cord injuries include both paraplegics and tetraplegics. First year treatment costs for tetraplegia are $625,000 with annual costs thereafter of $113,000 and lifetime costs of $2.4 million if that individual is about twenty-five years old at time of injury. This last example is introduced to make a very deliberate point. All our prior examples were about the costs of saving lives and life years. In this case the life-saving costs represent only a small portion of total costs, the bulk of which will be rehabilitation costs aimed at yielding a more functional satisfying life. Should those costs have lower priority than any costs associated with saving or prolonging lives? Would we rightly think of ourselves as acting in a morally acceptable manner if we 'only' expended resources on saving the lives of these individuals and doing nothing to improve the functioning or quality of those lives?

Here is one final challenge to libertarians, egalitarians, and utilitarians regarding health care justice and the emerging elderly population. We have to deal with the historical oddity of the post World War II 'baby boom' generation in the US. Roughly 78 million Americans were born in the period 1946–62, which created a very large population bulge. Currently 13% of the US population is over age sixty-five. That will increase to 21% by 2030. The economic significance of this is that the current elderly use 35% of all health dollars spent annually. That percentage and the dollar volume it represents would increase massively by 2030, thereby creating the potential for yet more challenges to our understanding of health care justice. The basic story is this: Our recent medical successes in dramatically prolonging lives afflicted with cancer and heart disease and all manner of other life-threatening chronic illnesses means that the total burden of chronic illness in the elderly has been steadily increasing (along with the relevant costs). If that same dynamic is sustained over the next twenty years, then the 'baby boom' generation will make massive claims on health resources through Medicare. They will claim more health resources than the current elderly generation, but they will contend they have a just claim to these resources because they have greater health needs (again reminding the reader of Callahan's point about the connection of health needs to emerging medical technologies). Further, they will contend that it would be unjustly discriminatory if, as elderly individuals, they were denied health treatments for the same medical problems treated in the non-elderly. Also, they will actively resist on moral grounds any health care rationing efforts because they will contend they have 'already paid' for this benefit through the 3.5% Medicare payroll deduction during their working lives. This can be taken as a libertarian argument; this was part of the social contract they signed on to forty years ago. Also, a very substantial number will have endured being uninsured (due to job loss) during the late stages of their working lives, which would make them even more resistant to 'sacrificing' any more in the way of needed health care once they were eligible for Medicare. But in many circumstances specific medical interventions will not yield as much medical benefit in many elderly individuals as in the non-elderly; and it will often cost much more (because of complicating medical conditions) to achieve those smaller benefits in the elderly. Those would be utilitarian considerations for diminishing the just claims of the elderly to some costly medical interventions. As for some aspects of the libertarian argument, the elderly have not really paid for all their Medicare benefits because Medicare failed to collect enough money for all the new medical interventions they failed to anticipate. So, the elderly do not really have a right to *everything* medicine might offer.

Let me summarise the main line of argument thus far. Hundreds of emerging medical technologies have driven health costs up inexorably and at an unsustainable rate that threatens other social priorities. The need to control escalating health costs and to make rationing decisions is inescapable. But the fragmentation of the financing of the US health care system is such that it is practically impossible to achieve either fair or effective cost control or rationing. We are also faced with moral fragmentation: there is not a widely shared conception of health care justice. Instead, there are multiple reasonable concepts of justice in relation to health care without agreement as to the morally appropriate scope and limits and contextual application of each of them. Hence, the actual distribution of access to needed health care is mostly a product of political and economic power with a self-serving patina of moral argument. All forms of health care rationing are resisted through a vague appeal to our obligation to be responsive to health needs when we have beneficial medical technologies that can address those needs, even if the benefits are very small or very improbable. Callahan's explication of the 'ragged edge' speaks directly to that problem. In addition, the heterogeneity and seeming incomparability of health needs, along with the enormous variation in lifetime health needs from individual to individual and across the span of life, make social judgments about the fair allocation of health resources (including fair rationing decisions) seemingly impossible. The net result is that those who are least well off health-wise and wealth-wise will generally have the least secure access to needed health care. How then should a society that aspires to be 'just' and 'caring' respond to this last state of affairs, given limited resources and virtually unlimited health needs?

We turn then to a discussion of the limits of moral theory and the need for rational democratic deliberation to address this question.

(3) Moral Theory and Rational Democratic Deliberation

Let us take as a working hypothesis that there are several conceptions of health care justice that are reasonable. It does not take that much effort to render this hypothesis plausible. What we have to show is: (1) that considerations of justice in some sense are relevant in a range of circumstances to how health care is distributed, and (2) that very different conceptions of justice (libertarian, utilitarian or egalitarian) in specific limited circumstances yield more just and more reasonable outcomes than in other circumstances where a competing conception seems morally superior, and (3) that the need for health care rationing is inescapable because we have only limited social resources for meeting virtually unlimited health needs. I remind the reader that health care rationing is universally regarded in advanced Western nations as being politically painful because it necessarily involves denying individuals what those individuals regard as needed and beneficial health care (albeit very marginally beneficial so far as life-prolongation or quality of life are concerned) for essentially economic reasons (as opposed to reasons of absolute scarcity).[21]

Why should access to needed health care be seen as a matter of justice? One short answer would be that serious threats to health represent a threat to virtually any life plan someone might have. In that respect effective health care can be seen as a *primary good* in Rawls's sense. Hence (following Rawls), the basic structure of a just society ought to be such that there will be a fair distribution of these primary goods (determined by principles of justice chosen from behind a veil of ignorance). It is relatively easy to determine what will be a fair distribution of most primary goods, but health care is complex and problematic due to both its inherent heterogeneity and huge variation of health need (however that is defined) from individual to individual. Thus, if everyone in the US were given a voucher for $6400 (per capita health spending in the US for 2005) to pay for needed health care for a year, then for the vast majority of very healthy individuals less than $1000 would be used. Others, however, would be faced with health expenses above $100,000 (and could not begin to cover those with a $6400 voucher). So, just access to needed health care must be relativised to something.

Daniels (1985), picking up on Rawls' fair equality of opportunity principle, has argued that principle provides us with a mechanism for determining justly differentiated access to needed health care. More precisely, individuals will have a prima facie just claim to effective health care that can restore or protect their access to the 'normal opportunity range' characteristic of our society. Put in another way, individual talents should not be denied the opportunity for realization due to injury or illness when a society has effective medical interventions that can cure or ameliorate that illness or injury. Daniels' account would seem to have two major virtues. First, it gives us an objective reference point for determining the content of a basic package of health benefits that ought to be guaranteed to all in our society. Second, it gives us an objective reference point for making some rationing decisions fairly. Not everything that someone will label a health need will generate content for a basic health benefit package; justice-relevant needs will have to be linked to protecting fair equality of opportunity. Thus, we would have no moral obligation to provide expensive life-prolonging medical care

[21] See Morreim (1991) for a fuller account of this point.

to patients with end-stage dementia or in a persistent vegetative state because they no longer have any access to any portion of the normal opportunity range.[22] Likewise, we would have no moral obligation to provide $100,000 worth of growth hormone to a five-foot six-inch adolescent to gain three extra inches of height since they are already in the normal opportunity range (though the parents of such a child would be free to spend their own money if that result were important to them).

Finally, the health care system itself (medical knowledge, medical institutions, and medical technology) is a product of massive public investment, taxes paid by virtually everyone. It would be prima facie unjust to extract resources from individuals to construct this system and then deny them access when they had a serious treatable medical need. Someone might object that libertarians would be opposed to the very idea of using taxes to construct the system in the first place, arguing that that should be left entirely to private enterprise freely agreed to. However, the health care system as we know it today represents a classic public goods/free rider problem. No one would be rationally motivated to do the basic medical research that must precede effective therapeutic technologies because others could freely appropriate the results of that effort. Without public investment to create that public good we would have a much less sophisticated and much less effective health care system. We all have the opportunity to benefit in very substantial ways from that public investment, including libertarians. More precisely, that benefit can be correctly described as being liberty-enhancing in numerous respects, both with regard to individuals whose life plans and liberties would be completely frustrated by a preventable premature death and with regard to the interests of the larger society that would lose millions of productive members as a result of uncontrolled epidemics (think of either the 1918 flu pandemic or AIDS). It would be irrational (from a libertarian perspective) to resist these investments.

Libertarians will resist any claim that there are justice-based social obligations to assure access to needed health care for anyone. I will posit for the sake of argument that this position can be consistently defended (i.e. there is nothing internally inconsistent about this view). Nevertheless, it is impossible to imagine any libertarian who is not pure intellect accepting the *practical* consequences of this view for themselves or anyone they care about. How many libertarians would accept the risk of death for their children when they (as parents) lose health insurance because they lost their job as a result of an enterprising capitalist ship-

---

[22] Note that these are judgments that utilitarians and libertarians would embrace as well, though the libertarians would want to permit families to pay for such care from their own resources if they wished, which is a conclusion Rawls and Daniels could accept as not unjust.

ping those jobs to another country? Think of all the childhood illnesses that are not preventable but that are treatable at great expense, such as serious asthma, or cystic fibrosis, or congenital heart defects, or childhood cancers etc. Or imagine a well-insured middle class libertarian in the earliest stages of recovery in an ICU for a massive heart attack. But ICU beds are scarce at the moment, and a wealthy libertarian with a serious heart attack offers the hospital ten times the normal rate for that ICU bed now occupied by the middle class libertarian. From a libertarian perspective the hospital is free to take that offer and transfer the middle class libertarian to a regular hospital bed where his risk of non-survival will be quadrupled. One might desperately hope for reputational reasons that a hospital would never do such a thing, but from the perspective of libertarian theory nothing prevents the hospital from so acting. The patient does not own the bed; the patient does not even have a contract to 'rent' the bed for any specific period of time. Everything depends upon the free choices of the doctors and the hospital. Would middle class libertarians chose a libertarian basic structure for society from behind the veil of ignorance if the above states of affairs would have to be accepted as just outcomes?

Regarding this scenario, Allen Buchanan (1998) has made an interesting argument. He notes the frequency with which middle class patients in managed care organizations in the US get extremely angry because they are 'unjustly' denied the care they have a right to. He asks these patients what conception of justice they are appealing to as the basis for these claims? He then points out that there seems to be no shared social understanding of what health care justice requires in the way of assured access to needed health care. Instead, there are only contractual generalities which these managed care organizations are free to interpret as they wish (since they wrote the contracts and have the lawyers to enforce their interpretation). Consequently, these middle class patients are only spouting empty rhetoric when they cry 'unjust.' Buchanan is not an anti-justice philosopher. On the contrary, his actual point is that the insured middle class has been indifferent to the plight of the uninsured in the US, in effect saying their plight is unfortunate but not unjust. If that is what they truly believe, however, then Buchanan is saying to the insured middle class that they too are merely unfortunate when economically powerful insurers deny them needed health care on the basis of their reading of these contracts. Buchanan's real take-home message is that Americans need to engage in public conversations aimed at articulating and legitimating a shared understanding of health care justice. Though space does not permit a full argument on this point, I will contend that a moderately egalitarian conception of health care justice will yield a more expansive and secure and effective set of liberties for all with regard to access to needed health care than a classical libertarian position (Nozick, 1974; Engelhardt, 1996).

What we want to show is that each of the major conceptions of health care justice has fruitful applicability. But each of them, if used exclusively to address the *entire* range of problems of justice in our health care system, will yield outcomes that all but the ideologically blinkered will recognize as being unreasonable or unjust. We can quickly consider some illustrative examples.

One aspect of the moral and political appeal of libertarianism is that individuals make rationing decisions for themselves. However, the moral and political reality is that such *effective* liberty is limited to those who are healthy and well insured and economically well off. Few will voluntarily invite into their health plans those with costly chronic illnesses, which means those who are least well off health-wise are also least likely to have secure access to the care they need. They have no effective liberty in this regard. Engelhardt (1996) will see fair negotiation and agreement as the key mechanism for the just distribution of goods in a respectful libertarian society. Fair negotiation is supposed to be uncoerced negotiation. What should 'uncoerced' mean? Imagine a health care world divided into two radically distinct systems: a superior health care system for the healthy and wealthy and a much inferior system for the poor and chronically ill. Imagine a wealthy individual, Mr Tromp, in the early stages of heart failure. He needs a heart transplant. He finds a poor individual, Mr Bill, with failing kidneys faced with imminent death because he cannot afford dialysis. He negotiates. He will pay for dialysis for three years for Mr Bill if he in turn agrees to surrender his heart for transplantation in three years. Mr Bill can refuse the offer and die next month, thereby exercising his liberty and showing he has not been coerced. Then Mr Tromp moves on to Mr Will. This looks like exploitation, even if it technically does not involve coercion. What reasonable libertarian would want to embrace this as an acceptable outcome of a libertarian conception of health care justice? Are there moral resources within libertarianism that would prevent such outcomes? I cannot find them. But our libertarian intuitions need to be constrained, most likely by some sort of egalitarian considerations. Daniels' fair equality of opportunity account of health care justice is one reasonable effort in that direction; it does involve a balancing of libertarian and egalitarian considerations.

Still, in the most universal and egalitarian (all are assured a substantial package of health benefits) health care system that is feasible, health care costs will need to be controlled. There will be limits; some health care needs will not be met. We can imagine a society with universal health care deciding to only fund artificial hearts for those below age 70, or those who had a confident predicted life expectancy of three years or more. Or we can imagine funding only 100,000 implantable defibrillators per year at $40K each. In both cases the core moral justification would be that such expenditures yielded too little benefit at too great a social cost (the appeal here is utilitarian), and other higher priority health needs would go unmet if those dollars were diverted to these other goals. Under such circumstances wealthier individuals denied these interventions at social expense could nevertheless purchase them with their own resources, *and this would not be unjust.* This is radically different from our Mr Tromp example. No one would be made less well off in a justice-relevant sense as a result of permitting such wealth-related purchases, as long as everyone has had the opportunity to have their health sustained earlier in life by a substantial package of guaranteed health services. Neither artificial hearts nor ICDs are absolutely scarce items, so the poor are not denied them because the rich outbid them. Also, we have a considered societal judgment that these interventions in these medical circumstances are cost-ineffective.[23] Libertarianism offers a reasonable moral justification for permitting such purchases. To this extent such libertarian moral judgments are justifiably included in a comprehensive conception of health care justice.

Utilitarian considerations will also necessarily have to be part of a comprehensive conception of health care justice. When health care resources are scarce relative to need, it is not unreasonable to maximize the health good obtained for each dollar spent. However, an unfettered maximization principle yields familiar injustices. If our goal with artificial hearts is to maximize the number of life-years saved at the lowest cost, then we will often be giving these devices to otherwise vigorous ninety year olds who were already genetically favoured for long life, thus giving them a yet longer life (another ten years, say) while we deny the artificial heart to a fifty year old with a prospect of only three more years due to bad luck in the genetic lottery. If our society can only afford so many artificial hearts, most people would be morally troubled that a ninety year old would be favoured over a fifty year old. The seven extra life-years saved would just not be seen as such a weighty moral factor. It is not obvious that most people would see even flipping a coin here as a morally reasonable option. Still, the virtue of utilitarianism is that effectiveness matters. We are forced to ask ourselves whether a cancer drug that costs $70,000 for a course of treatment and an average gain in life expectancy of 5.5 months represents a wise and just social investment. Likewise, we are forced to ask ourselves whether we should be implanting more than 100,000 ICDs annually, given the remote and diminishing likelihood of benefit as we move above the 100,000 level.

---

[23] See David Eddy's work on this point, nicely collected in *Clinical Decision Making* (1996).

A strict egalitarianism (Veatch, 1986) will also necessarily have to be part of a comprehensive conception of health care justice. Individuals with the same medical condition (a life-threatening but treatable form of cancer or heart disease) ought to have equal access to the same medical care. This intuition was essential to the ESRD program for patients in kidney failure. It was very much a rebuke of the Swedish Covenant committee in Seattle in the late 1960s that used social worth criteria to determine who would have access to a dialysis slot. These are the intuitions to which we appeal when we criticize the fragmentation of the US health care system that results in extraordinarily unequal treatment for patients with essentially the same medical problems. However, these same intuitions leave us without the moral resources needed to address fairly and effectively the health care cost containment problem. Strict egalitarians would seem to require that we provide ICDs to end-stage Alzheimer's patients, and that we either implant 600,000 ICDs annually in the US or else no ICDs. Their reasoning would be that we are otherwise making invidious quality of life judgments about Alzheimer's patients. That is, we are denying their equal worth as persons; we are saying that it is not worth it to society to save those lives from a premature death. As for ICDs in the aggregate, there is no invidious social worth judgment in implanting none or implanting 600,000. However, both those options seem unreasonable. Utilitarian and moderate egalitarian considerations would likely yield a more reasonable social judgment regarding ICDs, but a strict egalitarian would resist such a compromise. Likewise, I would contend that the strict egalitarian has few moral resources for putting limits on the care that Mr Diaz receives as well as most other cases where we need decisions regarding 'last chance therapies' (Fleck, 2002).

A moderate egalitarianism would seem to provide a more promising and reasonable approach to our rationing problems. One of its moral virtues is the Rawlsian bias of choosing health policies for cost control and rationing that favour to some degree the 'medically least well off.' A moderate egalitarianism will require that a just and caring society provide dialysis to patients in end-stage kidney failure (otherwise faced with premature death). The same will be true for AIDS patients needing expensive protease inhibitors and later fusion inhibitors (Fleck, 1999). But a moderate egalitarian will stumble when having to deal with the 'last chance therapy' problem in all its complexity. All those patients would seem to be among the 'medically least well off' because they are faced with a terminal outcome unless they are given access to some very expensive medical intervention that will marginally prolong their lives, as with the very expensive cancer drugs mentioned earlier. Note that 'all those patients' would include Mr Diaz. No doubt a strong justice argument could be made for providing last chance therapies to *some* of these patients. But which ones would have the strongest just claims? What precisely would be the moral resources within a moderate egalitarianism that would allow such distinctions to be made justly and *cost-effectively*? How precisely would moderate egalitarians judge who the 'medically least well off' were?[24] Would such a phrase always include reference to life-threatening medical problems? Could someone with a very severe form of arthritis relievable only by some very expensive medication be included among the 'least well off'? And would a moderate egalitarian judge that if there were a conflict between meeting the needs of severe arthritis sufferers and the needs of patients like Mr. Diaz that the arthritis sufferers had the stronger just claim?

Again, our major point is that other strands of a comprehensive conception of health care justice would be needed to address these issues. But our additional point is that very often all these strands together will not provide the intellectual resources needed to yield a morally compelling answer to a specific rationing problem. Imagine the case of Alice and Betty, forty-two and forty-four years old, each with terminal liver failure and a two-month life expectancy. We have one liver that becomes available for transplant purposes. Who should get it? The two are similar to one another in all morally relevant respects, except that Alice would have only a two-year predicted life expectancy because of other medical problems while Betty would have a predicted life expectancy of twenty years. From a utilitarian perspective we clearly maximize cost-effectiveness by giving the liver to Betty. But such a decision would seem contrary to our societal egalitarian commitments. Each individual has a right to 'the rest of her life', no matter how long or short that might be. So the egalitarian might insist that the only fair way of resolving this problem is through the use of a lottery mechanism.

To my mind neither resolution seems unreasonable or unjust. I would add that neither argument seems so morally compelling that it clearly trumps the other. But we need a decision, and we need a stable and consistent decision to protect fairness at least within a health plan. That implies that we ought to reject the idea of simply allowing each transplant surgeon to go with her own moral intuitions. Even though neither choice in itself would be open to moral criticism, this method would certainly cause rejected patients to wonder whether some morally questionable factor tipped the balance one way rather than the other in the case of their transplant surgeon.[25] A better approach, I argue, would be a

---

[24] I discuss the moral and conceptual complexities behind this question in a paper I presented in Amsterdam (Fleck, 2005) under the title 'Priority-Setting, Health Care Justice, and the Least Well Off.'

[25] It needs to be kept in mind that a *social* resource is being allocated, which is why the personal moral intuitions of a given transplant surgeon are not an appropriate

process of rational democratic deliberation that yielded a societal rule for addressing such questions. I have in fact posed the Alice/Betty problem to dozens of audiences of health professionals and lay people whom I have equipped with audience response devices that permit anonymous responding. I remind them that all of us are vulnerable to liver failure for many possible medical reasons, and that a future possible version of ourselves might be either Alice-like or Betty-like. We have no way of knowing now who we might be; we are as a practical matter behind a Rawlsian veil of ignorance in this regard. What should our social rule be? Virtually without exception 80% or more of every audience to whom I have posed this question will choose to maximize life-years saved in this situation. (If Betty's predicted life expectancy is reduced to the four to six year range, then the audience will shift toward a more egalitarian choice.) Morally speaking, it really does not matter which choice prevails through this deliberative process since there are sound justice-relevant considerations to support both. Still, the deliberative process itself is morally and politically necessary.

Flipping a coin to get a decision would not have the same moral or political value as the deliberative process. The deliberative process itself contributes to the development of what Rawls calls 'public reason' (Rawls, 1993). These are the moral capacities essential to peaceful problem-solving in any liberal pluralistic democratic society. Public reason requires that we give reasons to one another, especially with regard to 'constitutional essentials', that are independent of commitment to some comprehensive religious or philosophical doctrine, since all of us (with our very different deep commitments) must still live with one another under a single set of basic rules.[26] The deliberative process also contributes to the articulation of a richer pool of shared considered moral judgments (in a way analogous to the way in which scientific knowledge is generated and tested), available in this case for addressing more thoughtfully and confidently in the future emerging problems of health care rationing. In the short term, the moral virtue of the deliberative process is that it is public, contrary to the hidden and invisible approaches to health care rationing that dominate in both the US and UK (Aaron and

basis for making that decision. This would be a requirement of our publicity principle, which would be one of our constitutional principles of health care justice.

[26]   I will contend that the deliberative process in matters of health care rationing and priority-setting must also reflect a commitment to public reason. Thus, if we were to move in the direction of some form of national health insurance, we could not refuse to fund contraceptives as part of that plan because it was contrary to Roman Catholic doctrine. There may be other reasons for refusing to fund contraceptives in the plan, i.e., if they were not cost-effective. That sort of reason is not attached to any comprehensive doctrine.

Schwartz, 2006; Fleck, 1987). The deliberative process is also rational in that *morally relevant reasons* need to be given to one another for legitimating one rationing decision rather than another (See Daniels and Sabin, 2002). It is not political or economic power that shapes decisions, nor interest group politics.[27] Finally, the deliberative process yields an outcome correctly described as self-imposed rationing. All will have to live with the implications of the rationing decisions they have legitimated.[28]

Someone may argue that it is misleading to describe the outcome as self-imposed rationing, when, as in our example of Alice and Betty, 20% reject the outcome. However, our primary concern has to be the question of whether those 20% are being treated unjustly, as when the healthy and wealthy impose rationing protocols upon the sick and the poor as a way of protecting their own advantages. This is clearly not the case. At least some portion of that 20% will end up benefiting as a result of this rule. That is, they will be in the position of Betty when their livers fail. Some, of course, will be in Alice's position and see themselves as being harmed. However, the same will be true for the same proportion of the 80% who approved the rule. In both cases the harm is correctly described, morally speaking, as unfortunate, not unjust. Further, it is not as if the rule was an outcome of a tyrannical democratic majority. The members of the majority had nothing in common other than the fact that they individually came to endorse a set of reasons supporting the maximizing option. Neither did they manipulate or distort the deliberative process in order to arrive at a pre-arranged outcome. We might be tempted to say that a liberty-respecting society ought to give the 20% an opt-out option, as when we said it was not unjust for the wealthy to purchase their own ICDs if a rationing protocol would otherwise deny them

[27] Over the past fifteen years a very substantial literature has developed around rational democratic deliberation, in part in reaction to the corruption associated with interest group politics or the distortions of public judgment associated with polling. Deliberative democracy is intended to offer an alternative vision of what our political life ought to look like. The goal is to satisfy the Rawlsian ideal of a political system that represents a fair system of social cooperation. Cohen (an early articulator of the ideal) writes, 'When properly conducted, then, democratic politics involves *public deliberation focused on the common good*, requires some form of *manifest equality* among citizens, and *shapes the identity and interests of citizens* in ways that contribute to the formation of a public conception of common good.' (1989, p.19) See also Bohman (1996).

[28] One of our other constitutional principles of health care justice would be an autonomy principle. It may be formulated this way: Individuals must have a reasonable and effective opportunity to decide for themselves which rationing / cost-control / priority-setting policies and practices are rationally acceptable to them. A properly managed deliberative process will satisfy this principle. In another essay (Fleck, 2006, pp. 265-82) I have explicated in considerable detail fifteen norms for assessing the quality and legitimacy of a democratic deliberative process.

one at public expense. But livers are absolutely scarce. If any of the 20% obtained a liver outside the maximizing rule, the necessary implication would be that someone acting under the rule would end up dying for lack of a liver transplant. That would be unjust.

We need to step back from this very detailed example to sketch the large picture of the deliberative process that I imagine is necessary for addressing the rationing problem as part of a broader health reform strategy in the US. We need to start with the concept of deliberative space. My own judgment is that the vast majority of rationing issues we will need to address in the real world can be properly addressed in this deliberative space. That is, there will be multiple morally permissible options we might choose for purposes of resolving a particular rationing challenge. None of the options will be unarguably morally superior to all the others. All will represent non-ideally just resolutions of a particular rationing problem. All will have reasonable considerations of justice that give them sufficient prima facie moral legitimacy such that they deserve to be deliberatively considered. But the deliberative space has boundaries, which I describe somewhat metaphorically as 'constitutional principles of health care justice' (Fleck, 1992, 1994a, 2002). If some particular rationing proposal violates one of these constitutional rules, then it is automatically excluded from the deliberative process.[29] One such principle would be an equal respect and treatment principle whose goal would be to outlaw rationing protocols that unjustly discriminated, such as the $5,000 lifetime limit placed on care for HIV-positive patients

---

[29] What I refer to as 'constitutional principles of health care justice' would be derived from the various strands that make up our pluralistic comprehensive conception of health care justice. That is, the task of carefully articulating, clarifying and critically assessing these principles, as well as specifying and balancing them in relation to one another, would be the task of philosophers (or others with comparable skills). Wide reflective equilibrium would be the method by which these latter tasks would be accomplished (see Daniels, 1996). The kind of reasoning associated with the work of the US Supreme Court would offer a good analogy with what I have in mind. That court only takes cases where it is believed some interpretive adjustment might need to be made in our understanding of constitutional matters in order to get a reasonable answer to that case. We can imagine cases in which in some very specific respect the constitutionally protected values of privacy and procreative liberty might be in conflict with one another. Some health care rationing problems could raise comparable challenges that would need to be resolved at that constitutional level rather than through the normal democratic deliberative processes I describe. Disability advocates could raise the question (and have) as to whether patients in a persistent vegetative state or end-stage dementia had a right to just as much in the way of aggressive life-sustaining care as someone with the same medical problem who was otherwise cognitively intact. They might claim that such care was required by the 'equal respect' constitutional principle.

by one employer in Texas (with no such limits for any other costly disease).[30]

Consider further the case of HIV-positive patients. Is a just and caring society morally obligated to cover the costs of protease inhibitors at $20K per person per year? I believe an easy affirmative answer can be given to this question. These are usually relatively younger individuals and the drugs in question are very effective in reining in the effects of HIV and helping the immune system to rebuild itself as a defence against opportunistic infections. Also, we already spend $55K per person per year for patients on dialysis, and this is generally an older population. Many of the protease inhibitor combinations have been defeated by the mutating HIV virus, so fusion inhibitors have been added to the drug mix, which brings the cost of therapy to $35K per person per year. These drugs may give many of these individuals as much as twenty years of life they otherwise would have been denied, but the aggregate cost of that might be more than $700K per person. If all these drug combinations ultimately fail, then an AIDS patient will face deadly opportunistic infections again. Last year of life costs (trying to fight these infections) might be $127K. Is a just and caring society morally obligated to cover these costs as well? Could we have a rationing protocol that said we would fund only palliative care when an AIDS patient had less than a 10% chance of surviving another year with maximal medical therapy? Prima facie, this does not appear to be an unreasonable proposal, given what society had already spent to sustain the lives of these individuals. Nevertheless, a constitutional concern would have to be raised if this rationing proposal were this narrowly crafted since it would look like it reflected discrimination against HIV-positive patients. On the other hand, if we took a broad view of patients with advanced heart disease and end-stage cancers and other costly end-stage chronic illnesses for which society had provided comparable expenditures for individuals, and if we crafted a 'last year of life' rationing protocol with this sort of breadth, then it is not obvious that any constitutional principle of health care justice would be violated. Such a proposal could be the focus of a deliberative conversation. The core idea would be that we would be willing to expend somewhat extraordinary sums to sustain higher quality life-years for our future possible self in the earlier and middle stages of a chronic illness in exchange for giving up the very high costs associ-

[30] I served on the White house Task Force for Health Care Reform in 1993, Working Group Number 17, which was charged with articulating the ethical principles that ought to be used to assess any proposal for health care reform in the US. We identified fourteen such principles, which are summarized and discussed by Brock and Daniels (1994). These very same principles are useful for informing and guiding the democratic deliberations I imagine regarding health care rationing and priority-setting.

ated with 'last chance, last year of life' interventions that our future possible self might also need.

The solution proposed above is both prudent and just enough (the assumption being that this reasoning is what prevailed in the deliberative process). It is congruent with a limited utility perspective as well as a number of egalitarian intuitions. It is respectful of individual liberty because individuals who wish to purchase such marginally beneficial last-year of life interventions may do so, as long as such purchases do not deny resources to which others are justly entitled, such as the last bed in the ICU. We cannot say that this resolution is 'the best', and it is doubtful that any such resolution could be identified in this case. There are simply too many considerations that need to be taken into account, and our ethical theories are incapable of this very fine-grained sort of discrimination.[31] We should also note the essential value of the deliberative process itself in this case. In our earlier Alice/Betty example we simply proposed two choices for consideration. Few rationing problems in the real world are that simple. There is need for creative problem solving. The diversity of perspectives and background knowledge cultivated and engaged through the deliberative process makes such social creativity possible.

In the past several years a number of critics have emerged of such social deliberative processes. Space does not permit responding to all those criticisms. In general they identify any number of factors that can subvert or pervert the deliberative process in such a way that we could have no confidence that the results of the deliberative process were 'just enough.' Those are honest criticisms. However, when we are socially mindful of such threats to the deliberative process we can put in place safeguards that would minimize the risk of such corruption. With regard to democratic deliberation in the context of health care rationing, a common contention is that disease interest groups will hijack the process in some fashion to gain resources for their favoured disease state. However, a small amount of reflection will show that this would be very imprudent for such self-interested groups beyond the very short term.

Again, I remind the reader of our post World War II 'baby boom' generation problem. I myself am at the leading edge of that generation. I know two things: I want to live to a ripe old age, and I want to have the money to enjoy life in my last years. I do not want that money extracted as taxes to support patients in their ninth decade in the late stages of Alzheimer's with artificial hearts or $100,000 cancer drugs. What our fundamental commitments to moral equality require is that any such rationing protocol I would impose on these others would also have to be imposed upon my future possible self if I were similarly situated. Our concern

---

[31]   This is what Rawls has described as the 'burdens of judgment' (see Rawls, 1993).

now is with some interest group of 'baby boomers' shaping the deliberative process for future health advantage. However, the vast majority of 'baby boomers' are in very good health as yet and have no idea what their future health needs might be. They are behind an actual Rawlsian veil of ignorance (partial, but opaque enough to be useful). They may be worried about heart disease in their family, but they remain as vulnerable as anyone else to cancer or stroke or automobile accidents and so on. And if we do not want disproportionate shares of our money devoted to purchasing very costly, very marginally beneficial health services, then we will want to deliberate honestly with one another to identify a most reasonable and affordable and 'just enough' set of health services for whichever future possible elderly person we turn out to be.[32]

As noted earlier, our constitutional principles of health care justice constrain the deliberative process and serve to 'de-legitimate' an outcome that should not have been legitimated through a democratic deliberative process. I have no idea precisely how many such principles there are or precisely how we ought to see them related to one another. I have sketched them more fully in an earlier paper (1994a), and this problem is the focus of a book length manuscript for Oxford University Press. What I do know is that a practical and socially essential task for philosophers today is to more fully identify and articulate and clarify these principles. Such principles are by no means the mere invention of philosophers; rather, they are already present in our social and political life, inchoately and confusedly, as is also the case with those 'strands' discussed above that are part of a comprehensive conception of health care justice. The task of philosophers in both cases is to clarify and justify the legitimate scope of application for each principle and its relationship with all the others. Philosophers should be guided in this task by the method of wide reflective equilibrium. But we also recognize that these principles must be dynamically related to political, economic, scientific, technological and organizational facts about the world. There would be no major problem of health care rationing in the US if health care costs had not been growing at 7% per year for the past thirty years, mostly as a result of enormous technological innovation. And if all that innovation yielded

---

[32] There are many possible models for a reasonable and fair deliberative process. In a nation of 300 million individuals we will have to resort to representative forums. But given the Internet and numerous other forms of mass communication we can effectively engage as large a portion of the population as chooses to become engaged. Ultimately, for practical reasons, any particular deliberative effort must end. Consensus will be a rare event, and consequently, we will need to rely upon a voting mechanism to yield an authoritative result. If the deliberative process has been fairly and honestly managed in accord with the fifteen norms I have identified (Fleck, 2006), then the vote will itself reflect that fairness and honesty (and hence should not be seen as a failure of deliberation).

substantial unequivocal health benefits at reasonable costs, then that would reduce substantially the moral complexity of the problem of health care rationing. Instead, we are faced with these very costly marginal benefits in complex clinical circumstances. Ultimately, it will not be sufficient that philosophers give their approval to any particular balancing among any particular constitutional principles of health care justice. Any particular balancing or re-balancing will also require some form of rational democratic deliberative legitimation.

(4) Just Health Care Reform: A Sketch

In this concluding portion of the essay I want to sketch the implications of the argument for health care reform in the US. My central claim has been that we cannot expect to achieve fair or effective or stable health reform unless we have a strategy for addressing fairly the problem of health care cost containment and health care rationing. But we cannot resolve that problem unless we have a unified (non-fragmented) system for financing health care that is universal in scope. That means we cannot have 46 million uninsured along with all the variable forms of health coverage associated with individual employers and the fifty forms of Medicaid coverage. Rather, our starting point must be a fairly comprehensive package of health benefits guaranteed to every citizen of the US (here following Brock and Daniels, 1994). A comprehensive benefits package means 'that health care services should address the full range of health care needs and respect the relative importance of meeting them under reasonable resource constraints' (Brock and Daniels, 1994, p. 1193). Comprehensive coverage will be based on needs (constrained by that relation to protecting fair equality of opportunity) and will take into account the effectiveness of various interventions in typical clinical circumstances. The actual content ought to be the product of democratic deliberative processes.[33]

There are two morally relevant considerations that justify this starting point, as well as one very strong practical consideration. One morally relevant consideration is that assuring universal access to the same comprehensive benefit package is a way of operationalising our social commitment to the equal value of each citizen. The other is that our rationing protocols will apply to everyone (with the understanding that individu-

[33] The reader might imagine endless deliberation, but the fact of the matter is that the very large core of such a package would be quickly settled since we would find most of it in current health insurance contracts for the middle class. Serious deliberation would be around the fringes of the content of that package with the help of medical experts. In Great Britain the range of issues addressed by NICE reflect well the issues that are at the fringe of that benefit package, such as the year-long debate occurring around Alzheimer's drugs (see Rawlins and Culyer, 2004).

als have the right to purchase with their own resources that which from a social point of view is marginally beneficial non-costworthy health care, so long as such purchases do not result in injustices to those within the system). The additional morally relevant implication of this is that savings achieved as a result of various rationing or cost control strategies are captured by the system and can be redeployed to meet what society has judged through a democratic deliberative process to be other higher priority health needs. One of the major injustices of our current fragmented system is that savings achieved through rationing decisions now can easily flow out of health care to fund higher CEO salaries or better returns for stockholders or lower premiums for employers. That is, patients make the sacrifices (by being denied marginally beneficial care), but non-patients reap the benefits.[34] In a seamless health care system patients will sometimes be the beneficiaries of the savings generated by a specific rationing protocol and at other times they will be sacrificing marginal benefits for themselves (having to risk a 1% chance of a fatal arrhythmia because they are denied an ICD).

The very strong practical consideration that warrants creating universal access and seamless financing as a starting point for health reform is that this achieves very large administrative savings (see Woolhandler et al, 2003), perhaps in the vicinity of $200 billion per year. Those dollars (if they can be captured) provide the resources necessary to buy the universal comprehensive benefit package for the currently uninsured and underinsured.

As for the democratic deliberative process, it is difficult to see how that would get off the ground, practically speaking, without everyone having the same benefit package and the same basic financing, cost control, and rationing mechanisms to live with. That gives everyone in the deliberative process a common interest and a common set of problems to address. Democratic deliberators can act as good thoughtful citizens cooperating to solve common problems rather than self-interested competitors seeking to gain personal or group advantage. Again, it needs to be kept in mind that deliberators are largely behind a practical veil of ignorance in that few of us have adequate knowledge of our future health needs. I might have some indications of heart disease right now, but I would certainly be vulnerable to cancer or stroke or kidney failure, which would mean it would be foolish for me to be an unconstrained advocate for every medical advance related to heart disease.

Libertarians have proposed as an alternative to these reforms Health Savings Accounts (HSAs). Individuals would be given by their employers a fixed sum of money for health care for a year; say, $5,000. They

---

[34] Daniels (1986) has called our attention to this very important deficiency in our current system for financing health care and trying to control health care costs.

would use about $2000 of that to purchase a catastrophic health insurance plan with a very high deductible, say $5–10,000. The rest of the money would go into a savings account to purchase non-catastrophic health services for the year. Money at the end of the year could be rolled over to the next year. The theory is that individuals would be motivated to make prudent spending decisions. That is, they would make rationing decisions for themselves by denying themselves what they judged (from their own point of view) to be marginally beneficial non-costworthy health care. But I would argue that a scheme such as this is hardly a reform from a moral point of view. On the contrary, it would simply magnify and make worse the most unjust features of our current health care system.

With HSAs the very healthy would be very fortunate and save substantial sums for themselves every year, which would represent a net loss of care-oriented income to the health care system. Administrative expenses would be greater for this system because everyone would be entering the market as an individual. No one would be guaranteed the right to buy this catastrophic insurance, which would mean individuals who were most likely to need health care would not have assured access to it (on the principle that insurers are not charities). As things are now, at least some individuals are protected from that outcome if they are part of a large employer group; they would not have that protection with HSAs. Further, individuals would lose large group buying power relative to service providers. They would have to accept whatever fees providers regarded as reasonable. In addition, one of the sad outcomes of the RAND experiment (which tested the effects of different co-payment and deductible schemes as cost-control mechanisms [Newhouse, 1993]) was that consumers making their own personal care-denial judgments were as likely to make wise as unwise judgments. Again, those in the lower income ranges would be faced with these risks more often than those in higher income ranges just because they saw the HSA as 'their money.' Overall, this 'reform' scheme would better protect the interests and liberties of the healthy, the wealthy, service providers, and insurers. Those who were least well off health-wise or wealth-wise would be made even worse off than under our present system, both in terms of their welfare and access to effective liberty. HSAs hardly look like a reform from either the perspectives of justice or liberty if the interests of all are supposed to count, morally speaking.

In short, a reformed health care system in the US will require a collective social response based upon a shared understanding of health care justice. To accomplish that, we need to create working models of rational democratic deliberation that are accessible to average citizens in our society. And we need to educate citizens as to the utility and need for these deliberative forums, especially in connection with the problem of health care rationing. If just rationing policies must be public and self-imposed as a minimal condition for being 'just enough', then that will necessitate these democratic deliberative processes for the articulation and legitimation of those rationing protocols. As things are now, the public perception is that such protocols are imposed by bureaucrats or insurance administrators or hospital administrators or 'experts' or physicians, all of whom are seen as having self-interested reasons for imposing these care denials. The problem is with 'them', not 'us.' That, however, is mistaken. When we are taxpayers or insurance premium payers we ourselves demand cost control; when we are patients we demand everything medicine can offer at no cost to ourselves. Recognizing that simple truth puts the problem squarely within ourselves and among ourselves, which is why we need public deliberation, not demonization.

Margaret M. and C.A.J. (Tony) Coady

The Ethics of Access to Health Care in Australia

Introduction

The phrase 'distributing health care' could call up images of an already existing amount of money to be distributed in the way a pie might be cut, and its equity or otherwise being established through a pie chart visually demonstrating that distribution. Equity in health care is much more complex than that image would suggest. Actual health systems are the result of a balancing of those groups who have an interest in the operation of the system. In the case of Australia, the major groups are the medical providers, the clients/patients, the government and the businesses that could benefit (mainly insurance companies and pharmaceutical companies). Though sporadic attempts to establish a health scheme began in the 1940s, the real attempt at a universal system took place in the 1970s when a Labor government was returned to power after twenty-three years and established a national health insurance scheme in 1975 called Medibank. This was interrupted by a return to power of a more conservative government in the same year, but resurrected with adjustments by another Labor government and renamed Medicare in 1984. Medicare was to be financed by a compulsory levy on taxable income, originally 1%, increased in 1995 to 1.5%. Low incomes were exempt, and at a later stage those who had incomes over $100,000 paid a 1% surcharge if they did not have private insurance.

There are three key foci of the health system: out-of-hospital medical services; in hospital care; and access to pharmaceuticals. All these raise issues of access, but access to pharmaceuticals will be described separately since it is a separate system. Medicare covers both in and out-of-hospital medical care.

Medicare: Hospital and Out-of Hospital Medical Care

In introducing Medicare to the Parliament, the Health Minister in 1983 described it as providing 'universality of cover', and as being 'desirable from an equity point of view' (cited in Biggs 2003). These ideals are elaborated in some of the legislation governing the health system in what are called the three Medicare Principles. The first principle has to do with choice of services: 'Eligible persons must be given the choice to receive public hospital services free of charge as public patients'. The second concerns universality: 'Access to public hospital services is to be on the basis of clinical need'. The third is the equity principle: 'To the maximum practicable extent, a State will ensure the provision of public hospital services equitably to all eligible persons, regardless of their geographical location' (Health Insurance Act, section 26). The specification of geographical location is interesting. Presumably the equity principle is also meant to apply to other aspects or circumstances of eligible persons, such as age, ethnic background and gender. But these are not mentioned in the principles. The special place of geography in the principle arises from the fact that geographical location is an important factor in Australia due to the size of the country and the fact that most people live in big coastal cities, leaving rural dwellers as a minority and subject to potential neglect because of their relative lack of electoral power.

Medicare provides free in-hospital accommodation and medical services for patients who choose to be treated as public patients in public hospitals. The funding for these services comes from Australian Health Care Agreements between the Australian Federal Government and the governments of the states and territories. With regard to out-of-hospital medical care a Medical Schedule of Fees drawn up by the Federal Government in consultation with the medical profession is declared. Doctors are free to charge what they like. Their patients will generally pay the doctor's fee and receive back from Medicare 85% of the scheduled fee. The medical practitioner can decide to 'bulk bill' the patient, accepting only the 85% of the scheduled fee as payment, thus in effect giving the patient free service, but ensuring prompt and efficient recovery of payment.

In its original conception Medicare was intended to balance competing interests. The patient was interested in good quality, affordable, timely care. The medical providers, no doubt also interested in quality of care, had the additional interest of being paid for their services. Doctors believed the quality of their service depended in part on their clinical and professional autonomy, which involved not only freedom to make decisions about what treatment to give a patient but also freedom to determine how much to charge. Talk within the medical profession of the sanctity of 'the doctor/patient relationship' had both a caring and a financial aspect, both real and defensible in different ways, but with a tendency of the former to cloak the latter. While Medicare left the medical practitioners free to charge what they liked, the declaring of a scheduled fee and tying reimbursements to this fee meant that some rein was effectively put on medical charges.

Private health insurance exists alongside Medicare, providing cover for private hospital treatment and choice of doctor in hospital. Lavelle (2006) claims 'there is absolutely no evidence you'll get any better treatment in a private hospital than in a public hospital.' The only advantages of being treated in a private hospital are that the patient could be more comfortable in matters such as décor and possibly individual rooms, she may not have to wait so long for elective surgery, and she will have choice of doctor. It is hard to estimate how important choice of doctor is since there is no public knowledge of particular doctors' success rates, and so choice depends largely on hearsay-based reputation or on the knowledge of the general practitioner who must refer the patient to the specialist surgeon or physician. More will be said about waiting lists for elective surgery in the public hospitals later.

From 1984 until the late 1990s private insurance declined, possibly indicating popular satisfaction with the services offered through Medicare. When the conservative Coalition government came to power in 1996, Liberal Party Minister Brendan Nelson acknowledged that opinion polls demonstrated 'overwhelming support by Australians for Medicare and the universal access to public health services this entails.' He went on to add:

> If you want to touch a broad nerve in public opinion polling then any politician just has to suggest some sort of change to universal and/or so-called free access to health care (Quoted in Gray, 2003, p. 32).

In the face of this popularity the Coalition government, in spite of the hostility of many of its members to the system while in opposition, promised to retain Medicare. Of course its popularity does not necessarily indicate the equitable or ethical nature of Medicare.

Over the last ten years there have been small but significant changes which affect the balance of interests of those with a stake in the system. These will be discussed in greater length later in this chapter. However it is worth noting that the intention of those introducing the original Medibank in 1975 was not to achieve the balance of interests we have indicated is one of the noteworthy aspects of the health system in Australia. The intention of the framers of the 1970s legislation was simply to break the connection between ability to pay and the obtaining of medical care. Gough Whitlam, the Prime Minister who brought in the 1975 changes, intended to adopt a National Health System of the U.K. model (Elliot, 2003, p. 2). However, as Whitlam revealed in his account of his

period of government, the barrier to this simple plan was the 'civil con-
scription' clause in the Australian constitution preventing conscripting
of medical doctors (Whitlam, 1985, pp. 331-32). It was believed that this
clause ruled out forcing doctors to bulk-bill. Thus, the more complex
system giving doctors autonomy in determining their fees but with
some incentive to bulk-bill was born.

Pharmaceutical Benefits Scheme

Access to medicines is at least as important as access to doctors in a discussion of the distribution of medical resources. Although it is seen as
closely aligned with Medicare, it has in fact a longer history; indeed,
some form of it has existed since the late 1940s. A key date was the establishment of the Pharmaceutical Benefits Advisory Committee in 1953.
This is a statutory body whose membership includes medical specialists, health economists, clinical pharmacologists, general practitioners
and consumers. After drugs have been passed for safety, quality and
efficacy by the Australian Drug Evaluation Committee, the Pharmaceutical Benefits Advisory Committee makes recommendations to the Minister for Health and Ageing about which drugs should be listed under
the Pharmaceutical Benefits Scheme (PBS). After approval by the Minister a drug will be referred to the Pharmaceutical Benefits Pricing
Authority which negotiates a price with the manufacturer before the
drug is listed on the PBS. If a drug is listed on the PBS it is available for
Australian residents (and visitors from some specified countries) for a
co-payment currently (2007) set at A\$30.70 for general patients and
A\$4.90 for concession patients. The co-payment may be greater when a
patient requires a particular brand of the same drug, or where the price
of a particular drug is above the benchmark price for its particular therapeutic group of drugs. A Safety Net Threshold exists which means that
when general patients reach A\$1059 in payments under the scheme, the
co-payment will reduce to the concessionary amount. Similarly, when
concessionary patients reach A\$274.40 their co-payment is abolished.

The PBS has been the fastest growing area of health expenditure for
the Federal Government. Suggested reasons for this are: increasingly
expensive new drugs; over-prescribing; increased consumer expectations; the ageing of the population; and the influence of the pharmaceutical industry on prescribers. It would be a mistake, however, to judge
the financial viability of the Pharmaceutical Benefits Scheme in isolation
from the other aspects of the health system, since much of the budget is
spent on preventative drugs which should relieve pressure on the medical budget elsewhere. Anti-inflammatory drugs, anti-smoking drugs,
and cholesterol lowering drugs have put most strain on the budget.
However within the system there are measures which counter some of
these inflationary effects. For example, there are restrictions on the phar-

maceutical industry advertising direct to consumers; there are checks on individual doctors' prescribing patterns; doctors are urged to advise patients to try dietary means of controlling cholesterol before resorting to statins, and then only to prescribe statins if patients have a certain combination of risk factors (with one factor being diabetes). The actual cost of the drug (often many times more than the cost to the patient) is now included on the drug packaging, so that patients will realise they are being subsidised. Various other regulatory devices (such as the Federal Government's National Prescribing Service) have been tried, mostly aimed at 'educating' prescribers so that costs may be reduced. Most importantly, the PBS is the only large purchaser of drugs in Australia from both local and foreign manufacturers. As such, it can and does exert pressure on manufacturers to lower prices.

While in 2006 the financial demands on the PBS have been lessened, there is still concern for the future of the Scheme based on speculation about the effects of the US-Australia Free Trade Agreement of January 2005 (Rickard 2004a). The scheme is certainly not a free market, since decisions about drugs are made by a committee acting under administrative rules, and the Pharmaceutical Pricing Authority has monopoly-like powers. However the government has declared that the only changes that will occur are changes in process: the reasons for recommendations of the Pharmaceutical Advisory Committee to put medicines on the PBS will be published, and there will be a review mechanism for medicines which have been rejected. The effect of these changes is yet to be seen.

Pressure to list new drugs on the PBS is exerted not only by consumers and medical practitioners, but also by the organisation 'Medicines Australia', which represents 'research-based pharmaceutical companies who discover, develop and manufacture prescription medicines' (Medicines Australia, 2006). This body also declares its support of the Pharmaceutical Benefits Scheme.

Complications of Federalism

So far this chapter has concentrated on the two big schemes emanating from the Federal Government, namely Medicare and the Pharmaceutical Benefits scheme. Yet it is the states and territories (six states and two territories - the Northern Territory and the Australian Capital Territory) that have constitutional responsibility for health. A major part of this responsibility is for the hospitals, funded as described earlier. But it also includes licensing or regulating private hospitals, doctors, and other health professionals. There seems little doubt that this sharing of responsibilities between states and Federal Government leads to overlapping services, gaps in services, cost-shifting and other inefficiencies. A single-payer system would avoid these problems.

Another factor contributing to a low level of medical care for some groups, particularly rural dwellers, is scarcity of medical personnel. Many Australian states have recruiting campaigns, both overseas and within Australia, for doctors and nurses. A recent matter of dispute affecting the size of the workforce concerned the number of specialists being trained each year. The Australian Competition and Consumer Commission (ACCC) determined that governments, presumably both state and federal, should make decisions about the number of specialists being trained each year since they funded the places. This finding carries the suggestion that decisions made by the College of Surgeons had underestimated the number of specialists required, and fuelled speculation that the self-interest of specialist bodies had contributed to a state of scarcity in order to maintain high fees.

Changes to the Balance of Interests

Though the present Federal Government is maintaining Medicare and the Pharmaceutical Benefits Scheme, probably because of popular pressure to do so, there have been changes over the last decade which are viewed by some as compromising the principles on which the original systems were based. One of the more significant changes was the removal of the previous ban on the provision of private insurance to cover the cost of what is known popularly as 'the gap', i.e. the difference between the schedule fee paid through Medicare and what the doctor actually charges for in-hospital services. The most notable and unusual Federal Government move was in 1999 to give a 30% rebate on taxation of the amount paid in private health insurance. The argument for this was to encourage the uptake of private health insurance which had fallen to a low of 30.5% in June 1998. Gray points out that the fact that private insurance companies can now provide insurance for 'the gap' has the effect of 'increasing the cost of health care for the community as a whole and increasing the cost to general taxpayers who meet 30% of the cost of private health insurance premiums' (Gray, 2003, p. 41).

The most important of the Medicare principles is that of universal access, and the debate on whether Medicare was ever and is now a universal service revolved around the issue of bulk-billing. This is the system where the doctor accepts only the government rebate and the patient does not directly pay for that treatment. The percentage of medical services bulkbilled increased progressively from the beginning of Medicare in 1984 until 1996 (Elliot, 2003). More recently the number of bulk-billed services has varied from year to year and there is evidence at present of a drop in such services. From 1994, incentives have been paid to doctors to bulkbill services to low-income families and to children in non-urban areas and Tasmania. Later this incentive was extended to selected urban areas and large regional areas.

The setting of a schedule fee has been one of the central levers available to the government to counterbalance the possible inflationary effects of the ability of the doctor to determine the fees charged. Over the last decade the schedule fee has increased but not sufficiently to keep doctors' incomes rising at the same rate as average weekly earnings (McAuley, 2004). This gives doctors the incentive or reason to ask for a co-payment, at least from their better off patients, to maintain their salary levels relative to other members of the community. Many continue to bulk-bill for children and for those whom the doctors judge to be in financial need. In case the paternalistic altruism of the doctors wanes, the Federal Government has put in place a number of incentives for doctors to bulkbill for children and holders of Commonwealth concession cards. The other lever used by the government is to put in place a 'safety net' to lessen the impact of medical costs on the less well off. So the consciences of the doctors and those of the general public may be salved by the thought that those most in need will still have access. The current safety net is extremely complex. When any Medicare card-holder has paid $345.50 in the calendar year in differences between the benefit received under Medicare and the schedule fee, the benefit will move from 85% to 100% of the schedule fee for the rest of the calendar year. Since doctors are free to charge what they like, there is still normally a gap between the schedule fee and what the patient actually pays. A more significant recent change is the provision that when a patient has paid $1000 in any year in differences between the Medicare benefit and the schedule fee, Medicare will refund 80% of *out of pocket costs* for out-of-hospital services. This is significant in that once this amount is reached the schedule fee becomes irrelevant. Tying Medicare benefits to the schedule fee is a way of controlling inflation of costs in the medical system. Tying benefits to the amount actually charged is described by one economist (McAuley, 2004) as 'extraordinary public policy' since it provides open-ended subsidies of the doctors' fees. When the policy was first introduced in 2004, the threshold amount was $500 before out of pocket costs rather than the scheduled fee became the basis for the refund. The cost of this was quickly seen. More Australians than had been calculated reached the $500 threshold, so a quick doubling of that amount to $1000 occurred in 2006.

While this open-ended subsidy of doctors' fees may be 'extraordinary policy' it is in keeping with the policy mentioned earlier of subsidising of health insurance companies through the taxation rebate of 30% of fees paid to such companies. In both cases more money is being directed to the private interests involved in the medical system—the doctors and the insurance companies.

It is clear that the social philosophy behind the system has changed. As Elliot (2003) points out, the system was never universal in providing bulk-billed services to all Australians. Doctors were always free to charge what they liked. Nevertheless the system is universal in the sense that everyone has the right to the Medicare rebate. However, if the rebate becomes a less considerable proportion of the total doctor's bill, 'access to medical services increasingly relies on an individual's capacity to pay rather than on their health needs' (Elliot, 2003). The original Medibank system was a universal system in that it provided a service where ability to pay was not an issue in obtaining medical care, where the whole community, through a specific levy on income tax, took responsibility for the access of everyone to medical services. In this, it resembled the drive behind the UK National Health Service where, as even Mrs. Thatcher put it, 'The National Health Service will continue to be available to all, regardless of income, and to be financed mainly out of taxation' (quoted by Howard Glennerster in Chapter 3, p. 92 above). Though the levy is still in place, the system has been evolving towards one that is more like a residual welfare system where the individual is basically responsible for paying for her own medical care, and a safety net is provided for those in need. This development has, however, met with considerable community and political resistance.

Senate considerations

In 2004 a Senate Select Committee was set up to enquire into the proposed changes to Medicare. A number of arguments were canvassed in favour of maintaining a universal system. Bulk-billing, it was argued, is important even for wealthy Australians since it encouraged regular checkups and was thus good preventive medicine (Dwyer, 2004, p. 11). The economist McAuley (2004, pp. 11–12) argued that for reasons of social cohesion it was necessary to see health care as a 'universal shared good'. The wealthier get less from the current system because people on high incomes are generally healthier. But McAuley argues that if health care is redefined as a charity rather than a 'universal shared good' this may lead to what has been called 'downward envy', where the wealthier resent having to pay taxes in order to benefit the less well off.

One of the Government senators, Senator Knowles, expressed surprise at the evidence that 'people somehow think health should be free and bulk-billed' but are prepared to pay to get their DVD fixed and for other services (Knowles, 2004, p. 15). Professor Dwyer's response was vehement:

> The big difference here is that through progressive taxation, through indexing contributions to our income, we have a system that overridingly is equitable and by which Australia, the lucky country, is able to supply its citizens — or should be able to supply its citizens — with quality health care independent of ones' personal or financial circumstances. That is ideological;

it is a principle that I am absolutely convinced Australians hold dear. Health is different. (Dwyer, 2004, p. 15)

Philip Davies, Deputy Secretary of the Department of Health and Ageing represented the government's position at the Senate Committee (Davies, 2004, p. 27). He pointed to government decisions to increase the number of doctors and nurses. Davies anticipated that this would have a downward pressure on doctors' fees, and possibly increase the rate of bulkbilling. He went on to argue that universality would be maintained because 'all Australians will continue to receive the same level of Medicare rebate, and all Australians will continue to be eligible to be bulk-billed.' But he reasserted that 'Decisions on when and who to bulk-bill remain a matter between individual doctors and their patients'. Davies' evidence to the Senate Committee provides another example of the hybrid nature of the Australian healthcare system. On the one hand the government has a degree of control over supply of doctors, particularly in its funding of training places, but at the same time it defers to the individual doctor's judgment at least in determining fees.

Quality

There seems little point in talking about equity if the good to which people have equity of access is of low quality. There is a practical point as well as a philosophical point to this claim. For if the quality of health care is low in a country, then the better off can travel in order to gain better quality care. Quality in a health system is hard to determine. There are certain elements which can be measured, such as life expectancy, infant mortality, and number of medical personnel per capita. On all these measures Australia does well. Life expectancy for Australians (OECD Health Data) is high, at 83 for females born in 2004 and 78.1 for males, in each case well above the OECD average. More significant is the healthy life expectancy, which is the 'equivalent number of years in full health a newborn infant can expect to live based on current mortality rates and prevalence distribution of health states in the population' (OECD Health Data) In these terms Australia falls behind only Japan, markedly, and Sweden, Italy and France, marginally. In the area of infant mortality Australia does slightly less well with 4.7 deaths per 1000 births which is in the middle third of OECD countries. The number of doctors per capita is 2.6 which compares favourably with most English-speaking countries but which is behind France, Greece and Italy (OECD Health Data). Likewise the number of nurses, 10.4 per 1000, is high in comparison with most countries.

In terms of equity it seems important that the facility to which all have free access, namely the public hospital, is of high quality. This may have been achieved through a number of circumstances. These circumstances include the fact that the public hospitals are generally teaching hospitals and connected with University departments of medicine, and that the majority of accident and emergency departments are in public hospitals. The Doctors Reform Society was fond of repeating the story of the then wealthiest man in Australia, Kerry Packer, who in the 1990s suffered a heart attack while playing polo. He was rushed to a public hospital and after being stabilised was transferred to a private hospital (Doctors Reform Society, 2004, p.1). The claim is made that even the wealthiest Australian is dependent on the quality of the public hospitals. Is there some kind of Rawlsian calculation here? No matter what our ethnic background or financial resources, we may find ourselves dependent on a public hospital in an emergency, so they had better be good.

The major complaint about the public hospitals is not about the quality of treatment but about the fact that they have long waiting lists for what is described as elective treatment. This elective surgery can cover any condition which is not immediately life-threatening. For many people there is no alternative but to wait in pain and possibly be unable to work or carry out normal activities but if a person has private insurance she can choose to have the surgery in a private hospital with a surgeon of her choice.

Podger (2006, p. 3) claims that waiting lists for emergency departments are shorter than for the U.S., Canada and the U.K. and waiting lists for surgery are shorter than for Canada, N.Z. and the U.K. Nevertheless a survey of one hundred general practitioners in Victoria in 2006 (AMAVic, 2006) found that 79% of surgical patients' access to public hospitals was poor or very poor. Waiting lists, with the apparent solidity given by numbers and statistics, can paint a picture of a health system in crisis and provide great political weapons for opposition parties. However Mann (2006) has pointed out that the figures are both manipulable for political reasons and produced by medical judgment which can vary widely. Elective surgery is categorised into three groups: urgent, which should receive treatment within 30 days; semi-urgent within ninety days; and non-urgent with no stated target. But the triage system driving the categorisation can vary tremendously from doctor to doctor and hospital to hospital. Hospitals can be subject to financial disincentives if the category of urgent patients is too long. But the professional judgment of the doctor making the decision about the degree of urgency seems to be the most powerful factor. A former Minister of Health in the Federal Government tells the story of a long waiting list for eye surgery in Broken Hill, a small city in central Australia with a large indigenous population.

> So they sent up an eye specialist from Adelaide and he reduced the waiting list by a whole lot, maybe by two-thirds. Now you could say he got it wrong, or maybe the original bloke got it wrong. And, you know, it doesn't really

matter. Because it's a matter of personal professional judgment. The bloke from Adelaide decided those people didn't need operations (cited in Mann, 2006).

Mann's own conclusions about waiting lists is that they are a form of rationing of medical resources. But it is rationing which is controlled by doctors and not open to a great deal of scrutiny.

Excluded Groups

While the figures on life expectancy and infant mortality and so on may indicate quality, they are no measure of equitable access. A further analysis of the health statistics suggests some marked inequities. The most shocking of these is the difference in life expectancy between indigenous and non-indigenous Australians. Life expectancy at birth is estimated as 59 years for indigenous men and 65 years for indigenous women. (Oxfam Australia, 2006, p.3), approximately 17 years less than non-indigenous Australians. It also compares badly with life expectancy of indigenous people in Canada and in New Zealand. Infant mortality in the indigenous population similarly compares badly with infant mortality in the non-indigenous population. The Australian Medical Association (Australian Medical Association, 2005) puts it bluntly: 'Each year 83 indigenous children die because they are indigenous.' Professor Ian Anderson, indigenous doctor and Director of VicHealth Koori Health Unit, University of Melbourne, raises the key question: 'We haven't seen the improvements in health outcomes that have been seen in other indigenous populations across the world and we have to ask the question 'why'.' (cited in Oxfam Australia, 2006, p. 3) The answer to that question is not apparent. The authors of the Oxfam Report (2006) suggest three answers:

> 1. Governments must provide resources to Aboriginal and Torres Strait islander health at a level that matches the dire level of need ... 2. Governments must support indigenous control and participation in the planning, management and delivery of health programs and services ... 3. Governments must support and enable a holistic approach to health, recognising the impact that broader social and economic factors have on health (Oxfam Australia, 2006, pp. 6-8).

The example of the health of indigenous Australians is instructive for several reasons. It is a dramatic example of the effect of wider social factors on health outcomes, thus showing the inadequacy of the simple pie chart approach to division of resources for health. Per capita spending on indigenous health is higher than for non-indigenous, but as the Productivity Commission states, 'this is against a background of much greater need, and service provision that generally occurs in more remote and costly settings.' (Productivity Commission, 2005, p.17) No doubt something could be achieved by spending more money on indigenous health, particularly targeted at areas of high need in the indigenous communities. However this is unlikely to solve the whole problem. There is a well-established connection between social class and health, indicated in the differing health outcomes and life expectancies of different suburbs of the large cities of Australia, and by the differences between health in city and rural areas. Judged in terms of health outcomes, rural dwellers and those of lower socio-economic class do not seem to receive equitable access to health resources. This suggests that if the aim is to achieve more equal health outcomes between groups, the answer may lie in achieving greater equality generally. But in the case of Australian indigenous communities, improvement of socio-economic status does not seem the complete answer. Many would argue that there is in addition the need to overcome the effects of racism and of destruction of culture through colonisation (Brennan, 2004, p. 5)

Disputed Access

There are a number of treatments where there are arguments about whether the treatment should be provided at all, or whether it should be provided only to a certain class of people, or whether it should be provided but not at the public expense. Abortion falls into the first category. Although there are many disputes about the practice of abortion it is available and attracts a Medicare benefit. Cosmetic surgery of a kind not considered medically necessary falls into the third category. It is available but not subsidised from the public purse. According to the Australian Society of Plastic Surgeons (2006) many people travel overseas to undergo cheaper cosmetic surgery than is available in Australia, with often unsuccessful results.

Various kinds of fertility treatments fall into the category of only being provided to some of those who want it. Australia is one of the more generous countries in funding infertility treatment (Smith, 2006, p.3) in that there is no cap on the number of cycles which will be funded, though there has been political discussion about such capping. But funding is only one factor affecting access. A more fundamental restriction of access occurs in regulations about fertility treatment which vary from state to state, with Victoria being the most stringently regulated. Until recently when there was a challenge under the Sex Discrimination Act, artificial reproductive technology in Victoria was only available to married women. Now it is available to both single and married women but the women must be infertile. Again the claim is that there is no 'medical need' for fertile women to have such treatment. One effect of the restrictions has been for one Victorian clinic to set up a branch just over the Victorian border in New South Wales and to encourage reproductive tourism to avoid the reach of the regulations.

Facing the Ethical Problems

It is obvious enough that justice in health care cannot be considered in isolation from the economic, political and practical problems involved in creating institutions for the delivery of such care. It should be equally obvious that money, politics and pragmatics are rudderless without a moral perspective within which they should operate. One need only recall the health policies of the Nazi regime towards the disabled (not to mention their 'health' policies towards Jews) or the Soviet Union's use of psychiatry against political dissidents to get the point.

Any discussion of a just or morally satisfactory health policy, especially in its access dimension, must begin by recognising that health is a basic human good. It is what Daniels calls 'a basic need', and he expands this with the description 'things we need to maintain species-typical normal functioning' (Daniels, 1985, p. 42). Daniels notes however that, for various theoretical reasons, John Rawls does not include health care as what he calls a 'primary social good'. These primary goods are focussed on certain liberties and their relation to income and wealth, and in Daniels' adaptation of Rawls to the case of health care, the moral necessity for such care emerges from the right to fair equality of opportunity. There are several things problematic about this approach, but the principal one is that, however well it fits the Rawlsian schema, there is something perverse in the idea that the good of health care is instrumental to the primacy of the opportunity to pursue careers which, Daniels thinks, is Rawls' primary concern (Daniels 1985, p. 43ff: for the point about Rawls' primary concern Daniels, 1985, p. 45.) There are many people who have no such interest, e.g., the very elderly, the very young, the very idle, the severely handicapped, and, by some accounts, certain unassimilated indigenous peoples. Yet all of these need a minimum level of healthy functioning, and the state they live in has some responsibility to ensure it. Of course, this objection to Daniels might be met by giving such notions as 'careers' a much broader reading than jobs or offices. We could disconnect 'career' from the option of competitive job-seeking and the construction of 'life plans' that are often found in such writings. Niall Maclean defends Daniels' approach in this sort of fashion (in a footnote to his chapter in this volume). This seems a departure from the spirit of such as Rawls, but it would make of health a more basic good than Daniels' own scheme seems to do, though still treating it as, in some degree, instrumental.

There is an interesting question about the ways in which some very fundamental values may nonetheless have some suggestion of instrumentality about them. It is usual to distinguish between intrinsic and instrumental goods, as between those that are valuable in themselves and those that are valuable only as means to other goods. But this can be misleading in several ways. One is that things valuable in themselves can *also* be valuable as means to other good things, as knowledge may be intrinsically good and also valuable as leading to prosperity or the admiration of others. Another is that what is valuable in itself may have that value in virtue of its complex relation to other goods with which it forms a valuable whole. So health may be good in itself precisely because it is a basic constituent in what could count as a good life. Both these thoughts are present in Aristotle's discussion of ethics and the good, and he particularly insists that fundamental goods are constitutive of eudaemonia or flourishing and not merely means to achieving it. Contemporary philosophers have recently elaborated the argument in different ways. Following some of the distinctions made by Korsgaard, and supported in different ways by Kagan (Kagan, 1998) and others, we might distinguish the range intrinsic/extrinsic from that of final/instrumental. Korsgaard does this because she thinks that some things may be valuable for themselves, i.e., not valuable for something else that they are instrumental in achieving, even though their value does not arise from their intrinsic properties. They may rather be valuable non-instrumentally because of some relational properties they instantiate. Thus, she would say, they have final value but not intrinsic value (Korsgaard, 1983). Some antique object, for instance, may be valuable primarily because of its rarity which is not a property intrinsic to it. Something similar may be true of other historical properties. Shelly Kagan gives the example of the pen that Abraham Lincoln used to sign the Emancipation Proclamation (Kagan, 1998, p. 285). It might be better to treat these arguments, if correct, as showing that there are different ways that goods and values may be intrinsic. Thus we could keep the traditional way of framing an important distinction but complicate the basis on which it is made. There is no doubt more to be said about this debate, but the distinctions envisaged do not seem to us to damage the idea that health is a fundamental value, whether we judge it final or intrinsic. As Henry Shue puts it, the right to reasonable health support is 'a basic right'. Shue argues that a right to 'the essentials for a reasonably healthy and active life' is part of the right to subsistence that is fundamental to the exercise of any other rights. (Shue, 1996, p. 24.) Shue is concerned with a basic minimum, but the provision of health care in any organised, advanced society creates needs that go well beyond that minimum, or, as it might better be put, the content of the minimum expands with advances in social structures and medical possibilities and the consequent creation of new needs. Whatever the difficulties of distinguishing needs from wants and other related states, such as preferences, it is useful (as Niall Maclean, following Wiggins, argues in his chapter) to think in terms of needs when we confront such basic human (or indeed animal) requirements as health.

Although good health is fundamental to human wellbeing (or in Aristotelian terms, human flourishing) practicalities and cultural factors can combine to produce divergent reactions to sickness. In communities that are desperately poor, badly governed, scientifically backward, and with minimal access even to charitable support, there must be little scope for the question we are concerned with about justice in provision of health care. What can be done by families, clans, and charitable (mostly religious) groups will be done, and there may well arise issues of priority and neglect that have a moral aspect just because health is such a basic value; nonetheless, the most serious questions, and those we are concerned with here, arise only when effective cures and preventions are available and effective state organization and authority exist. Where strong, central government is a mere prospect for the remote future, then questions about the state's role in providing health care to citizens and residents do not seriously arise.

Complexity in the Balancing of Competing Demands

Once such questions do arise, as they palpably do in economically advanced modern democracies such as Australia, then the concern of governments must be to meet the basic needs of their populations as best they can. This is not all they should do, but they should attempt at least this. Of course, although the need for good health is universal, there will be a degree of relativity about the specific form this need takes in different circumstances. Expectations about species typical functioning will often relate to scientific possibilities, specific genetic dispositions both toward immunities and disabilities, and to some extent cultural factors. Whether deafness needs curing, for example, is a matter hotly disputed amongst some elements in the deaf community, and in the wider community, homosexuality was once considered (and still is amongst some groups) as a disease needing treatment. We may allow that complications of this sort need attention, but they are peripheral to the key idea that health is a basic human need. A more pressing problem that immediately confronts governments is that of balancing the different basic needs against inevitably limited resources. We need education, housing, political and religious liberty, freedom from poverty, and security from attack or natural disaster as well as health. And we might add, though more contentiously, capacity for leisure, opportunity for economic improvement, and for aesthetic satisfaction. Support for all of these out of inevitably limited resources, even in rich societies, requires choosing between the degrees to which these needs are satisfied. This does not mean that the values involved are no longer crucial, as some seem to think. Values and ideals remain significant, and very importantly, remain as action-guiding, even where they cannot be fully realised in certain concrete circumstances. Here we seem to differ from Professor

Fleck, though the difference may be more apparent than real, more a matter of language than moral substance. When Fleck says 'we need ... a practical, non-ideal conception of health care justice' he makes it seem as if our ideals must be abandoned to concrete judgement, but if this is his idea (and other comments suggest it may not be) then it devalues the significance of aspiration, the importance of striving to transcend the pressures of the status quo and the restrictions of what has so far been acceptable. We need to make our ideals work and to take account of all the complexities, without denying their capacity to dynamise our efforts. Take the ideal of peace. The fact that the dismal conflict between Israel and the Palestinians seems at present intractable should not mean that we abandon the ideal of a peaceful resolution of the conflict. Indeed, it makes it all the more urgent that the rich moral and imaginative resources of that ideal are brought to bear upon the participants in the conflict to move it in the direction of a resolution. Similarly with justice in health care. The dynamic of the ideal of a just provision of health care not only can survive the limitations of complex practicalities, but should help guide the decisions that communities and individuals make about such provision, and help open up new possibilities.

Talk of balancing the needs of the population and the potential trade-offs between values and ideals with respect to them can obscure the important fact that the relationship between these is not necessarily one of conflict. We have a tendency at one level to concentrate upon the potential clashes between justice and efficiency, equality and productivity, or freedom and security while at another level stressing the tensions between providing resources for health or education, for prevention or cure. There are doubtless clashes and tensions, but there are also intimate connections between these various pairs, so that promoting one may very often be also a way of promoting the other. In philosophical theory, some value pluralists are so concerned to stress the potential for conflict between ultimate values or significant ideals that they ignore or downplay the fact that very often these 'great goods' as Isaiah Berlin calls them, are in supportive harmony. Berlin's rhetoric, in particular, sometimes obscures this reality. So, he says:

> The notion of the perfect whole, the ultimate solution, in which all good things coexist, seems to me to be not merely unattainable - that is a truism - but conceptually incoherent; I do not know what is meant by a harmony of this kind. Some among the Great Goods cannot live together (Berlin, 1997, p. 11).

Admitting that cohabitation is sometimes impossible and that perfect harmonies of any sort may be unattainable in the moral universe, nonetheless we should not accept a picture of the moral life as a zone of permanent conflict, nor overlook the many instances in which such 'great goods' as peace and justice, prudence and compassion, and many others support and reinforce one another. This insight is particularly appropriate to the topic of access to health care. There is, for instance, considerable evidence that more educated people tend to have better health, as do people with higher levels of income. Moreover, there is even evidence that higher levels of justice and equality in societies correlates with better health outcomes. As Dwyer (2004, p. 4) says in the course of discussing this in relation to poorer and wealthier parts of Sydney, 'In the western part of Sydney, you are five times more likely to die prematurely of a preventable disease than you are if you live on the north shore.' There is always room for intervening variables, such as natural disasters, climate, religion and culture, to play some part in broad statistical results; nonetheless, the evident interconnections are ignored at some peril.

What these linkages further suggest is that we should have a more complex focus upon access to health care, seeing it not merely in terms of the specific processes of delivering the care, important as that is, but also in terms of the broader social agenda related to other significant values. There is an immediate connection here with the vexed issue of the relationship between prevention and cure. If improved education, reduction of poverty, environmental protection, and better nutrition can improve health and ward off certain diseases, then funding devoted to these is itself health-related. This makes it clear that the common picture of health funding as mired in competition for resources, though understandable and realistic to a degree, nonetheless obscures the ways in which this competition is not zero-sum. Money that is taken from a narrowly defined health budget for these other purposes will often enough have positive impacts upon the betterment of health and the combating of disease. Measures to improve the amenities and self-respect of disadvantaged groups, or to provide the opportunities and resources for migrants to learn the local language seem far removed from local delivery of health care, but in fact they may make it far more effective in a variety of ways. Indeed, it has even been plausibly argued that, quite apart from such measures improving the health of the disadvantaged groups directly affected by them, the removal of socio-economic inequalities tends to improve the overall health of the whole community (Daniels, Kennedy and Kawachi, 2000).

A secondary problem is that of triage within the provision of health care, i.e., that of prioritising the provision of treatment for those who are ill in different ways and different circumstances. To take an example of Professor Fleck's, if we are forced to the choice between treating the ventilator-dependent sixty-nine-year-old demented Angel Diaz at very great expense when he contracts pneumonia, and treating the impoverished, uninsured college student Bud who cannot afford a simple and effective remedy, then it would seem scandalous to choose Diaz. At any rate, this would appear the right verdict if we are confronting the choice *ab initio*, i.e., whether to begin the treatment of one or the other. Indeed, if any one of us had a spare \$280,000 and could spend it on treating 1400 Buds rather than one Diaz, that would seem the right option. But, of course, such choices do not present themselves in that form since they arise not from one-off options presented to individuals with no background of prior commitment, but as the result of a system and the policies that it embodies. This raises important questions about the nature of the authority for medical decision-making, and here matters are very complex, in the Australian system as in any other. Both at this distributional level and at the more general level of federal and state health budgets, much of the rationing decisions (as economists tend to call them) remain to a considerable extent ad hoc and based on tradition. It is understandable that there should be some pressure to replace this with principles of distribution that are guided by rational and moral considerations.

Aside from the many political difficulties in the way of implementing such principles, there are certain obstacles within the sphere of the rational and moral. Before examining these, however, it is important to dispel one difficulty that can haunt the discussion, even if it not always explicitly mentioned. This is the clash between utility and duty, or more broadly between consequentialist and non-consequentialist approaches to ethics. There is undoubtedly the possibility of such conflict, but there are several points that need to be made in partial mitigation of it. (Utilitarianism is a narrower theory than consequentialism, but the points we are making apply to both, so we will talk only of utilitarianism for ease of exposition. We will also group the various non-utilitarian positions together under the title of 'intrinsicalist' since they are all concerned with features of action that are not extrinsic to the deed itself or the character of the agent.) The first is that utilitarianism is a theory concerned with judging right and wrong in terms of consequences, and that fact can make it seem as though its opponents cannot themselves have any recourse to consequences, and instead must judge solely in terms of rights, duties, virtues or the like. But this misstates the opposition. The crucial point of opposition is that utilitarianism is committed (ultimately) to considering *only* consequences whereas intrinsicalists hold that, in addition to the consequences of acts for good or ill, we must consider *also* the nature and quality of the acts, the motives for acting, the rights and duties involved in the act, and much else. Hence the fact that some policy may save more lives than another can be considered an important moral factor by utilitarian and non-utilitarian alike, just as the greater good (in health terms) produced by saving 1400 Buds for the cost of one Diaz must weigh with both sorts of theorists. In particular, where a decision about a government or community policy is involved many of the morally relevant partialities that intrinsicalists are otherwise concerned with (such as those engendered by friendship or family) are morally irrelevant. Whether from the perspective of general benevolence or that of justice, all citizens must initially receive equal, impartial consideration. This need not, however, mean that they must all get the same treatment or the same priority. For, instance, at an accident scene, it may be better overall for everyone if an injured doctor is treated first so that she can then assist in the treatment of other victims. And there are many other ways in which equal concern and equal respect need not translate into equal treatment. Nor need a genuine concern for the dignity and importance of individuals and the (often ambiguous) right to life translate into an obsession with prolonging individual lives whatever their state and whatever the costs, both financial and moral, to others.

A second respect in which the utilitarian/intrinsicalist contrast can be misleading is that the most defensible forms of utilitarianism are likely to be those that are indirect. Ever since J.S. Mill and Henry Sidgwick, it has been clear that a simple act utilitarianism faces major difficulties accounting for what Sidgwick called 'Common Sense Morality', and so Mill (1972, pp. 22–3) and Sidgwick in different ways sought to make utilitarianism match ordinary morality by showing that adherence to most of the rules, prohibitions and inhibitions of common sense morality was itself more likely most of the time to produce the best consequences. Sidgwick (1962) indeed held that, from a utilitarian point of view, it was best that utilitarianism not be adopted by the bulk of people. The adoption of indirect forms of utilitarianism means that the distance between utilitarian and intrinsicalist moral outlooks is in practice greatly reduced. Simple maximising of outcomes, either in terms of numbers of lives saved or dollar cost effectiveness, need not be the proper utilitarian response to a rationing problem.

Political, Rational and Moral Obstacles

After this theoretical detour, we may return to the political, rational and moral obstacles earlier foreshadowed. Decisions about health care priorities in the Australian context are governed by a mix of procedures and informal understandings in which there is relatively little in the way of formal direction from above. The situation is complicated by the workings of the Australian federal system in which the States have primary fiscal and supervisory responsibility for the hospitals and the Federal Government has the major role in out-of-hospital medical treatment. The division between public and private hospitals and various linkages between the two complicate matters further, as does the extensive role of the private insurance system. There are some procedures that most private plans do not fund, such as dental care (though special insurance can be arranged for some limited dental cover) but the restrictions are not yet as complex, extensive and even intrusive as is common in the United States. Critics complain nonetheless that things are gradually moving in that direction. The Federal Government has established various bodies, pre-eminently the AHMAC (Australian Health Ministers' Advisory Council), a Federal/State collaborative effort that has set up the National Health Priority Action Council. This body has developed seven National Health Priority Areas (NHPAs) and considers them in the light of the health burden of the disease or condition, the potential for health gain and progress through national collaboration, cost-effectiveness, sustainability and reduction of health inequalities. The seven areas are: cardiovascular health, cancer control, injury prevention and control, diabetes mellitus, mental health, asthma, and arthritis and muculoskeletal conditions. Nonetheless, it does not seem that these impinge strongly at the micro level of prioritising treatment options, though they have an effect on the shape of the overall health budget. At the micro level, the doctor, or the team, in combination with the hospital authorities have dominant discretion. As mentioned earlier, the regulation of the new artificial birth technologies has a more top-down policy emphasis in some states, notably Victoria, but several states have no legislative regulatory body for this area. Decisions about the value of treatments at the beginning of life and the advanced stages of life raise many problems, but these tend to be addressed by medical interests and judgements *in situ* rather than government decrees. One doctor told us that when he began practice heart transplants were never attempted on people over sixty-five whereas now people in their 80s have them. This is a function largely of improved techniques and drugs, but also of increased lifespans that make the prospects of an eighty year-old much brighter than before.

The question arises whether there *should* be more prescriptive policy guidelines or instructions from government or governmentally sponsored supervisory bodies. In favour, is the matter of consistency: it seems unreasonable that decisions on priorities and rationing are treated one way in some places and quite differently in others. As noted, different rules or practices on access to artificial reproduction in different states can lead to fertility tourism and other anomalies. Moreover, there is some confusion about the boundaries between state and federal responsibility and this sometimes creates gaps and overlaps that militate against reasonable outcomes. Against, there are several considerations. First, infertility treatment aside, it is unclear how much practices vary since professional education and mutual learning amongst medical professionals can promote a high degree of convergence in thinking about priorities. Second, the higher the level at which such rules are adopted the more they risk being too remote from the realities of clinical practice and experience. Whether this patient should be resuscitated or that, whether this patient's affliction deserves more urgent attention than that, and so on, are decisions that require highly specific information and judgement. Third, resort to measures such as QALYs and other devices aimed to quantify value of life are fraught with contestable value judgements about what makes a life worthwhile. All of us have the intuition that a life cut dramatically short is a terrible thing, whereas our regrets at the passing of someone who 'has had a good innings' are less severe. But it is a far cry from this to assess an elderly person's continued life (especially where they want to live it) as less in need of medical support than someone thirty years younger. Yet there is a tendency at present amongst some philosophers[1] and others to move in this direction, by invoking the idea that the elderly have made their contribution and have nothing left to contribute. Quite apart from the fact that this latter claim is often false, it betrays a work and product-centred conception of life that is highly disputable. Leaving aside vegetative states and embryonic or foetal life, there is a good case for a baseline assumption that all stages of life are equally valuable. There may well be catastrophic circumstances that make a life unendurable, but outsiders' judgements on the value of a life are fraught with difficulty in most other circumstances. Disabled people are quick to point to the enjoyments life has for them and to the contributions they can make to the wellbeing of others. Stephen Hawking is only one example of many that could be given of someone who has wrought a significant life from the most disabling condition. We are not arguing, as some would, that disabilities are a good thing in themselves or that they are merely 'socially constructed'; the point is only that the quantification of quality of life when dealing with the elderly, the very young, or the disabled is a hazardous thing to base treatment priorities upon.

Nonetheless, such priorities must be addressed and this pressure favours the idea that some prescriptive devices might be developed at a governmental level to make a more rational distribution of health care dollars. Niall Maclean in his chapter, extending a suggestion of Ronald Dworkin, favours a voucher system generated by an appeal to a hypothetical veil of ignorance situation in which participants choose an insurance scheme that fits their perceived health needs and priorities. We are reluctant to go down this path for several reasons. First, appeals to state of nature decision-making made popular by Rawls are, at best, most plausible for choosing just principles for the basic structure of a society. Even in that task, what rational agents would choose under conditions of partial ignorance is not only more debatable than such theorists allow, but is (we would argue) dictated by the value of the goods or principles

---

[1] The most thorough defence of this position we know is Douglas MacLean's 2006 unpublished paper *Longevity*.

chosen rather than the rationality of the agents choosing. In any case, once we reach the level of distributional detail involved in Maclean's extension of Dworkin's proposals, the rationality of heeding the weighted appropriations delivered by his proposal is far from compelling. In addition, there are well-known difficulties with voucher systems (Ladd, 2002) for such matters as education that would carry over to this scheme. Ladd describes the use of school vouchers in New Zealand. 'There is little doubt that the expansion of choice in that country exacerbated the problems of the schools at the bottom of that distribution and reduced the ability of those schools to provide an adequate education.' (Ladd, 2002, p.19) This highlights the dangers in fragmenting public pressures for quality public institutions. One need not be a full-blooded communitarian to see the value of community-driven approaches to the creation or preservation of such institutions. There are also significant issues in the real world of those individuals left behind through lack of full information.

The underlying problem with the approach suggested by Maclean seems to lie in the quest for a rationality that would be sufficiently neutral to 'meet the approval of nearly all citizens'. This seems to us an illusory quest. We therefore prefer the approach to the rationing problem later adopted by Daniels (Daniels and Sabin, 2002). Once the basic need of health care is acknowledged (whether by recourse to a Rawlsian state of nature argument or more directly) then the rationing problem should be met by a combination of the low-level experiential decision-making of medical professionals with the setting of guidelines and very broad policy parameters by open, democratic politics. Maclean worries that there is a disconnection between Daniels' principled approach to the creation of a health care system and his more pragmatic approach to the rationing problems, but it is unclear why this disjunction is problematic. One positive aspect of Rawls' position is that he restricts the application of his abstract justification of principles of justice to the basic structures of society, but the political implementation of the institutional details of the workings of a just (or nearly just) society are left to be determined by practical democratic procedures. This is no failure of moral nerve, since the case for democracy, open procedures and so on can be in large part a moral argument. An understandable concern for consensus or very widespread agreement can itself prove a barrier to the development of a morally sensitive politics in a pluralist society.

Endorsing the approach taken by Daniels is not tantamount to endorsing every detail he proposes. Detailed procedures must make reference to the actual traditions and political culture of the community in question. In the case of Australia, this must involve both the well-entrenched and publicly endorsed structures of governance and the animating ideals of public life. As to the former, there is a firm, though not unlimited, commitment to traditional freedoms and prerogatives of the medical profession, a commitment supported, as we noted earlier, by the Constitution. Respect for professional freedom and relative autonomy also suggests that some degree of self-regulation will have an important part to play, and there will be a complex interplay between self-regulation, government policy, and law. There are also the complexities and constraints of the federal system which might, and indeed have, changed with time, but need to be factored into any open, democratic procedures for determining or recommending health priorities. As to the animating ideals, there remains a prevailing egalitarian streak in Australian culture that underpins the repeated endorsements of 'equity' in the health system made by governments of all persuasions. This also supports the concern frequently expressed at efforts by overseas interests to undermine the PBS. The vast majority of Australians still believe that your health should be attended to on the same basis of need whether you are rich or poor, young or old, male or female, or dwelling in city or country. In view of these considerations, it is likely that concerted national rationing priorities, if developed at all, are likely to be framed mostly in terms of guidelines or recommendations, and that such guidelines will have a strong emphasis on equity. In addition, however, there are legal prohibitions that restrict what various groups concerned with health can do, and some of these are concerned with equity. For instance, under the restrictions known as 'community rating', the health insurance companies are prohibited from allowing considerations of age or state of health or claim history to affect their policies. (There is some minor flexibility in this, in that, for example, some differentiation is allowed on grounds of age of entry into the plan, a concession that has been designed to encourage more youth participation in private insurance in the face of dwindling membership.) There are also prohibitions on certain forms of research in the area of assisted reproduction, such as reproductive cloning and even on some forms of so-called therapeutic cloning.[2] On the other hand, in the delivery of assisted reproduction treatments, there are no top-down formal restrictions on many other matters, for instance, the age at which patients can be treated for infertility. The guidelines issued by RTAC (Reproductive Technology Accreditation Committee) contain no reference to age, so that the matter is left to clinical and institutional practice to decide. RTAC itself is not a government body but an instrument of the Fertility Society of Australia which was set up by medical professionals interested in advancing reproductive medicine and in

---

[2]   The funding of health and medical research is another element in the mix of health funding that has implications for access, but we cannot discuss it further here. It is worth noting, however, that AHMAC has a sub-committee that also sets priorities for health research.

self-regulation. It exerts considerable power since patients in the clinics will not receive medical benefits unless the clinics are accredited by RTAC, and RTAC also assists governmental authorities in the licensing process for clinics. Even in Victoria, where the Infertility Treatment Authority has a stronger role than elsewhere, the only external constraint on the clinics in respect of age comes in the form of licensing arrangements where the clinics voluntarily agree to flexible age limits. The usual stipulation is that an upper age limit on treatment will be the early forties, but there is room for variation at the discretion of the clinics. Other guidelines of RTAC, on the number of embryos that can be implanted at the same time, for instance, are not legal prohibitions, but have a great deal of informal force within the profession. A significant role is also played by the National Health and Medical Research Council which not only awards government grants for medical research, but produces very detailed ethical guidelines and statements for research that have considerable influence in reproductive medical practice as well as other areas. It is already the case that the Federal Government specifies broad national health priorities as mentioned earlier.

Conclusion

The pressures on the Australian health system are many and it is difficult to predict how they will be resolved. They might be summarised under the headings of sustainability, efficiency, and transparency. Because of the divisions of responsibility between state and federal authorities, there is a growing movement for a more dominant role for the Federal Government in both the funding of health services and, inevitably, the policies pertaining to such funding. The present federal health minister, Tony Abbott, has been loudest in urging that the Federal Government assume total responsibility for state hospitals. (As we go to press, a Federal election campaign is in progress in Australia and it is noteworthy that both major parties have expressed varying degrees of dissatisfaction with federal/state arrangements regarding hospitals. The Coalition government have taken over one hospital in Tasmania that the state government had been going to close, although this has been widely perceived as political opportunism in a swinging electorate; the Labor Opposition has spoken of using similar federal powers, if elected, where it deems that state governments are nor providing satisfactory hospital services.)

At the same time, there is a strong belief that the health system creates a strain on government resources that needs to be relieved by a continued, if not greater, role for private funds, most notably the medical insurance companies. One of the insurance funds, Medibank Private, is actually government-owned, but the present Federal Government is planning to privatise it, a plan that has created such community hostility that it is to be postponed until after the next federal election in 2007. Prominent in this debate is the free-market ideology that insists on the superior efficiency of private as opposed to government management, an ideology that is, in our view, sometimes more remarkable for a priori conviction than sensitivity to empirical facts. Nonetheless, freedom of choice is well established as a significant value in democratic societies and it has a role to play in the delivery of health care, even if it needs to be balanced against any consequent effects of dilution in the value of equity within the system, especially with regard to the quality of public hospital care. Quite apart from the claims of the values of free choice and efficiency, there is the argument that the public purse cannot provide enough funds to sustain an excellent system, so a greater role for the private sector is inevitable. In the past, Australians have not been averse to paying more taxes for better public services, so the 'public purse' argument may not have the weight it is generally believed to have. When the Australian Government initially proposed a further 1% tax levy to pay the costs of the military/political support to East Timor in its humanitarian crisis in1999, there was not the slightest murmur of dissent in the community. The levy proved unnecessary, but the response was indicative of a willingness that is barely acknowledged in current government's policies. Increasing the role of private insurance in the health system will inevitably create a two-tier system with significant loss of the advantages spelt out for universality.

As for transparency, it could be argued that too many of the decisions in the health sector as to access, priority of treatments, and drug regulation have been insufficiently subjected to open discussion and debate. Recent changes to the operation of the PBS require that its decisions on the listing of drugs should be accompanied by the publication of its reasons for decisions, and by an appeal procedure. There have also been increasing demands for public information about the 'success rates' of medical specialists, in order that patient choice, where it exists, can be more realistic.

The Australian Health system is in many respects an impressive attempt to provide fair, universal, quality cover while leaving a good deal of freedom to the medical profession and to patients. We have described the system, the ethical elements relevant to its assessment, and the various strains and difficulties to which it is exposed. The further tasks of predicting future developments or seeking to give them concrete shape in light of the ethical perspective sketched must be left for debate and discussion in the democratic forum.

Susan Cleary, Di McIntyre,
Okore Okorafor & Michael Thiede

Equity & the Ethics of the South African Health System

Introduction

The South African health system is characterised by lack of integration. An upper middle-income country with a per capita gross national income comparable to Turkey or Costa Rica, the South African economy reflects severe inequalities in the distribution of income and resources. Over 10 years after the first democratic elections, the apartheid legacy of inequality is still a striking feature of the economy despite the introduction of a range of redistributive instruments. There are major socio-economic differences in access to health care. The current health system is divided into a private sector catering for a minority and a public sector providing health services to the rest of the population. The distribution of resources between the private and the public sector does not mirror the population shares the sectors serve. The public sector is struggling with major resource and capacity constraints. In addition, the health system has to shoulder the burden of an HIV/AIDS epidemic that has grown into one of the worst in the world.

Concepts of Equity

It is necessary to specify the conceptualisation of equity that will be used to guide our analysis of the South African health system. We are guided by normative considerations (i.e. what definition ought we to use from a moral perspective), but are constrained by pragmatism. By this we mean that the definition that we choose needs to be useful in guiding policy. However, in taking this pragmatic approach, it becomes difficult to find a one-size fits all equity definition; instead we have drawn on a number of different approaches, both consequentialist and procedural in nature.

Access

A common approach taken in the literature and by policymakers is to define equity as equal access to health care for those with equal need (Mooney, 1983; Oliver and Mossialos, 2005). This would also seem a sensible approach for South Africa given that Section 27 of the South African Constitution of 1996 guarantees everyone the 'right to have access to health care services'. The constitutional mandate to ensure equitable access to health services is the basic premise under which the health system is intended to function. While there has been some debate about the interpretation of this mandate, the new democratic government has consistently highlighted the need to improve equity within the health system. Since 1994 different frameworks for health reform have been proposed. Common to all of them has been the vision of an equitable health system where resources are allocated fairly between population groups with different socio-economic backgrounds and different health care needs, relative to what has previously been the case. The solution is generally seen in a structure in which the public and private spheres of the health system are better integrated to provide universal coverage. Universal coverage does not necessarily mean a single collective financing mechanism, rather a system in which every citizen has access to an affordable and acceptable package of health care services (Carrin and James, 2004), independent of socio-economic or socio-demographic background. From an ethical perspective, this definition of universal coverage should be expanded to include a requirement that there should be minimal differentials in the 'acceptable package of care' between groups. Similarly, in the programmatic area of HIV-treatment, equity is commonly defined as universal access to antiretroviral treatment for all in need (World Health Organisation, 2004).

However, while the concept of access is a common feature of many equity definitions, the usefulness of this concept from a policy perspective is open to debate. Although access is not a clearly defined concept, access to health care is receiving increased attention in the health research literature (Gulliford and Morgan, 2003; Oliver and Mossialos, 2005; Ricketts and Goldsmith, 2005; Thiede, 2005; Thiede et al., 2007). Whether access is considered at the level of a programme addressing specific health care needs or at a systemic level with a view to the security of care and treatment, access is always a multi-dimensional phenomenon comprising at least three dimensions that are made up of multiple factors. One can think of these dimensions as the availability, the affordability and the acceptability of health services. Availability addresses the question of whether the medically appropriate health services are on hand in the right place and at the right time that they are needed. Affordability speaks to the relation between the costs of utilising health services, including non-medical costs (e.g. transport costs) as well as indirect costs (e.g. time off work), and the patient's socio-economic position. Acceptability encompasses perceptions and attitudes of providers and patients in relation to each other and the interactions between providers and patients, or in a wider sense between the health system and the lifeworld of the client, whereby lifeworld is understood as 'the sphere of shared cultural knowledge, valid norms and accountable motivations' (Habermas, 1989, p. 183). Acceptability touches on socio-cultural norms and beliefs.

The 'degree of fit' (Penchansky and Thomas, 1981) between the health system and its clients with regard to each of the dimensions determines the opportunity to use health services. However, access goes somewhat beyond this notion and includes whether the client is informed — where the individual as a citizen must be empowered to make an informed choice. This notion lies beyond mere opportunity (Thiede, 2005). In South Africa, the fragmented health system and the historical burden reflected in socio-economic inequalities in terms of income, education, and health (as well as the unequal geographical distribution of publicly provided services) places a moral duty on policy-makers to address all dimensions of access. In particular, it levies a moral duty to engage in communicative interaction with individuals and communities to empower clients to make informed choices on whether or not to use health services if needed. The individuals and communities hold a moral claim to access. It should be clear that access to health services does not necessarily translate into utilisation. The empowered individual remains in charge of the decision to use health care or not.

It is difficult to translate the goal of equal access into a clear-cut set of policy guidelines, partly because of heterogeneity in the health system and partly because many of the access dimensions cannot be captured through routinely available data. An alternative approach is to judge fairness according to the allocation of financial resources, or the inputs to health care. The allocation of resources across geographical areas in South Africa has been a question of particular concern in the light of historical patterns of wealth and deprivation.

At the programme level of antiretroviral treatment for HIV/AIDS, although (near) universal access by 2010 has been the stated equity goal of the United Nations General Assembly (UNGASS, 2006), severe resource constraints could make the achievement of universal access unlikely, particularly in the short to medium term. An alternative approach needs to be developed that promotes equity even if universal access is not possible.

Procedural Justice

Policy processes around the allocation of resources also warrant critical analysis from an ethical perspective. For example, in the context of HIV-treatment programmes, which form a key area of attention in the public sector of the South African health system, it becomes obvious that not enough work has been done on how to integrate ethical considerations into outcome measures in order to allow for a normative assessment of the success of the programmes. This is one strong reason why it is essential to recognise the relevance of procedural justice. This chapter will employ the concept of procedural justice to give a critical account of HIV/AIDS treatment, and also to underline the relevance of fair processes in the wider health system context.

Daniels (2004) argues that the central requirements of a fair process are:

- Publicity, i.e. transparent and publicly available rationales for any priorities set;
- Relevance, i.e. agreement by stakeholders that decisions have been based on appropriate reasons, principles and evidence;
- Revisability and appeals; and
- Enforcement or regulation to ensure that the previous three conditions are met.

The goal of securing adequate publicity is ambitious (Daniels, 2004). Frequently, resource allocation and priority setting decisions are taken behind closed doors. If the condition of publicity is to be met, the full rationales, resultant recommendations and any complaints or disputes related to these decisions would need to be in the public domain in a format that was comprehensible to a lay audience. Publicity is both intrinsically and instrumentally valuable. First, it gives legitimacy to decisions (Wailoo and Anand, 2005) and gives the public greater confidence in the process and the outcomes (Daniels, 2004). Secondly, people value knowing why decisions that affect their lives have been taken in the way they have (Litva et al., 2002; Daniels, 2004; Wailoo and Anand, 2005). Thirdly, a form of precedent emerges which assists in consistency over time. This has intrinsic value from an equity perspective as it ensures that like cases are treated in a like manner (Wailoo and Anand, 2005). Consistency also has instrumental value, since the setting of precedents assists in future decision-making, thereby improving the quality of decision-making over time.

The relevance condition, on the other hand, suggests that there should be restrictions on the kinds of rationales that are permitted to serve as a basis for decision-making and that these restrictions should be agreed by key stakeholders. These 'reasonable rationales' could be set with reference to the values of the community, where the community sets the 'structures, principles or rules on which to base the social welfare function...and hence the basis for priority setting in health care' (Mooney, 1998, p. 1173). Research has shown that the public finds intrinsic value in having a voice in decisions; allowing the community to set reasonable rationales provides one avenue for this voice (Litva et al., 2002; Wiseman et al., 2003; Wailoo and Anand, 2005).

The third requirement for fair process is revisability and appeals. A distributive decision will tend to be more acceptable if there are mechanisms which allow decisions to be challenged and reversed if required (Wailoo and Anand, 2005). This requirement also allows for the improvement and revisiting of policy over time as resource constraints and technologies change. Revisability and appeals are strongly related to the publicity condition because the transparency of the original decision, both in terms of rationales and ultimate recommendations, facilitates the identification of inappropriate decisions or errors of judgement. It also provides an avenue for parties affected by decisions to appeal. Even if unsuccessful, the appeals process gives voice to stakeholders who might not have been included in the original decision and adds to the body of precedents, thereby improving the quality of future decision making (Daniels, 2004).

The final requirement for a fair process is regulation and enforcement. A mechanism needs to be created to ensure that the process, in order to be fair, complies with the publicity, relevance, and revisability and appeals requirements set out above (Daniels, 2004).

Having outlined the concepts of equity that will be used in this chapter, the remainder will be devoted to analysing the South African health system through posing three questions:

1. What claims do South Africans have on health care?

2. How is health care currently distributed? What are the ethical implications?

3. What reforms could be implemented to enhance equity, both in terms of processes and outcomes?

These questions are posed at the macro level where inequalities in access to health care and in health outcomes are particularly significant for patients dependent on the public sector versus those dependent on the private sector, and through a case study of the distribution of health and health care to HIV-positive people.

What Claims do South Africans have on Health and Health Care?

One way of judging the degree of moral importance that ought to be attached to distributions of health and health care is through the notion of claims. This idea has been taken from Broome (1991) who argues that claims (as opposed to other reasons) are the object of fairness. If a person has a claim on health care, this is stronger than merely wanting health care because a claim includes the notion that there is an obligation on others to provide care. A number of criteria could be the constituents of claims, including the social context in which many South Africans live, whether or not people have personal responsibility in their health status, the need for health care, the impact of health care on the broader health of society, and the impact of health and health care on the social fabric. These claims on health and health care are summarised in Figure 1, which has been adapted from Olsen et al (2003) and Cleary (2007).

The question of to whom health and health care should be distributed considers whether the personal characteristics of people should be a basis for additional claims or for limitations of claims on the good, as illustrated through claims 1–3 in Figure 1. According to the concept of responsibility, a person's claim on health or health care could differ if the causes of her illness were exogenous as opposed to being partially determined by personal risky behaviour (Edgar et al., 1998; Olsen et al., 2003). This is illustrated by a free choice continuum at the top of Figure 1. The oval in the top left-hand corner relates to having no free choice in acquiring a particular illness. Examples include certain genetic disease and babies who become HIV-positive through mother to child transmission. It also captures any unexplained variation in susceptibility to disease or ill health. Thus claim 1 on the good relates to morally arbitrary bad luck. At the other end of the free choice continuum, it is presumably possible to have full responsibility for one's health status. However, given the likelihood of high levels of variation in personal susceptibility, most people have some 'level' of claim 1 on health and health care.

It is important to recognize that responsibility for one's health status is mediated via social context. What this means is that any argument that someone is less deserving of health care owing to personal responsibility would have to consider the social context and how this constrains free choice. Thus, the claim based on disadvantage could complement the claim based on compensation for morally arbitrary bad luck and offset any reduction in claims owing to personal responsibility. The oval entitled 'social context' draws attention to the socioeconomic circumstances of many South Africans. Campbell (2003) argues that two forms of social disadvantage can be key determinants of poor health. These are poverty and symbolic social exclusion caused by a lack of respect and recognition. Poverty can have a direct impact on health and susceptibility to various diseases and can limit a person's access to health-related information. Symbolic social exclusion can limit health enhancing behaviour through reducing a person's feelings of self-adequacy and self-control (Evans and Stoddart, 1990). Although South Africa is an

Figure 1: A Framework for Considering the Claims of South Africans on Health and Health Care.

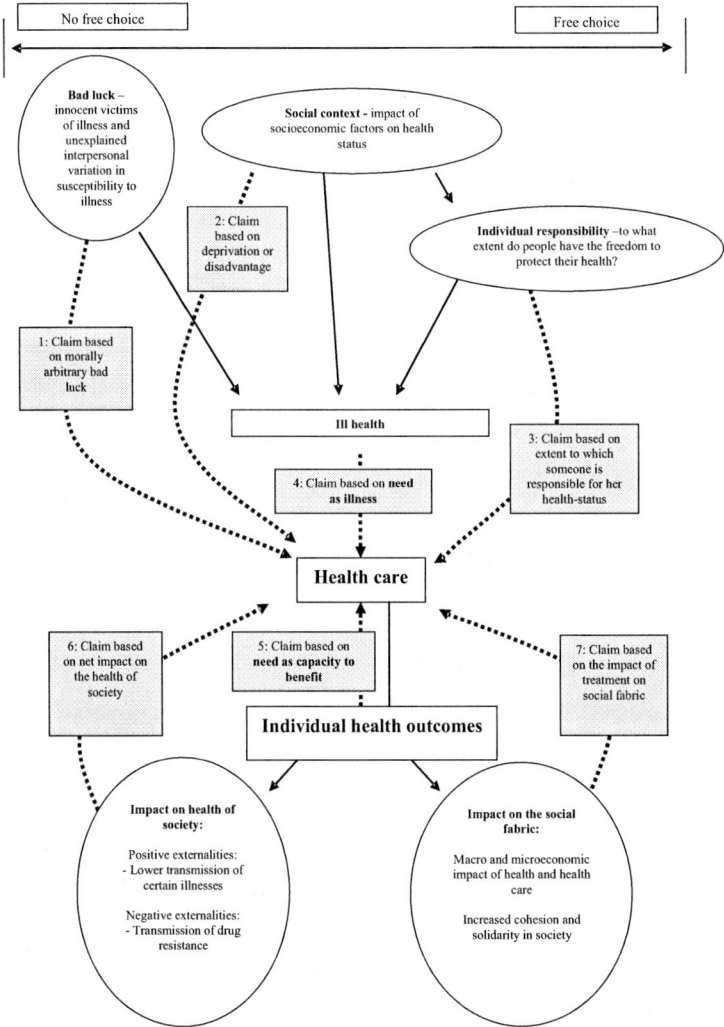

Solid arrows show the causes of illness and consequences of health care.
Dotted arrows show claims on the good.

upper middle income country, it also has high rates of unemployment, abject poverty among more than 50% of the population, sharp inequalities in the distribution of income, property and opportunities and high levels of crime and violence (Terreblanche, 2002). Particularly striking is the strong racial bias in these inequalities.[1] For example, in 1995, the average per capita income of whites was 7.4 times higher than that of Africans. While 6.7% of whites were unemployed, the corresponding figure was 46% for Africans.[2] By 1993, estimated real per capita social spending on Africans was just over half the level of social spending on whites (Terreblanche, 2002). Health policy, like other government social policy, served the objective of maintaining economic and political power for whites (McIntyre and Gilson, 2002; McIntyre et al., 2006). In the early 1990s this bias translated into infant mortality rates that were nearly 11.5 times higher for Africans than for whites and maternal mortality rates that were 31 times higher for African than for white women (McIntyre and Gilson, 2002).

This social context has a direct bearing on the extent to which a person can be deemed to have personal responsibility for his or her health status. Roemer (1993; 1996) argues that equality of opportunity for X (e.g. health care) has been achieved if X is equalised for all those who exercised a comparable degree of responsibility, regardless of their circumstances. The argument rests on the assumption that there is a core of human nature that is common to everyone. Except for social context and genetic factors, people have the capacity to exercise equal levels of responsibility, but will actually exercise different degrees of responsibility because of circumstances or because of effort. Fairness allows our life paths to diverge through our own effort, but not because of circumstances that are out of our control.

While Roemer's approach might offer a possible way of assessing the strength of claims on a good according to personal responsibility, available data may be too crude to measure free choice accurately. This limits the usefulness of the theory for policy purposes, unless one is prepared to risk penalising people who have become unwell through no fault of their own (Williams and Cookson, 2000). Similarly, Kopelman (2002) argues that 'poverty, social norms, ignorance, temptation, compulsion, addiction and irrational views can create considerations of such com-

---

[1]   The use of the terms 'African', 'coloured', 'Indian' and 'white' reflects the stratification of the population into race groups in terms of the former Population Registration Act. The term 'blacks' refers to Africans, coloureds and Indians. While it is necessary to maintain these terms when discussing the legacy of Apartheid and resultant socioeconomic and health inequalities, this does not imply any legitimacy in these terms.

[2]   Unemployment is considered relative to an expanded definition of the labour force that includes both the formal and informal sectors.

plexity that untangling them to determine blame for illnesses seems hazardous' (p. 239).

Claims 4 and 5 are based on need. A certain amount of moral force is associated with the word need – to have a need for health care is different from wanting health care. For example, while someone might want a private bed in a hospital, that person does not need this if a bed in a multi-bed ward would be equally effective in terms of health gain. A need for health care is therefore premised on health improvements (Culyer and Wagstaff, 1993).

While it might be argued that need is at least one constituent of the claim on health care, there is some debate about how need should be defined (Culyer and Wagstaff, 1993). Two common definitions as shown in Figure 1 are need as ill-health and need as capacity to benefit from health care. Equating need to ill-health suggests that people who are more ill have a greater need. The shortcoming of this definition is that one cannot need health care unless health care is effective. Defining need as illness can lead to resource allocations that focus on the size of the problem as opposed to the amount of benefit that can be obtained from these allocations. Need as capacity to benefit is our preferred definition because it recognises that health care can only be needed if it contributes to health (Culyer and Wagstaff, 1993). However, if a disease exists that can be treated, this does not mean that it should be treated, or that it should be treated with the most effective treatment available. The opportunity cost of treating one need over another must be considered given scarcity of resources (Mooney, 2003). This issue is particularly relevant in the context of HIV/AIDS where resource scarcity means that many needs remain unmet.

Claim 6 assesses the impact of health care on the health of society, considering the positive and negative externalities associated with various interventions. For example, successfully treating one person's tuberculosis has positive externalities for the health of society in general, while unsuccessful treatment or poor adherence to treatment can lead to drug resistance with associated negative impacts. This claim therefore points to the importance of maintaining health care of an acceptable quality.

Claim 7 suggests that society should balance personal responsibility against the potential for health care to mitigate the impact of illness on the social fabric, which is defined following Haacker (2004) to include social and economic institutions such as households, companies and the government, and less tangible concepts such as social cohesiveness and solidarity. Before 1994 public sector health authorities were structured to address separately the 'African', 'coloured', 'Indian' and 'white' population groups. There was a geographic bias in service provision to favour historically 'white' areas, whilst rural areas, so-called 'homeland' areas, 'townships' and informal settlements were systematically under-funded. The public sector before 1994 also had a strong leaning towards hospital-based, curative care. Hospital facilities, however, were heavily concentrated in urban areas. Like all government action, health policy in the apartheid era was driven by the objective of sustaining a higher quality of life and preserving economic and political power for the 'white' minority (McIntyre and Gilson, 2002). As a social institution, the health care system has the potential to assist South Africa to become a society reflecting greater social solidarity, with positive spin-offs for social justice in general. On the other hand, if the health care system is perceived to be inequitable, levels of solidarity could decrease. Because of the need to develop solidarity in South Africa, the importance of claim 7 on health and health care requires urgent attention.

How is Health Care Currently Distributed?

Having outlined the claims that South Africans might have on health and health care and the importance of health care as a social institution, this section discusses the way in which health care is currently distributed in South Africa and the associated equity implications. The sub-section on public–private mix takes a view on the health system as a whole, while the sub-sections on the private sector, the public sector and the programmatic area of HIV-treatment identify the main challenges within these respective spheres.

The Public-Private Mix

The public sector health system has experienced a unifying shift since 1994, guided by the desire to overcome the inequities associated with the apartheid era. However, there is still little interaction between the public and private sectors. The divide between these two spheres has increased despite a number of equity-orientated policy initiatives over the last decade. The private sector currently exists as a completely separate structure from the public sector, mainly attracting people of higher socio-economic status. The lion's share of funding is generated through contributions to so-called medical schemes, private insurance companies offering community-rated benefit packages mainly to formal sector employees. Frequently, employers act as co-contributors. Less than 15% of the South African population are beneficiaries of such arrangements.

The stark inequalities implied by the resource dichotomy in the South African health system become apparent in an analysis of public and private health expenditure. Forty per cent of total health care funds in South Africa flow via public sector financing intermediaries — national, provincial and local Departments of Health — while sixty per cent flows via private intermediaries. Even if one takes into account the private sector out-of-pocket spending of people who are not beneficiaries of medical schemes, the difference in per capita health care spending between the minority of medical scheme beneficiaries and the more than 85% of the population who are mainly dependent on public sector health services is striking. In 2005, the average annual per capita health expenditure for a medical scheme beneficiary, in the form of medical scheme expenditure plus out-of-pocket payments, amounted to 9,700 ZAR (approximately 1,530 USD); the average annual equivalent for the uninsured who use public sector hospitals but with out-of-pocket expenditure in the private sector (mainly for private sector primary care and medicines) was 1,500 ZAR (235 USD); for the remaining 64.5% of the population who are entirely dependent on the public sector for all health care services, annual average spending per capita totalled less than 1,300 ZAR (205 USD) (McIntyre et al., 2007).

Since 1994, government has undertaken a series of initiatives to strengthen the health system according to its mission to 'improve health status through prevention and promotion of healthy lifestyles and to consistently improve the health care delivery system by focusing on access, equity, efficiency, quality and sustainability' (Department of Health South Africa, 2004a). Access to health services and the equity objective stand out as the two guiding ethical principles shaping the health system. In 1997 a White Paper emphasised the equity objective and defined key areas of attention. The main focus in health policy, as in other policy areas, remains redressing the historical inequities, whereby vulnerable groups (women, children, the elderly, the disabled and the poor) should receive priority (Department of Health South Africa, 1997). The South African government has put a particular emphasis on the role of health care financing in improving equity, highlighting the redistributive function of financing mechanisms both between socio-economic groups and across geographic areas. Already in the 1997 White Paper, social health insurance is mentioned as a mechanism for improving equity in health care financing. The more recent National Health Act, Section 2, highlights that a key objective is to 'provide uniformity in respect of health services across the nation'. (Government of South Africa, 2004)

Policies introduced since 1994 have encouraged risk- and income-related cross-subsidies within parts of the health system. The overall extent of these cross-subsidies, however, is still relatively insignificant and basically limited to individual medical schemes or closed entities within the health system. Whilst substantial improvements in overall health system cross-subsidies and thus promotion of social solidarity are only likely to become a reality in the medium-term, there are two broad areas that require immediate attention. At the macro level, the inequitable allocation of resources across geographic regions within

South Africa has become a pressing health policy issue, as geographical differences in the delivery of health services ranked among the very obvious features of health policy in the apartheid era. At the micro level, the inequitable distribution of benefits of health care across socio-economic groups and between the public and private sectors constitutes an obstacle to broader social progress within the country.

The Private Sector and its Role in Health Reform

The private sector has developed its own dynamics. Actors in the private sector face allegations of nurturing unethical processes both within and between sectors. The private sector is dominated by the medical scheme industry. Medical schemes undertake liability in return for a premium in order to make provision for obtaining health services. The schemes are private not-for-profit organisations offering community-rated benefit packages, although the administrators responsible for their management are for-profit companies. There are three types of schemes: restricted membership schemes that can restrict membership to employment characteristics or professional associations; open schemes that unite the largest number of beneficiaries (about two thirds of all medical scheme beneficiaries); and so-called bargaining council schemes, which are exempted from certain sections of the Medical Schemes Act (Government of South Africa, 1998) and tend to offer limited benefits, often restricted to primary health care delivered by salaried or panel doctors. Out of a total population of more than forty-seven million South Africans, less than seven million are beneficiaries of medical schemes. The breadth and depth of services covered by individual benefit packages varies broadly. Across the (roughly 130) schemes, there are a few hundred different options available. There is not only variation in coverage between schemes; many schemes offer a broad variety of packages at different premiums. Many schemes offer medical savings accounts in addition to a basic package. These accounts can be used to pay for day-to-day expenses so that health expenditure beyond the plan's coverage is covered via these accumulated contributions. Any part of the account that is not used in a year can be rolled over to the next year. The individualised nature of these accounts compromises risk-pooling within schemes. Medical savings accounts do not allow for any cross-subsidisation between scheme members. Plans for reforms to limit the use of medical savings accounts are in the policy pipeline. The general benefit packages emphasise coverage of hospital services and the major chronic diseases, and many contracts exclude primary care. More than a third of medical scheme expenditure relates to hospital services. Medical scheme premiums and expenditure by medical schemes have both increased dramatically over the last decade. Contributions to medical schemes have increasingly become unaffordable to many.

Hospital expenditure has seen the most dramatic increases over recent years, based on both volume increases as well as escalating prices. This development is facilitated by the oligopolistic structure of the hospital market, with three groups dominating the private hospital industry. The hospital sector is but one example of an area that is inappropriately regulated to enable it to function within an equity-orientated system. The dichotomous structure of the South African health system, in which there is hardly any link between public and private health care, is plainly in conflict with fundamental equity principles. Moreover, within the spheres there is a range of issues to be addressed in the light of health system ethics.

Over the last decade, steps have been taken to improve equity within the medical scheme environment. Measures have facilitated risk-related cross-subsidies and laid the foundation for income-related cross-subsidies. These two dimensions of cross-subsidies within a social group (and more importantly across groups) form the core elements of an environment of solidarity. The 1998 Medical Schemes Act, which came into effect in January 2000, signified an important move towards strengthening social solidarity within the medical schemes environment (Government of South Africa, 1998). Open enrolment, i.e. an environment in which all open schemes must accept (at standard rates) anyone who wants to become a member, combined with community-rated contributions, have allowed for some cross-subsidisation within individual schemes' risk pools. Community-rating implies that everyone must be charged the same standard rate for a specified benefit package, regardless of age or state of health. Prior to the implementation of the Act, schemes were legally permitted to discriminate against the elderly and chronically ill through risk-rating of premiums and the denial of membership to particular applicants. These discriminatory practices resulted from the deregulation of the industry in the late 1980s and early 1990s. One of the main aims of the Act was to abolish these discriminatory practices and ensure non-discriminatory open access to medical scheme coverage through community-rating of premiums and open enrolment of applicants in line with the requirements of the type of scheme. In this community-rated environment there should be some level of cross-subsidy from the healthy to the sick — but practice shows that this depends on the type of scheme. In addition, risk cross-subsidies are reduced by the existence of a number of different 'options' within each scheme, which often effectively segment membership along socio-economic lines (albeit, within the upper middle-income and high income groups).

Furthermore, the Act introduced so-called Prescribed Minimum Benefits (PMBs) as a policy instrument for defining minimum required levels of medical scheme cover. The PMBs, a list of 270 (hospital-based) diagnosis and treatment pairs that must be provided by each scheme as part of every benefit package, came into effect on 1 January 2000. This list was then complemented by 25 chronic conditions, the Chronic Diseases List (CDL), with effect from 1 January 2004. The defined benefits must be provided without financial limits or co-payments, and in at least one provider setting. Whilst the medical scheme industry still offers a range of benefit options both between and within individual medical schemes, there is thus a guaranteed minimum level of cover included in every option. From an ethical perspective, two aspects ought to be highlighted. Firstly, beneficiaries can rely on full coverage for a comprehensive list of disease events that could translate into catastrophic expenditure — irrespective of the size of their contributions. Secondly, the existence of a minimum package that is comparable across schemes is a necessary condition for risk-related cross-subsidies between the schemes.

The package will form the basis of a mechanism for risk equalisation between medical schemes. The impending introduction of a risk equalisation fund on the basis of a set of risk-adjusters including age, birth rate (but not gender), and measures of chronic disease burden means that the incentives for schemes to compete on the basis of risk selection, particularly with respect to the age and health profile of the beneficiaries they attract, will be reduced. Competition will be on the basis of cost-effective health care delivery. Despite these measures to address some inequities within the medical scheme environment, there is a need to take the policies further and initiate strategies for the integration of the private sector.

The private sector is not fully represented by the medical scheme environment. Nearly a quarter of health care expenditure in the private sector is made up by households' out-of-pocket payments (including public sector user fees and medical scheme members' co-payments). A large share of this is spent on medicines. Out-of-pocket expenditure tends to be the most regressive form of health care financing, meaning that people from lower socio-economic strata contribute a relatively larger share of their income to health care than the better-off. There are manifold reasons in the South African health system that drive people into a care environment where they have to pay out of their own pocket, often beyond their ability to pay.

By regulating prices for medicines, the South African government has tried to address the problem of affordability of health care in a sector characterised by rapidly increasing prices over an extended period. Medicine prices in the private sector have been a key target for regulation, as uncontrolled price increases were seen as a growing barrier to access for many. Medical schemes have excluded acute medicines from many benefit packages, so that patients either pay out of their medical savings accounts or out-of-pocket. With a clear equity target, government regulation has introduced a so-called single exit price for medicines that in the future will be benchmarked against medicine prices from a basket of other countries. Further, regulations around distribution margins have been introduced and dispensing fees at the retail level have been regulated. Different elements of the regulations around medicine prices have brought about court action initiated by different stakeholders. The future of medicine pricing in South Africa is therefore still uncertain. However, the determination the South African government has demonstrated in the context of medicine pricing indicates that there is a strong commitment to regulate the private sector in the interests of a more equitable health system.

Allocation of Resources in the Public Sector

Despite the general provision of services through the public sector, which is fully tax-funded, and the presence of a separate private sector, the health system is far from providing what could be called universal coverage. The public sector requires close attention in order to address some of the key barriers to equitable and universal health care. At the time of the first democratic elections, the key challenges facing the public health sector included allocative inefficiencies and geographic inequities. There was an inefficient distribution of resources between levels of care, with hospitals accounting for nearly 89% of expenditure on the major categories of health services and non-hospital primary care accounting for only 11% (McIntyre et al., 1995). This relative distribution has shifted significantly. By 2005, the share for primary care had already more than doubled (National Treasury South Africa, 2007).

Public health care, however, is facing enormous capacity challenges at different levels. First, public sector health care is seriously under-funded despite significant real increases in government health care expenditure over the last few years. Health care currently accounts for about 11% of government spending. Secondly, the absorptive capacity, reflected by the ability of the public sector to design, disburse, coordinate, control, and monitor public spending (Gottret and Schieber, 2006), is low at provincial level, meaning that part of government health sector resources are either not used efficiently or are not used at all. Thirdly, at the provider level the public sector is confronted with infrastructural problems as well as a human resource crisis in the form of a multi-level migration of health workers: rural to urban, public to private sector, and out of the country.

South Africa's 1996 Constitution established three separate, independent and interrelated spheres of government: first, the level of national government; secondly, nine provincial governments; and thirdly 284 local governments. Each sphere is assigned its own powers, functions and responsibilities, with the national government responsible for managing the country's affairs while sharing the responsibility for providing basic social services with the sub-national governments. The provinces are mandated to deliver most basic services including education and health. Local governments are responsible for certain local services and infrastructure such as water, sanitation and electricity. The national government's intervention in provincial and local government decisions is defined and limited by the Constitution.

Fiscal decentralisation aims to provide a framework for the efficient provision of public services by aligning expenditure with regionally based priorities. This fiscal structure thus defines the nature and process of the allocation of resources to the public health sector. With the introduction of fiscal federalism, provinces have been assigned significant spending autonomy with regard to their assigned functions.

Revenue raising powers still remain highly centralised in the national government. The most productive taxes such as personal and corporate income tax and value added tax (VAT) are collected at national level because administration is deemed more efficient if centralised. Provincial revenue stems from fees, such as road traffic fees or hospital patient fees, as well as gambling levies and other one-off revenues. These sources amount to less than 5% of provincial budgets. Given the substantial expenditure responsibilities of the provincial governments and their relatively low revenue generating capacity, provinces receive a share from nationally collected revenue to bridge this revenue-expenditure gap. These transfers take two forms: 'Conditional grants' and 'equitable shares'.

'Conditional grants' are meant to support national priorities, particularly in the social sectors. These grants are direct transfers from national government to provinces (and local governments) and are tied to specific functions or services and cannot be used for other purposes. Within the health sector, conditional grants comprise the following (National Treasury, 2007):

- Comprehensive HIV and AIDS Grant;
- Forensic Pathology Services Grant;
- Health Professionals Training and Development Grant;
- Hospital Revitalisation Grant;
- National Tertiary Services Grant.

Effectively, even though the provinces are tasked with providing the relevant services, they do not have any autonomy to review the use of funds that are transferred as conditional grants. These grants are earmarked for specific services as indicated by their name, e.g. for implementing the comprehensive programme for preventing and treating HIV/AIDS. The provincial health departments have to fulfil certain conditions before the resources are released to them, e.g. develop a business plan for the use of the funds.

The majority of central funds are allocated to the nine provinces and local governments via the 'equitable shares' process. Provinces and local governments then have autonomy in deciding on the allocation of these resources between different sectors. Equitable shares to provinces are determined according to a formula that is updated annually, taking into account the recommendations of the Financial and Fiscal Commission (FFC).[3] For the 2007 budget, the equitable shares formula has six components. The components of the formula are designed to capture the relative demand for services between provinces, while taking into account particular provincial circumstances. The distribution of weights is as follows:

- The education share (51%) is based on the size of the school-age population (ages 5 to 17) and the number of learners enrolled in public ordinary schools;
- The health share (26%) is based on the proportion of the population with and without access to medical scheme cover;
- A basic share (14%) is derived from each province's share of the national population;
- An institutional component (5%) is divided equally between the nine provinces;
- A poverty component (3%) reinforces the redistributive bias of the formula.

The components of the formula are neither indicative budgets nor guidelines as to how much should be spent on the respective functions. Rather, the education and health components are weighted broadly in line with expenditure patterns to provide an indication of relative need for these services. Provincial executive councils have discretion regarding the determination of allocations for each service function, taking into account the priorities that underpin the division of revenue (National Treasury South Africa, 2007).

The budgeting process for national and provincial governments occurs within a three-year rolling expenditure and revenue plan called the Medium Term Expenditure Framework (MTEF). This takes into account the macro-economic realities, expected revenues and longer-term needs of programmes as well as government's spending poli-

---

[3]   The Financial and Fiscal Commission was established in 1997. It is a statutory institution separate from the government and has the mandate to make recommendations on financial and fiscal matters to parliament, the provincial legislatures, and other institutions of government when necessary.

cies (National Treasury South Africa, 2000). For the annual budgeting process, each department and spending agency within government prepares budget proposals, which may include revisions to the three year MTEF baselines. The Budget Council considers the division of revenue across the three spheres of government, in line with submitted budget proposals from departments and spending agencies within these spheres of government. Budget proposals from departments and spending agencies, and the division of revenue across spheres of government, are aligned before they are approved by the cabinet (National Treasury South Africa, 2006).

The National Department of Health works with the nine provincial departments in priority setting and defining overall policy objectives. In this process, equity within the health sector is considered a fundamental goal (Okorafor et al., 2003). However, once provinces have received their share of national revenue, they have significant autonomy in deciding how much to allocate to the health sector. This process has effectively undermined the national Department of Health's attempt to work towards an equitable allocation of health care resources across provinces. Between 1994 and 1996, significant progress had been made in redressing the inequities in health care resources across regions. During this period, a health sector formula that supported re-allocations of budgets between provinces on the basis of population size weighted by need was used under the direction of the national Department of Health and the Functions Committee (Gilson et al., 1999). With the introduction of fiscal federalism in 1997, there have been concerns that the decentralisation of sectoral allocation to the province level would leave allocations to the health sector hostage to provincial politics. Thomas and Muirhead (2000) observed that the allocations to health within provinces are subject to competition from other sectors. Indeed, disparities in provincial level health care budgets widened (McIntyre et al., 1998). However, while such disparities still exist, there has been a gradual convergence of public health care expenditure per capita in recent years (McIntyre et al., 2007). As indicated in Figure 2, there is still a need for progress in promoting inter-provincial equity in public sector health care expenditure.

Consequently, there is a perception that a centrally managed resource allocation system for the health sector may be preferable in the light of inter-provincial equity. There are strong arguments in favour of arrangements in which the ultimate responsibility for redistribution and equity lies with the central government (Shah, 1998). Yet there is strong potential for fiscal federalism to achieve substantial gains in terms of both efficiency and equity — more so where the responsibility for each type of public expenditure is assigned to the level of government that most closely represents the beneficiaries of the expenditure outlays

(Bird and Vaillancourt, 1999; de Mello, 2000; Ter-Minassian, 1997). A key question then is whether provincial government is the level of government that most closely represents health care expenditure beneficiaries. Undoubtedly, provincial governments are closer to the beneficiaries of health expenditure than the national government, and therefore (theoretically) should be more responsive to the needs of the communities within their jurisdiction. Following this line of thought, differences in the needs and preferences of populations within provinces should result in differences in the allocation of resources for health (and other services) and in expenditure patterns across provinces.

Figure 2: Health Care Expenditure in Each Province, Per Person Dependent on Public Sector Services (2005/06)

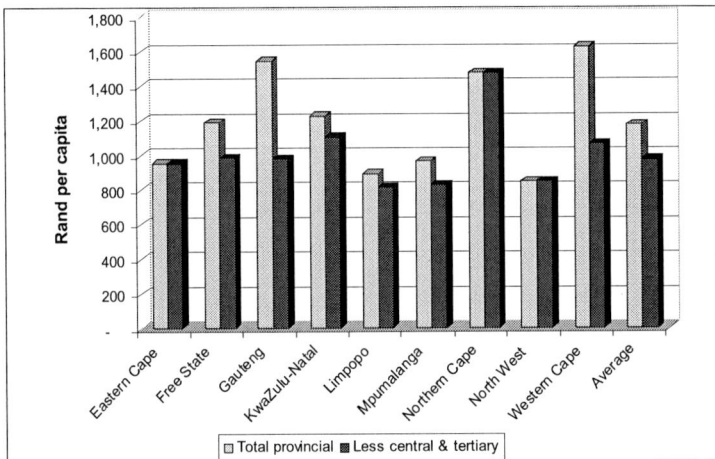

Source: McIntyre et al. (2007). Note: The Northern Cape has a very low population density and hence a much higher cost of health service provision. It is thus regarded as a 'special case' and is explicitly allocated a relatively greater share of resources than its population size suggests it should receive.

Possibly even more concerning, there are considerable inequities in resource allocation within provinces and across districts (McIntyre et al., 1998; Thomas et al., 2005). Resource allocation within provinces is largely driven by incremental budgeting based on historical expenditure. This has only created inertia in the move towards a more equitable allocation of health resources. Also, the low levels of managerial capacity and a lack of medical personnel have severely reduced the capacity of under funded health districts to utilise additional allocations made to them (McIntyre et al., 1999; Okorafor et al., 2005).

The South African government recognises the importance of community participation in identifying health priorities for planning the financing and delivery of health services. This is evidenced by the establishment of clinic committees and district health forums in some provinces. However, not very much has been documented concerning the effectiveness of these institutions in bringing the voice of communities to bear on the policy agenda. There have been other initiatives, such as the use of Integrated Development Planning (IDP), to elicit community preferences. While the recognition of the importance of community participation in decision making for health financing and provision is a positive move in the context of implementing fair processes in resource allocation, the predominance of incremental budgeting based on historical expenditure is unlikely to allow for resource allocation based on elicited community preferences in the near future.

Thus, if we focus on resource allocation within the public sector, we find mixed approaches in dealing with a clearly identified need to address differential claims on health care. The allocation of resources consists of different stages, each on its own well justified but which together contribute to the fragmentation of the process, which ultimately appears to inhibit the achievement of both an overall fair process and an equitable allocation.

Antiretroviral Treatment for HIV/AIDS

Having outlined how health care is currently distributed in the public and private spheres of the South African health system, this section describes how health care is allocated within the programmatic area of HIV-treatment, and comments on the ethical implications. The need to respond equitably to the HIV-epidemic is clearly one of the largest challenges facing the South African democracy. According to projections by the Actuarial Society of South Africa, the country has experienced a rapidly growing HIV epidemic since the mid 1980s, with a peak in incidence at 781,000 new infections during 1998 (ASSA, 2007).[4] In 2005, there were approximately six million HIV-infected people and over 400,000 HIV-related deaths. At least 1.8 million people have died of HIV-related causes during the twenty years since the start of the epidemic. Because of this, life expectancy has declined from a high of 62.9 years in 1989 to

[4]   The Actuarial Society of South Africa (ASSA) is the pre-eminent body undertaking demographic modelling of the South African HIV epidemic. The demographic data in this article have been extracted from the most recent version of the ASSA suite of models, the ASSA2003lite AIDS and Demographic Model (release 24 November 2005).

49.2 years in 2005, and HIV-related deaths currently exceed deaths from all other single causes. A relatively large population coupled with high prevalence has meant that South Africa has the highest number of HIV-infected people in the world.

In recent years, antiretroviral treatment (ART) has been shown to be effective in reducing morbidity and mortality in patients infected with HIV in developing countries (ART-LINC and ART-CC, 2006), and the feasibility of providing this treatment has been demonstrated in pilot projects (Coetzee et al., 2004). Treatment in the South African public health system consists of combinations of three to four antiretroviral agents, structured into first-line and second-line regimens. Once the first-line regimen has failed, the patient is switched to the second-line agents. The discounted (3% annual rate) lifetime costs and outcomes of first-line therapy are estimated to be US$5,779 for six quality adjusted life years (QALYs) while the corresponding figures for a patient receiving both first and second-line therapy is US$9,435 for eight QALYs (Cleary, 2007).

Although South Africa had started over 100,000 people on ART in the public sector by the middle of 2006, only approximately 25% of people who clinically qualified for treatment during this period were able to use it (Cleary, 2007). The challenge over the next ten years will be to increase coverage rapidly; if treatment scale-up is successful, millions of South Africans will be receiving ART in the short to medium term. Providing ART is an example of resource allocation in the face of scarcity that is particularly ethically charged. First, without ART HIV-positive people will die a premature death. If no effective treatment were available these deaths would be a tragedy, but because effective treatment is feasible ongoing HIV-related deaths have been argued to constitute a moral outrage (Nattrass, 2004). Secondly, HIV/AIDS is a new and complex disease. Because infection is associated with immune system decline, HIV-treatment is not restricted to controlling the spread of the virus in the body, but also requires knowledge and capacity in the treatment of opportunistic and HIV-related infections and events, many of which were previously rare. In addition, because HIV mainly affects prime-age adults, defined at those between 15 and 49 years old, it can be expected to have a significant impact on the demand for health care in these age groups and for the country in total (Over, 2004). Without a commensurate increase in health care supply, providing HIV treatment can be expected to crowd out existing health care interventions. The allocation of resources to HIV treatment is therefore not about changing the scale at which the treatment programme is operating, but about the creation of a new health care programme with associated training of health personnel, investments in infrastructure and medical equipment and the development of drug procurement and delivery systems. Thirdly, treatment as currently proposed is relatively costly and the majority of this cost is associated with recurrent expenditure on medicines that need to be taken for the duration of a patient's lifetime (Cleary et al., 2006).

In South Africa, priority setting for ART involves agreement on broad goals and coverage targets within a multi-sectoral National Strategic Plan (NSP). The latest plan, covering the period from 2007 to 2011, was developed through an intensive and inclusive process of drafting, collection and collation of inputs from a wide range of stakeholders through emails, workshops, meetings, and a national consultative conference. The South African National AIDS Council (SANAC) had an opportunity to interrogate drafts on three separate occasions.[5] SANAC approved the plan on 30 April 2007 and it was adopted by the South African Government Cabinet a few days later. This plan has been described as a 'watershed document' (Hoboyi and Geffen, 2007, p.27) by the Treatment Action Campaign, one of the key activist movements in South Africa. It is hoped that its adoption could end a long period of recrimination, conflict and confusion in HIV/AIDS policy. The wide consultative process and high levels of support suggests that many aspects of procedural justice were respected in the creation of the NSP.

The plan contains goals and targets that are described as ambitious but realistic (National Department of Health South Africa, 2007). In terms of treatment, the goal is to incrementally increase access in order ultimately to provide treatment to 80% of all patients needing it by 2011.[6] The implication is that approximately 1.7 million patients would be started on ART between 2004 and 2011, of whom between 1.2 and 1.4 million could be alive and remaining in care by the start of 2012 (Cleary et al., 2007). As has been explained, meeting up to 80% of new need during each period is generally regarded as the achievement of universal access to HIV-treatment.

The new NSP appears highly equitable. It respects procedural justice since key aspects of fair process (Daniels, 2004) have been manifested in its creation and adoption. In addition, it aims to provide universal access to HIV treatment by 2011. Universal access has been described by partic-

---

[5] SANAC is the highest national body that provides strategic and political guidance as well as support and monitoring of sector programmes. The Deputy President, Mrs Phumzile Mlambo-Ngcuka, is the Chairperson of SANAC.

[6] The 'National Antiretroviral Treatment Guidelines' (Department of Health South Africa, 2004b) specify that treatment is initiated in patients with an AIDS diagnosis or a CD4 count of less than 200 cells/μl. Patients failing the first-line regimen (on virological, immunological or clinical grounds) are switched to the second-line regimen. There are however indications that the treatment initiation criteria will be expanded to include patients with CD4 greater than 200 cells/μl, which obviously has implications for the numbers of patients in need.

ipants at a World Health Organisation consultation as the 'only truly ethical outcome' (World Health Organisation, 2004, p. 8).

Yet there is room for improvement. Although the process of decision-making around the latest NSP might meet the criteria of fair process, there is a danger that the resulting outcomes will be inequitable. This is because ambitious treatment targets have been set without adequate consideration of the feasibility of meeting these targets. Although the costs of the NSP were assessed, there was no discussion of whether the proposed resources would be available. Whitehead (1992) argues that health inequity relates to differences in health status that are avoidable and unfair. Any definition of 'avoidable' in this context has to be a function of the availability of resources. Without due consideration given to resource needs, it is possible that the end result will be implicit rationing of treatment with negative implications for equity. This is because implicit rationing, which is what happens when HIV-treatment targets are missed, is less likely to be consistent and fair and is less transparent and open to review than is the case with explicit priority setting (Bennett and Chanfreau, 2005). To be equitable in HIV treatment does not mean that equal access to ART for all in need is the only possibility. Given resource scarcity, unequal access might be unavoidable.

Moving Towards Ethical Objectives — Ambitious Reform Plans

Health Care Financing Reform

Moving towards a more equitable health care system is to a certain extent contingent upon the values of South African society and the level of compassion that wealthier South Africans have for the poor. South Africa's history of oppression of one group by another and the more recent adoption of a neo-liberal capitalist economic system (Terreblanche, 2002) makes it uncertain that this commitment will be forthcoming.[7] According to Coburn (2000), neo-liberalism produces higher income inequality and lowered social cohesion, partly through undermining the welfare state. If the economy, the state and civil society are inextricably linked, then a neo-liberal economic system will create a more individualistic society (Coburn, 2000). According to Terreblanche (2002), in South Africa's neo-liberal system, members of the 'upper class' profit handsomely from mainstream economic activity while about half of the population is increasingly pauperised. While many societies

---

[7] Neo-liberalism is characterised by the dominance of markets and market models in the economy, by the assumption that societies are collections of autonomous individuals motivated chiefly by economic considerations, and by the belief that competition is the major vehicle for innovation (Coburn, 2000).

might consider South Africa's inequalities in health status and access to health care as inequitable, it is not clear that South Africans (especially the elite) share this view. Instead, South Africa's elite might view the public provision of health services to the poor in terms of 'we are paying for them' as opposed to 'we are paying for our health service' (Mooney, 2002). Given these constraints, it seems pragmatic to take a more moderate view regarding the reforms that might be achievable in the short to medium term.

Social health insurance is seen by many stakeholders as a medium-term goal (with the ultimate goal being an all-encompassing form of national health insurance). Changes to health care financing mechanisms have been proposed, in order to address some of the equity and sustainability challenges facing the South African health system. Early proposals suggesting the introduction of mandatory health insurance date back to the early 1990s. The African National Congress, which won the first democratic elections, presented the first formal policy-related document on a consolidated health system (African National Congress, 1994). Since then, different committees and working groups have drafted proposals to overcome the fragmentation of the health system and the lack of income- and risk-related cross-subsidies across the population.

Regarding the aim of fairness in health care financing, the proposals currently under discussion (Ministerial Task Team, 2004) include a mandatory social health insurance tax to be levied on all payers of income tax. Community-rated contributions to medical schemes would initially still be voluntary but possibly made mandatory at a later stage. There is a strong sense that an all-embracing approach can only be achieved via an evolutionary process. A standardised basic benefit package would be universal and cover those goods that in the medical schemes environment are currently known as prescribed minimum benefits (PMBs), as well as primary care services. These benefits could be 'topped-up' for beneficiaries of medical schemes. The basic benefit package would be the basis for risk equalisation between funding entities as well as for risk-adjusted subsidies. In contrast with earlier proposals, the current discussions do not suggest any changes to provider payment. In a system that tries to bring together a private and a public sector that have hardly had any overlap, principles of provider payment should be a concern, not only in the greater interest of harmonisation, but principally in the interest of equity in service delivery. It is envisaged that services will be provided via public facilities for non-contributors and those on low-incomes. Medical scheme members will be eligible to choose public or private services.

Incrementally, elements are being introduced into the South African health system that have the potential to act as catalysts towards increased risk-related and income-related cross-subsidies. We characterised the envisaged risk equalisation fund as a crucial first step towards achieving risk-related cross-subsidies within the current medical schemes environment, and therefore as an important tool to improve equity within that setting. The introduction of this tool has experienced delays at various levels of the policy process. Once implemented it will have limited power to 'equalise risks' as its basis is restricted to the PMBs. The medium-term goal would be to base risk-equalisation on the standardised basic benefit package that is being proposed. At that stage, there will be significant progress regarding risk-related cross-subsidisation. Yet income-related cross-subsidisation would require a completely separate set of tools. Here, the proposed mandatory social health insurance tax would constitute the big breakthrough. Both modes of cross-subsidisation are necessary elements of a health system that promotes equal access to health care within the South African social context, interpreting access as a multi-dimensional concept covering availability, affordability and acceptability. An integrative reform of the health system is thus a necessary step on the path towards social justice and at the same time a precondition to appropriately addressing South Africans' claims on health and health care.

Allocation of Public Sector Health Care Resources

In the absence of national health insurance that integrates both mandatory insurance contributions and general tax funds into a single financing pool, there will continue to be a need to promote an equitable allocation of government health care resources between and within provinces. Over the years, various proposals have been put forward. From an early stage, the Financial and Fiscal Commission suggested that conditional grants should focus on basic health services (not dissimilar to the abovementioned basic benefit package), particularly those provided at the health district level (Financial and Fiscal Commission, 1996). Thus, instead of focussing on earmarking allocations for tertiary services as at present, it may be more appropriate from an equity perspective to protect allocations for a basic benefit package through conditional grants. The key problem with this approach is that conditional grants do reduce the degree of autonomy in inter-sectoral resource allocation decision making of those spheres of government to which service delivery responsibility has been devolved.

An alternative approach is the development of norms and standards. The South African constitution allows for national government to legislate minimum norms and standards to ensure *'uniformity across the nation'* (Act 108 of 1996; Section 146(2b)) (Government of South Africa, 1996). The form that norms and standards take is flexible; for example they may specify the type, quantity and quality of health services that each province must fund and provide. Such norms and standards will apply pressure to provinces to fund health services adequately, but still allow provincial discretion about the exact mode of service delivery (McIntyre et al., 1999).

Even in the absence of efforts to promote equity in the inter-provincial allocation of health care resources, there is considerable scope for individual provinces to make dramatic progress in the equitable allocation of government health care resources within their jurisdictions. Each province has complete autonomy over the allocation of the provincial health budget between health districts and facilities. Moving away from historical budgeting processes towards resource allocation mechanisms that take account of the relative need for health care in different districts, and which reflect societal preferences in relation to who should receive priority in the allocation of government resources, is long overdue.

HIV-Treatment

In the case of HIV-treatment, any ethical reform demands a thorough discussion of resource needs and resource availability (i.e. budget constraints) within the NSP process. Unless budget constraints are considered the tendency is to set ambitious targets in order to attain consensus from stakeholders. However, as has been argued, this tendency could have negative implications for equity.

Knowledge of budgetary constraints within the NSP process would also assist in the choice of treatment strategies. For example, while South Africa offers both first and second-line ART with relatively frequent patient follow-up and laboratory monitoring, other African countries have opted for a much less resource intensive approach (Harries et al., 2006). Research indicates that a first-line only approach is more cost-effective than offering first and second-line; this means that access to a first-line only approach would be higher than access to first and second-line if the budget were insufficient for universal access to first and second-line ART (Cleary, 2007). Similarly, a less resource-intensive approach to patient follow-up and laboratory monitoring could also increase cost-effectiveness (Cleary et al., 2006). On the other hand, while it is more effective to initiate patients on ART with CD4 counts that are greater than 200 cells/μl, this is also more costly (Badri et al., 2006). If national antiretroviral treatment guidelines are revised to include patients with higher CD4 counts, this could also have negative implications for equitable access. Ultimately, stakeholders would need to decide whether they were in favour of more limited health gains to a higher proportion of people in need or higher health gains to the few.

Conclusions

The current state of health and health care in South Africa raises a number of ethical issues, most of which are closely linked to the country's pervasive socio-economic inequalities. The health system is still marked by the legacy of apartheid. Although the first decade of democracy has brought about progress in addressing the key obstacles towards a more equitable health care system, the differential resource constraints in the fragmented health system coupled with skewed distributions of wealth and health in an environment loaded with historical sensitivities makes it extremely difficult to propose a simple way forward to achieve an ethically superior situation. Alternative plans for comprehensive reforms have been proposed but health policy finalisation and implementation has been patchy. Possibly the greatest problem is the lack of an explicit, comprehensive and coherent vision for the overall health system.

Problems of inequity exist within the public sector, as has been illustrated using the example of resource allocation in geographical contexts. In the private sector, a cost spiral has triggered problems of service affordability. In the medical schemes environment a large number of separate risk pools, combined with lack of transparency and a multitude of benefit package options, leads to unfairness in contributions. Most importantly, however, inequities exist between the public and private sectors. Without a reform that integrates the two sectors, this key challenge will not be addressed. Risk- and income-related cross-subsidies are key elements of social solidarity. They are crucial for integrative and redistributive processes within the health system. As expressed above, we hold the view that the health system could potentially serve as a tool to strengthen the social fabric beyond the realm of health care.

Despite the existence of different proposals pointing in a similar direction, the debate about systemic reform has slowed down over the last few years after some initial progress, mainly within the private sector. There is a worry that the window of opportunity for large-scale reforms, which certainly existed in the immediate years after the first democratic elections, may be closing. It appears necessary to remind stakeholders at this time of the importance of completing systemic reform, especially in light of the objective of promoting social justice in South Africa.

In the area of HIV-treatment, the past year has seen a shift in policy towards a stronger commitment to ART, as evidenced by the latest national strategic plan which outlines a framework for a dramatically increased response. This framework has also been created in a process that meets many of Daniels' criteria for procedural justice. However, responding to the HIV-epidemic is just one of the many challenges currently facing the South African democracy. Whether this response becomes a 'resource for democracy' (Fassin and Schneider, 2003, p.497) or whether it undermines social cohesiveness within poor communities and between rich and poor communities will be partially determined by the steps that are taken during the next years. Implicit rationing of treatment, where overly optimistic treatment targets are set and subsequently missed, is less equitable and less likely to generate a socially reproducible return than explicit priority setting.

To conclude, fragmentation in the South African health care system mirrors many of the nation's historical divides. With appropriate reforms, the health care system, as a social institution, has the potential to be a key mechanism for breaching these divides and for creating social solidarity.

References

Aaron, H. J. and Schwartz, W. B (1984) *The Painful Prescription: Rationing Hospital Care* (Washington: The Brookings Institution).

Aaron, H. J. and Schwartz, W.B. with Cox, M. (2005) *Can We Say No? The challenge of rationing health care* (Washington: The Brookings Institution).

Acheson Report (1998) *Independent Inquiry into Inequalities in Health: Report* (London: The Stationery Office).

Adamson, J., Ben-Shlomo, Y., Chaturvedi, N. and Donovan, J. (2003) 'Ethnicity, socioeconomic position and gender - do they affect reported health-seeking behaviour?', *Social Science and Medicine*, 57 (5).

Alexander, Z. (1999) *Study of Black, Asian and ethnic minority issues* (London: Department of Health).

Alford, K. (2005) *Comparing Australian with Canadian and New Zealand Primary Health Care Systems in Relation to Indigenous Populations: Literature Review and Analysis* (Melbourne: Onemda VicHealth Koori Health Unit Discussion Paper No. 13).

Alvarez-Rosete, A, Bevan, G. Mays N. and Dixon, J. (2005) 'Effect of diverging policy across the NHS', *British Medical Journal*, 331 (7522).

Anand, G. (2003) 'Who Gets Health Care? Rationing in an Age of Rising Costs', *Wall Street Journal*, (Sept. 12, at A1).

Anderson, G.F., Frogner, B.K., Johns, R.A. and Reinhardt, U.E. (2006) 'Health Care Spending And Use of Information Technology in OECD Countries', *Health Affairs*, 25 (819).

Aristotle, *Nicomachean Ethics* (1966) ed. and trans. David Ross (London: Oxford University Press).

ART-LINC and ART-CC (2006) 'Mortality of HIV-1-infected Patients in the First Year of Antiretroviral Therapy: Comparison Between Low-Income and High-Income Countries', *Lancet*, 367 (9513).

ASSA (2007) 'ASSA2003lite AIDS and Demographic Model (released November 25, 2005)'. Available at: www.assa.org.za (Accessed: March 1, 2007).

Australian Bureau of Statistics (2006) *4102.0: Australian Social Trends* (Canberra: Australian Bureau of Statistics).

Australian Medical Association (2005a) 'Lifting the Weight – Low Birth Weight Babies: An Indigenous Health Burden That Must Be Lifted'. Available at:

www.ama.com.au/web.nsf/doc/WEENGB4BW/$file/Indigenous%20 Report.pdf (Accessed: July 15, 2006).

Australian Medical Association (2005b) 'Federal Budget Submission 2006-7'. Available at: http://www.ama.com.au/web.nsf/doc/WEEN-6J58VL/$file/AMA/ Federal Budget Submission 2006-07-Simple Steps to a Healthier Population.pdf (Accessed: July 27, 2006).

Australian Medical Association Victorian Branch (AMA Vic) (2006) 'Media Release 31 July 2006'. Available at: www.amavic.com.au/page/Media/Media_Releases/2006/_The_hidd en_waiting_list_is_hurting_Victorians/ (Accessed: March 31, 2007).

Australian Society of Plastic Surgeons (2006) 'Latest News, January 16, 2006'. Available at: www.plasticsurgery.org.au/public/aspsframe.asp (Accessed: July 10, 2006).

Badri, M., Cleary, S., Maartens, G., Pitt, J., Bekker, L-G., Orrell, C. and Wood, R. (2006) 'When to Initiate HAART in Sub-Saharan Africa? A South African Cost-Effectiveness Study', *Antiviral Therapy,* 11 (1).

Banks, G.T. (1979) 'Programme Budgeting in the DHSS' in *Planning for Welfare: Social Policy and the Expenditure Process,* ed. T.A. Booth (Oxford: Blackwell and Robertson).

Barry, B. (1965) *Political Argument* (London: Routledge and Kegan Paul).

Beauchamp, D. (2004a) 'Public Health Law: Legal Moralism and Public Health,' *Encyclopedia of Bioethics,* ed. S. G. Post (New York: Macmillan).

Beauchamp, D. (2004b) 'Public Health: Philosophy,' *Encyclopedia of Bioethics,* ed. S. G. Post (New York: Macmillan).

Bennett, S. and Chanfreau, C. (2005) 'Approaches to Rationing Antiretroviral Treatment: Ethical and Equity Implications', *Bulletin of the World Health Organisation,* 83 (7).

Benzeval, M. and Judge, K. (1994) 'The determinants of hospital utilisation: implications for resource allocation in England', *Health Economics,* 3 (2).

Berlin, I. (1997) *The Proper Study of Mankind* (London: Chatto & Windus).

Biggs, A. (2003) 'The Pharmaceutical Benefits Scheme – An Overview' (Parliamentary Brief, Parliament of Australia). Available at: http://www.aph.gov.au/library/intguide/sp/pbs.htm (Accessed: June 20, 2006).

Biggs, A. (2004) 'Medicare Background Brief E-Brief'. Available at: www.aph.gov.au/library/intguide/SP/medicare.htm#history (Accessed: July 10, 2006).

Bill and Melinda Gates Foundation, 'Global Health.' Available at: www.gatesfoundation.org/globalhealth (Accessed: August 15, 2006).

Bird, R. and Vaillancourt, F. (eds.) (1999) *Fiscal Decentralization in Developing Countries* (Cambridge: Cambridge University Press).

Bleichrodt, H., Diecidue, E. and Quiggin, J. (2004) 'Equity weights in the allocation of health care: the rank-dependent QALY model', *Journal of Health Economics,* 23.

Bloch, S. and Reddawy, P. (1984) *Soviet Psychiatric Abuse: The Shadow over World Psychiatry* (London: Gollancz).

Bodenheimer, T. S. and Grumbach, K. (2005) *Understanding Health Policy: A Clinical Approach* (4th ed.) (New York: Lange Medical Books).

Bohman, J. (1996) *Public Deliberation: Pluralism, Complexity, and Democracy* (Cambridge, MA: MIT Press).

Borger, C., Smith, S., Truffer, C., Keehan, S., Sisko, A., Poisal, J., and Clemens, M.K. (2006) 'Health Spending Projections Through 2015: Changes on the Horizon', *Health Affairs* (Web Supplement for January to June 2006), 25 (W61). Available at:
http://www.healthaffairs.org/content/vol25/issue2/ (Accessed: March 23, 2007).

Brennan, S. (2004) 'Could a Treaty Make a Practical Difference in People's Lives? The Question of Health and Well-being', Gilbert & Tobin Centre of Public Law, University of New South Wales, The Treaty Project Issues Paper No. 4. Available at:
www.gtcentre.unsw.edu.au/publications/docs/treatyPapers/Issues_P aper4.pdf (Accessed: July 11, 2006).

Breslow, L. (2004) 'Public Health: Determinants,' in *Encyclopedia of Bioethics*, ed. S. G. Post, (New York: Macmillan).

Brock, D. (1988) 'Ethical Issues in Recipient Selection for Organ Transplantation' in *Organ Substitution Technology: Ethical, Legal, and Public Policy Issues*, ed. D. Mathieu (Boulder, CO, and London: Westview).

Brock, D. (2004a) 'Ethical Issues in the Use of Cost Effectiveness Analysis for the Prioritisation of Health Care Resources' in *Public Health, Ethics and Equity*, ed. S. Anand, P. Fabienne and A. Sen (Oxford: Oxford University Press).

Brock, D. (2004b) 'Public Health Law: Legal Moralism and Public Health,' in *Encyclopedia of Bioethics*, ed. S. G. Post (New York: Macmillan).

Brock, D. and Daniels, N. (1994) 'Ethical Foundations of the Clinton Administration's Proposed Health Care System', *Journal of the American Medical Association*, 271 (1189).

Brooks, P. M., Lapsley, H.M. and Butt, D.B. (2003) 'Medical Workforce Issues in Australia: "Tomorrow's doctors – too few, too far"', *Medical Journal of Australia*, 179 (4).

Broome, J. (1988) 'Goodness, fairness and QALYs' in *Philosophy and Medical Welfare*, ed. M. Bell and S. Mendus (Cambridge: Cambridge University Press).

Broome, J. (1991a) 'Fairness', *Proceedings of the Aristotelian Society*, 91 (1).

Broome, J. (1991b) *Weighing Goods: Equality, Uncertainty and Time* (Oxford: Basil Blackwell).

Buchanan, A. (1983)'The Right to a Decent Minimum of Health Care' in *Securing Access To Health Care (Vol. II)*, President's Commission for the Study of Ethical Problems in Medicine and Biomedical and Behavioural Research (Washington, D.C.: US Government Printing Office).

Buchanan, A. (1998) 'Managed Care: Rationing Without Justice, But Not Unjustly', *Journal of Health Politics, Policy, and Law*, 23 (617).

Cabinet Office (2005) *Regulatory Impact Assessment Guidance (updated 2005)*, (London: Cabinet Office). Available at:
www.cabinetoffice.gov.uk/regulation/ria/ria_guidance/index.asp (Accessed: May 30, 2006).

Calebresi G. and Bobbitt, P. (1978) *Tragic Choices* (New York: Norton).

Callahan, D. (1990) *What Kind of Life: The Limits of Medical Progress* (New York: Simon and Schuster).

Campbell, C. (2003) *Letting Them Die: How HIV/AIDS Prevention Programmes Often Fail* (Bloomington: Indiana University Press).

Carrick, P. (2001) *Medical Ethics in the Ancient World* (Washington, D.C.: Georgetown University Press).

Carrin, G. and James, C. (2004) *Reaching Universal Coverage Via Social Health Insurance: Key Design Features in the Transition Period* (Geneva: World Health Organisation).

Chave, S. P. W. (1986) 'The Origins and Development of Public Health' in *Oxford Textbook of Public Health*, ed. W. W. Holland, R. Detel, and G. Knox, (Oxford: Oxford University Press).

Cleary, S. (2007a) 'Equity and Efficiency in Health and Health Care for HIV-positive Adults in South Africa'. Unpublished Doctoral Thesis, University of Cape Town.

Cleary, S. (2007b) *The Costs of the National Strategic Plan on HIV/AIDS and STIs 2007-2011* (Cape Town: Health Economics Unit, University of Cape Town).

Cleary, S., McIntyre, D. and Boulle, A. (2006) 'The Cost-Effectiveness of Antiretroviral Treatment in Khayelitsha, South Africa: A primary data analysis', *Cost Effectiveness and Resource Allocation*, 4 (20).

Cm 555 (1989) *Working for Patients* (London: HMSO).

Cm 3807 (1997) *The New NHS: Modern, dependable* (London: The Stationery Office).

Coburn, D. (2000) 'Income Inequality, Social Cohesion and the Health Status of Populations: The Role of Neo-Liberalism', *Social Science and Medicine*, 51 (1).

Coetzee, D., Hildebrand, K., Boulle, A., Maartens, G., Louis, F., Labatala, V., Reuter, H., Ntwana, N. and Goemaere, E. (2004) 'Outcomes After Two Years of Providing Antiretroviral Treatment in Khayelitsha, South Africa', *AIDS*, 18 (6).

Cohen, J. (1989) 'Deliberation and Democratic Legitimacy' in *The Good Polity*, ed. A. Hamlin and P. Pettit (Oxford: Blackwell).

Consumers International (2006) *Branding the Cure: A Consumer Perspective on Corporate Social Responsibility, Drug Promotion and the Pharmaceutical Industry in Europe*, (London: Consumers International).

Cooter, R, and Pickstone, J., eds. (2000) *Medicine in the Twentieth Century* (Singapore: Harwood Academic Publishers).

Copleston, F. (1962) *A History of Philosophy* (Vol. 1, Part II) (New York: Image Books).

Culyer, A. and Wagstaff, A. (1993) 'Equity and Equality in Health and Health Care', *Journal of Health Economics*, 12 (4).

Daniels, N. (1985) *Just Health Care* (Oxford: Oxford University Press).

Daniels, N. (1986) 'Why Saying No to Patients in the United States is so Hard', *New England Journal of Medicine*, 314 (1381).

Daniels, N. (1995) *Seeking Fair Treatment: From the AIDS Epidemic to National Health Care Reform* (Oxford: Oxford University Press).

Daniels, N. (1996) *Justice and Justification* (Cambridge: Cambridge University Press).

Daniels, N. (1998) 'Kamm's moral methods', *Philosophy and Phenomenological Research*, 58 (4).

Daniels, N. (not dated) 'Justice, Health, and Health Care' (unpublished essay). Available at: www.hsph.harvard.edu/benchmark/ndaniels/pdf/justice_health.pdf (Accessed: August 18, 2006).

Daniels, N., Kennedy, B., and Kawachi, I. (eds.) (2000) *Is Inequality Bad For Our Health?* (Boston: Beacon Press).

Daniels, N. and Sabin, J.E. (1997) 'Limits to Healthcare: Fair Procedures, Democratic Deliberation, and the Legitimacy Problem for Insurers', *Philosophy and Public Affairs*, 26 (4).

Daniels, N. and Sabin, J. E. (2002) *Setting Limits Fairly: Can We Learn to Share Medical Resources?* (Oxford: Oxford University Press).

Davies, P. (2004) 'Evidence before the Senate Select Committee on Medicare', January 20, 2004 (Canberra: Official Committee Hansard, Commonwealth of Australia).

Davis, L. (1979) *Theory of Action* (Englewood Cliffs, NJ: Prentice Hall).

Davoren, P. (2001) 'Why Private Health Insurance Initiatives Don't Help Public Hospitals', *New Doctor*, 75 (Winter).

Day, C. and Gray, A. (2005) 'Health and Health Indicators' in *South African Health Review 2005*. ed. P. Ijumba and P. Barron (Durban: Health Systems Trust).

de Mello, L. (2000) 'Fiscal Decentralisation and Intergovernmental Fiscal Relations: A Cross-Country Analysis', *World Development*, 28 (2).

Department of Health (2003a) *Resource allocation: Weighted capitation formula* (London: Department of Health).

Department of Health (2003b) *Investing in General Practice: The New General Medical Services Contract* (London: Department of Health). Available at: www.dh.gov.uk/assetRoot/04/07/86/58/04078658.pdf (Accessed: May 30, 2006).

Department of Health (2005a) *Resource Allocation: Weighted Capitation Formula* (Leeds: Department of Health).

Department of Health (2005b) *Tackling Health Inequalities: Status Report on the Programme for Action* (London: Department of Health).

Department of Health, 'National programme budget project'. Available at: www.dh.gov.uk/PolicyAndGuidance/OrganisationPolicy/FinanceAndPlanning/ProgrammeBudgeting/fs/en (Accessed: May 30, 2006).

Department of Health and Social Security (1976a) *Priorities for Health and Social Services in England* (London: HMSO).

Department of Health and Social Security (1976b) *Sharing Resources for Health in England* (London: HMSO).

Department of Health South Africa (1997) *White Paper for the Transformation of the Health System in South Africa* (Pretoria: Government Printer).

Department of Health South Africa (2004a) *Strategic Priorities for the National Health System: 2004-2009* (Pretoria: Department of Health).

Department of Health South Africa (2004b) *National Antiretroviral Treatment Guidelines* (Pretoria: Department of Health).

Devlin, N. and Parkin, D. (2004) 'Does NICE have a cost-effectiveness threshold and what other factors influence its decisions?', *Health Economics*, 13 (5).

Dixon, A., Le Grand, J., Henderson, J., Murray, R. and Poteliakhoff, E. (2003) 'Is the NHS equitable? A review of the evidence', LSE Health and Social Care Discussion paper No. 11, (London: London School of Economics).

Dobson, A., DaVanzo, J. and Sen, N. (2006) 'The Cost-Shift Payment "Hydraulic": Foundation, History, and Implications', *Health Affairs*, 25 (22).

Doctors Reform Society (2004) 'Media Release (February 17, 2004)'. Available at: www.drs.org.au/media/2004/media170204.htm (Accessed: October 25, 2007).

Dolan, P. (1998) 'The measurement of individual utility and social welfare', *Journal of Health Economics*, 17 (1).

Donaldson,L.(2006) *On the State of the Public Health: Annual Report of the Chief Medical Office 2005* (London: Department of Health).

Duffy, J.(1993) *From Humors to Medical Science: A History of American Medicine* (Chicago, IL: University of Illinois Press).

Duffy, J. (2004) 'Public Health: History' *in Encyclopedia of Bioethics*, ed. S. G. Post (New York: Macmillan).

Duru, G., Auray, J.P., Beresniak, A., Lamure, M., Paine, A., Nicoloyannis, N. (2002) 'Limitations of the methods used for calculating quality-adjusted life-year values', *Pharmacoeconomics*, 20(7).

Dworkin, R. (1985) *A Matter of Principle* (Cambridge, MA: Harvard University Press).

Dworkin, R. (1993) 'Justice in the Distribution of Health Care', *McGill Law Journal*, 38 (4).

Dworkin , R.(2000) *Sovereign Virtue* (Cambridge, MA: Harvard University Press).

Dwyer, J.M. (2004) 'Evidence before the Senate Select Committee on Medicare', January 19, 2004 (Canberra: Official Committee Hansard, Commonwealth of Australia).

The Economist (2006, February 25) 'Inescapable trade-offs'.

Eddy, D. (1996) *Clinical Decision Making: From Theory to Practice* (Boston: Jones and Bartlett).

Edelstein, L. E. (1967) *Ancient Medicine: Selected Papers of Ludwig Edelstein*, eds. O. Temkin and C. L. Temkin (Baltimore, MD: Johns Hopkins University Press).

Edgar, A., Salek, S., Shickle, S., Cohen, D., (1998) *The Ethical QALY: Ethical Issues in Healthcare Resource Allocation* (Haslemere: Euromed Communications).

Editorial (2006) 'Costly New drugs Raise Ethical Questions', *St. Louis Post-Dispatch*, (February 19).

Elliot, A. (2003) 'Is Medicare Universal?' (Research Note No. 37, 2002-3) (Canberra: Parliamentary Library).

Employee Benefits Research Institute (2006). Available at: http://www.ebri.org/pdf/publications/facts/0204fact.pdf (Accessed: April 25, 2006).

Engelhardt, H.T. (1996) *The Foundations of Bioethics* (Oxford: Oxford University Press).

Enthoven, A. and Kronick, R. (1989) 'A Consumer Choice Health Plan for the 1990s', *Journal of the American Medical Association*, 320 (29).

European Court of Justice (2006) Press Release: Available at: www.curia.europa.eu/en/actu/communiques/cp06/aff/cp060042en. pdf (Accessed: May 30, 2005).

Evans, R. (2004) 'Epidemics' in *Encyclopedia of Bioethics*, ed. S. G. Post (New York: Macmillan).

Evans, R. and Stoddart, G. (1990) 'Producing Health, Consuming Health Care', *Social Science & Medicine*, 31 (12).

Fassin, D. and Schneider, H. (2003) 'The Politics of AIDS in South Africa: Beyond the Controversies', *British Medical Journal*, 326 (7387).

Financial and Fiscal Commission (1996) *The Financial and Fiscal Commission's Recommendations for the Allocation of Financial Resources to the National and Provincial Governments for the 1997/98 Financial Year* (Midrand: FFC).

Fleck, L.M. (1987)'DRGs: Justice and the Invisible Rationing of Health Care Resources', *Journal of Medicine and Philosophy*, 12 (165).

Fleck, L.M. (1990)'Pricing Human Life: The Moral Costs of Medical Progress', *Centennial Review*, 34 (227).

Fleck, L.M. (1992) 'Just Health Care Rationing: A Democratic Decision-Making Approach', *University of Pennsylvania Law Review*, 140 (1597).

Fleck, L.M. (1994a)'Just Caring: Oregon, Health Care Rationing, and Informed Democratic Deliberation', *Journal of Medicine and Philosophy*, 19 (367).

Fleck, L.M. (1994b)'Just Caring: Health Reform and Health Care Rationing', *Journal of Medicine and Philosophy*, 19 (435).

Fleck, L.M. (1999) 'Just Caring: Managed Care and Protease Inhibitors' in *Ethical Issues in Modern Medicine* (5th edn.), ed. J. Arras and B. Steinbock (Mountainview, CA: Mayfield Publishing).

Fleck, L.M. (2002) 'Last Chance Therapies: Can a Just and Caring Society Do Health Care Rationing When Life Itself is at Stake?', *Yale Journal of Health Policy, Law, and Ethics*, 2 (255).

Fleck, L.M. (2005)'Priority-Setting, Health Care Justice, and the Least Well Off', paper presented at the David Thomasma International Bioethics Retreat, Amsterdam.

Fleck, L.M. (2006)'Creating Public Conversation About Behavioural Genetics' in *Wrestling With Behavioural Genetics: Science, Ethics, and Public Conversation*, ed. E. Parens, A. Chapman, and N. Press (Baltimore: Johns Hopkins University Press).

Foot, M. (1975) *Aneurin Bevan 1945-60* (St Albans: Paladin).

Garrison, F. H. (1929) *An Introduction to the History of Medicine* (Philadelphia, PA: W. B. Saunders).

Gerdtham, U.G. and Jonsson B. (2000) 'Cross country studies of health care expenditure' in *The Handbook of Health Economics*, ed. A.J. Culyer and J. Newhouse (Amsterdam: North Holland).

Gilson, L., Doherty, J., McIntyre, D., Thomas, S., Brijlal, V., Bowa, C. and Mbatsha, S. (1999) *The Dynamics of Policy Change: Health Care Financing in South Africa 1994-99 (Monograph No. 66)* (Cape Town: Health Economics Unit, University of Cape Town, and Johannesburg: Centre for Health Policy, University of the Witwatersrand).

Glennerster H. (1974) *Social Service Budgets and Social Policy* (London: Allen and Unwin).

Glennerster, H. (2005) 'The Health and Welfare Legacy' in *The Blair Effect 2001-5*, ed. A. Seldon and D. Kavanagh (Cambridge: Cambridge University Press).

Glennerster, H (2006) *British Social Policy: 1945 to the Present* (Oxford: Blackwell).

Glennerster, H., with Korman, N. and Marslen-Wilson, F. (1983) *Planning for Priority Groups* (Oxford: Martin Robertson).

Glennerster, H., Hills, J. and Travers, T. (2000) *Paying for Health, Education and Housing: How does the Centre Pull the Purse Strings?* (Oxford: Oxford University Press).

Goldberger, Z., and Lampert, R. (2006) 'Implantable Cardioverter-Defibrillators: Expanding Indications and Technologies', *Journal of the American Medical Association*, 295 (809).

Gottret, P. and Schieber, G. (2006) *Health Financing Revisited: A Practitioner's Guide* (Washington DC: The World Bank).

Government of South Africa (1996) Constitution of the Republic of South Africa (Pretoria: Act No.108 of 1996).

Government of South Africa (1998) Medical Schemes Act (Pretoria: Act No. 131 of 1998).

Government of South Africa (2004) National Health Act (Cape Town: Act No. 61 of 2003).

Grad, F. P. (2004) 'Public Health Law: The Law of Public Health' in *Encyclopedia of Bioethics,* ed. S. G. Post (New York: Macmillan).

Gravelle, H., Sutton, M., Morris, S., Windmeijer, F., Leyland, A., Dibben, C., Muirhead, M. (2003) 'Modelling supply and demand influences on the use of health care: implications for deriving a needs-based capitation formula', *Health Economics* 12 (12).

Gray, G. (2003) *The Politics of Medicare: Who Gets What, When and How* (Sydney: University of New South Wales Press).

The Guardian (2001, August 7) 'MS drugs likely to stay off health service list'. Available at:
   http://www.guardian.co.uk/uk_news/story/0,,533132,00.html (Accessed: May 2, 2006).

Guillebaud Committee (1956) *Committee of enquiry into the cost of the National Health Service* (London: HMSO).

Gulliford, M. and Morgan, M. (eds.) (2003) *Access to Health Care* (London: Routledge).

Gutmann, A. and Thompson D. (2004) *Why Deliberative Democracy?* (Princeton, NJ:
Princeton University Press).

Haacker, M. (ed.) (2004) *The Macroeconomics of HIV/AIDS* (Washington, D.C: International Monetary Fund).

Habermas, J. (1989) *The Theory of Communicative Action, Volume 1: Reason and the Rationalization of Society* (Boston: Beacon Press).

Hall, S. (2006) 'Cholesterol Drug Available to Extra 3M', *The Guardian,* (Jan 25).

Harries, A., Schouten, E. and Libamba, E. (2006) 'Scaling Up Antiretroviral Treatment in Resource-Poor Settings', *Lancet*, 367 (9525).

Harrison, A. and Appleby, J. (2005) *The war on waiting for hospital treatment: What has Labour achieved and what challenges remain?* (London: King's Fund).

Hartnack, J. (1962) *Wittgenstein and Modern Philosophy* (Garden City, NY: Anchor Books).

Health Insurance Act (1973) (Canberra: Commonwealth Consolidated Acts).

Henry J. Kaiser Family Foundation (2006) 'Health Coverage & Uninsured'. Available at: http://www.statehealthfacts.org/cgi-bin/healthfacts.cgi (Accessed: November 12, 2006).

H.M. Treasury (2002) *Securing our Future Health : Taking a Long Term View* (London: The Stationery Office).

H.M. Treasury (2003) *Green book: Appraisal and evaluation in central government* (London: The Stationery Office). Available at: www.greenbook.treasury.gov.uk/ (Accessed: May 30, 2006).

H.M. Treasury (2004a) *2004 Spending Review – New Public Spending Plans 2005 -2008* (London: The Stationery Office).

H.M Treasury (2004b) *Securing good health for the whole population* (London: The Stationery Office).

H.M. Treasury (2006) *2006 Budget* (London: The Stationery Office).

H.M. Treasury (2007) *2007 Pre-Budget Report and Comprehensive Spending Review* (London: The Stationery Office).

Hoboyi, N. and Geffen, N. (eds.) (2007) *Equal Treatment* (Cape Town: Treatment Action Campaign).

Human Rights and Equal Opportunity Commission Aboriginal and Torres Strait Islander Social Justice Commissioner (HREOC) (2005) *Social Justice Report 2005* (Sydney: Human Rights and Equal Opportunity Commission). Available at: www.humanrights.gov.au/socila%5Fjustice/sjreport05/ (Accessed: July 25, 2006).

The Independent (2006, April 2) 'Cancer: There are life-saving drugs. So why can't we have them?'. Available at: http://news.independent.co.uk/uk/health_medical/article355173.ece (Accessed: May 2, 2006).

Kagan, S. (1998) 'Rethinking Intrinsic Value', *Journal of Ethics*, 2 (4).

Kamm, F. (1993) *Morality, Mortality: Death and Whom to Save From it:* Vol. 1 (Oxford: Oxford University Press).

Kant, I (1783, 1964) *Groundwork of the Metaphysic of Morals,* trans. H. J. Paton (New York: Harper Torchbook).

Klein, R., Day, P. and Redmayne, S. (1996) *Managing Scarcity: Priority setting and rationing the National Health Service* (Buckingham: Open University Press).

Knowles, S. Senator (2004) *Select Committee on Medicare* (Canberra: Official Committee Hansard, Commonwealth of Australia).

Kopelman, L. M. (2002) 'If HIV/AIDS is Punishment, Who is Bad?', *Journal of Medicine and Philosophy*, 27 (2).

Korsgaard, C. (1983) 'Two Distinctions of Goodness', *Philosophical Review*, 92 (2).

Kuttner, R. (2005) 'Medicare Misery', *The American Prospect,* (January 5).

Ladd, H.F. (2002) 'School Vouchers: A Critical View', *The Journal of Economic Perspectives,* 16 (4).

Lavelle, P., 'Private Health Insurance', Health Matters Consumer Guides, Australian Broadcasting Commission. Available at: www.abc.net.au/health/cguides/privatehealthins.htm (Accessed: July 22, 2006).

Lawrence, S. C. (1996) *Charitable Knowledge: Hospital Pupils and Practitioners in Eighteenth Century London* (Cambridge: Cambridge University Press).

Levi-Strauss, C. (1969) *The Elementary Structures of Kinship* (London: Eyre and Spottiswoode).

Litva, A., Coast, J., Donovan, J., Eyles, J., Shepherd, M., Tacchi, J., Abelson, J. and Morgan, K. (2002) '"The Public is Too Subjective": Public Involvement at Different Levels of Health Care Decision Making', *Social Science and Medicine,* 54 (12).

Local Government Finance Act (1982) *Public General Statutes* (London: HMSO).

MacLean, Douglas (2006) 'Longevity', paper presented at the Centre for Applied Philosophy and Public Ethics seminar program (Melbourne division).

Mann, S. (2006) 'Lies, damned lies, and waiting lists'. *The Age* (Melbourne) (August 5).

Mano, M. (2006) 'The Burden of Scientific Progress: Growing Inequalities in the Delivery Of Cancer Care', *Acta Oncologica,* 45 (84).

Marx, K. (1848, 1963) *The Communist Manifesto,* trans. S. Moore (Chicago, IL: Regency Books).

McAuley, I. (2004) 'Evidence before Senate Select Committee on Medicare', January 19, 2004 (Canberra: Official Committee Hansard, Commonwealth of Australia).

McConnachie, A. and Sutton, M. (2004) *Report to the Standing Committee on Resource Allocation: Derivation of an adjustment to the Arbuthnott formula for socioeconomic inequities in health care.* Available at: www.gla.ac.uk/projects/platform/Derivation%20Report%20Feb%202 004.pdf (Accessed:August 28, 2006).

McIntyre, D., Baba, L. and Makan, B. (1998) 'Equity in Public Sector Health Care Financing and Expenditure in South Africa' in *South African Health Review 1998,* ed. A. Ntuli (Durban: Health Systems Trust and Henry J. Kaiser Family Foundation).

McIntyre, D. and Gilson, L. (2002) 'Putting Equity in Health Back Onto the Social Policy Agenda: Experience from South Africa', *Social Science and Medicine,* 54 (11).

McIntyre, D., Gilson, L., Wadee, H., Thiede, M. and Okorafor, O. (2006) 'Commercialisation and Extreme Inequality in Health: The Policy Challenges in South Africa', *Journal of International Development,* 18 (3).

McIntyre, D., Thiede, M., Nkosi, M., Mutyambizi, V., Castillo-Riquelme, M., Gilson, L., Erasmus, E. and Goudge, J. (2007) *A Critical Analysis of the Current South African Health System - SHIELD Work Package 1 Report* (Cape Town: Health Economics Unit, University of Cape Town, and Johannesburg: Centre for Health Policy, University of the Witwatersrand).

McIntyre, D., Thomas, S., Mbatsha, S., Baba, L. (1999) 'Public Sector Health Care Financing and Expenditure' in *South African Health Review 1999*, ed. N. Crisp and A. Ntuli (Durban: Health Systems Trust and Henry J. Kaiser Family Foundation).

McIntyre, D., Valentine, N. and Cornell, J. (1995) 'Private Sector Health Care Expenditure in South Africa', *South African Medical Journal*, 85 (3).

McKie, J. and Richardson, J. (2003) 'The Rule of Rescue', *Social Science and Medicine*, 56 (2003).

McLean, I. and McMillan, A. (2005) *The State of the Union* (Oxford: Oxford University Press).

Mechanic, D. (1997) 'Muddling through elegantly: finding the proper balance in rationing, *Health Affairs*, 16 (5).

Medicines Australia (2006) 'New PBS Investment as PBS Slows' (Media Release, 21 June, 2006). Available at: www.medicinesaustralia.com.au/pages/view_news.asp?id=24 (Accessed: August 12, 2006).

Mill, J. S. (1859, 1971) *On Liberty* in *Essential Works of John Stuart Mill*, ed. M. Lerner (New York: Bantam Books).

Mill, J.S. (1972) 'Utilitarianism' in *Utilitarianism, On Liberty, and Considerations on Representative Government*, ed. H.B. Acton (London: J.M. Dent and Sons).

Miller, D. (1999) *Principles of Social Justice* (Cambridge, MA: Harvard University Press).

Miller, T. (2004) 'History of the Hospital: Medieval and Renaissance' in *Encyclopedia of Bioethics*, ed. S. G. Post (New York: Macmillan).

Ministerial Task Team (2004) *Final Recommendations Concerning the Implementation of Social Health Insurance in South Africa: Report 1* (Pretoria: Department of Health).

Mooney, G. (1983) 'Equity in Health Care: Confronting the Confusion', *Effective Health Care*, 1 (4).

Mooney, G. (1998) '"Communitarian Claims" as an Ethical Basis for Allocating Health Care Resources', *Social Science & Medicine*, 47(9).

Mooney, G. (2002) *Access and Service Delivery Issues* (Canberra: Health Policy Round Table).

Mooney, G. (2003) *Economics, Medicine and Health Care* (Harlow: Pearson Education Limited).

More, T. (1518, 1964) *Utopia,* ed. E. Surtz (New Haven, CT: Yale University Press).

Morreim, E.H. (1991) *Balancing Act: The New Medical Ethics of Medicine's New Economics* (Dordrecht: Kluwer Academic Publishers).

Morris, S., Sutton, M. and Gravelle, H. (2003) 'Inequity and inequality in the use of health care in England: An extended empirical investigation', Centre for Health Economics, Technical paper, No. 27 (York: University of York).

Moss, A.H. and Siegler, M. (1991) 'Should Alcoholics Compete Equally for Liver Transplantation', *Journal of the American Medical Association,* 265 (10).

Moss, R. (2006) 'Hype and Herceptin', *New Scientist,* (March 4).

Murillo, J. and Koeller, J. (2006) 'Chemotherapy Given Near the End of Life by Community Oncologists for Advanced Non-Small Cell Lung Cancer', *The Oncologist*, 11 (1095).

National Department of Health South Africa (2007) *National Strategic Plan for HIV and AIDS & STIs 2007-2011* (Pretoria: National Department of Health).

National Institute for Health and Clinical Excellence (2006) *Technology Appraisal 94* (London: NICE).

National Institute for Health and Clinical Excellence, 'About NICE Guidance: what does it mean for me?'. Available at: www.nice.org.uk/page.aspx?o=AboutGuidance (Accessed July 9, 2006).

National Institute for Health and Clinical Excellence, 'About Technology Appraisals'. Available at: www.nice.org.uk/page.aspx?o=202425 (Accessed July 9, 2006).

National Institute for Health and Clinical Excellence, 'Appraisal of Beta Interferon / Glatiramer for Multiple Sclerosis: Final Appraisal Determination'. Available at: www.nice.org.uk/pdf/betainterferonfad.pdf (Accessed: August 26, 2006).

National Treasury South Africa (2006) *Medium Term Expenditure Framework - Treasury Guidelines: Preparing Budget Proposals for the 2007 MTEF* (Pretoria: National Treasury).

National Treasury South Africa (2007) *2007 Budget Review* (Pretoria: National Treasury).

Nattrass, N. (2004) *The Moral Economy of AIDS in South Africa* (Cambridge: Cambridge University Press).

Newhouse, J.P. and the Insurance Experiment Group (1993) *Free for All? Lessons from the RAND Health Insurance Experiment* (Cambridge, MA: Harvard University Press).

Nord, E. (1999) *Cost-Value Analysis in Health Care: Making Sense out of QALYs* (Cambridge: Cambridge University Press).

Nozick, R. (1993) *Anarchy, State, and Utopia* (Oxford: Blackwell).

Number, R. L., and Amundsen, D. W., eds. (1986) *Caring and Curing: Health and Medicine in the Western Religious Traditions* (New York: Macmillan).

Nussbaum, N. (2000) *Women and Human Development: The Capabilities Approach* (Cambridge: Cambridge University Press).

OECD (2005a) *Health Data 2005* (Paris: Organisation for Economic Co-operation and Development).

OECD (2005b) *Health at a Glance: OECD Indicators 2005* (Paris: Organisation for Economic Co-operation and Development). OECD 'Health Data'. Available at: www.ecosante.fr/index2.php?base=OCDE&valeur (Accessed: March 31, 2007)

Okorafor, O., Thomas, S., Mbatsha, S., Gilson, L., Jikwana, S. and Mooney, G. (2005) *Protecting Resources for Primary Health Care: Options for Resource Allocation* (Cape Town: Health Economics Unit, University of Cape Town).

Okorafor, O., Thomas, S. and McIntyre, D. (2003) *An Evaluation of Public Primary Health Care Financing in South Africa: 1992/93 - 2002/03* (Cape Town: Health Economics Unit, University of Cape Town).

Oliver, A. and Mossialos, E. (2005) 'Equity of Access to Health Care: Outlining the Foundations for Action', *Journal of Epidemiology and Community Health,* 58 (5).

Olsen, J. A., Richardson, J., Dolan, P. and Menzel, P. (2003) 'The Moral Relevance of Personal Characteristics in Setting Health Care Priorities', *Social Science & Medicine,* 57 (7).

Over, M. (2004) 'Impact of the HIV/AIDS Epidemic on the Health Sectors of Developing Countries' in *The Macroeconomics of HIV/AIDS*, ed. M. Haacker (Washington, D.C.: International Monetary Fund).

Oxfam Australia (2006) *Commonwealth Games Briefing Paper: Aboriginal and Torres Strait Islander Health* (Melbourne: Oxfam).

Pauker, S., Ester, N., and Salem, D. (2005) 'Preventing Sudden Cardiac Death: Can We Afford The Benefit?', *Annals of Internal Medicine,* 142 (664).

Pear, R. (2006) 'States Intervene After Drug Plan Hits Snags', *New York Times,* (January 8).

Penchansky, R. and Thomas, J. (1981) 'The Concept of Access: Definition and Relationship to Consumer Satisfaction', *Medical Care,* 19 (2).

Podger, A. (2006) 'A Model Health System for Australia' (Inaugural Menzies Health Policy Lecture, March 3, 2006). Available at: www.ahpi.health.usyd.edu.au/pdfs/events2006/apodgerlecture.pdf (Accessed: October 25, 2007).

Porter, R. (1999) *The Greatest Benefit to Mankind: A Medical History of Humanity* (New York: W. W. Norton).

Porter, R. ed. (2000) *Cambridge Illustrated History of Medicine* (Cambridge: Cambridge University Press).

Productivity Commission (2005) 'The Health Workforce Productivity Commission Issues Paper May 2005'. Available at: www.racp.edu.au/hpu/workforce/ ProductivityCommission Issues.pdf (Accessed: July 5, 2006).

Rawlins, M.D. and Culyer, A.J. (2004) 'National Institute for Clinical Excellence and its Value Judgments', *British Medical Journal,* 329 (224).

Rawls, J. (1971) *A Theory of Justice* (Cambridge, MA: Harvard University Press).

Rawls, J. (1972) *A Theory of Justice* (Oxford: Oxford University Press).

Rawls, J. (1993) *Political Liberalism* (New York: Columbia University Press).

Rawls, J. (2001) *Justice as Fairness: A Restatement* (Cambridge, MA: Harvard University Press).

Rettig, R. (2002) 'Historical Perspective' in *Ethics and the Kidney*, ed. N. Levinsky
(Oxford: Oxford University Press).

Richardson, J. (2001) 'How Should We Decide Which Ethical Preferences to Include in The Economic Analyses of The Health Sector?' (West Heidelberg, Australia: Centre for Health Program Evaluation).

Rickard, M. (2002) 'The Pharmaceutical Benefits Scheme: Options for Cost Control'. Available at:

www.aph.gov.au/library/pubs/cib/2001-02/02cib12.htm (Accessed: June 20, 2006).

Rickard, M. (2004a) 'Free Trade Negotiations, the PBS and Pharmaceutical Prices' (Research Note No. 32) (Canberra: Parliamentary Library).

Rickard, M. (2004b) 'How Much Will the PBS cost?' (Research Note No. 29) (Canberra: Parliamentary Library).

Ricketts, T. and Goldsmith, L. (2005) 'Access in Health Services Research: The Battle of the Frameworks', *Nursing Outlook*, 53 (6).

Risse, G. B. (2004) 'History of the Hospital: Modern' in *Encyclopedia of Bioethics*, ed. S. G. Post (New York: Macmillan).

Roemer, J. (1993) 'A Pragmatic Theory of Responsibility for the Egalitarian Planner', *Philosophy and Public Affairs*, 22 (2).

Roemer, J. (1996) *Theories of Distributive Justice* (Cambridge, MA: Harvard University Press).

Rosen, G. (1958) *A History of Public Health* (New York: MD Publications).

Rosser, R.M. and Kind, P. (1978) 'A scale of valuations of states of illness – is there a social consensus ?, *International Journal of Epidemiology* (7).

Sainsbury Centre for Mental Health (2003) *Money for Mental Health* (London: The Sainsbury Centre for Mental Health).

Schackman, B., Gebo, K., Walensky, R., Losina, E., Muccio, T., Sax, P., Weinstein, M., Seage, G., Freedberg, K. (2006) 'The Lifetime Cost of Current Human Immunodeficiency Virus Care in the United States', *Medical Care*, 44 (990).

Scottish Executive (2000) *Fair Shares for All: Final Report; The National Review of Resource Allocation for the NHS in Scotland* (Edinburgh: Scottish Executive).

Sen, A. (1982) *Choice, Welfare, and Measurement* (Oxford: Blackwell).

Sen, A. (1992) *Inequality Reexamined* (Oxford: Clarendon Press).

Sen, A. (1993) 'Capability and Well-Being' in *The Quality of Life*, ed. M. Nussbaum and A. Sen (Oxford: Clarendon Press).

Shah, A. (1998) Fiscal Federalism and Macroeconomic Governance: For Better or For Worse? (Policy Research Working Paper Series 2005) (Washington DC: The World Bank).

Sheldon, T., Cullum, N., Lankshear, A., Lowson, K., Watt, I., West, P., Wright, D. and Wright J. (2004) 'What's the evidence that NICE guidance has been implemented? Results from a national evaluation using time series analysis, audit of patient notes, and interviews', *British Medical Journal*, 329 (7473).

Shryock, R. H. (1966) *Medicine in America: Historical Essays* (Baltimore, MD: Johns Hopkins University Press).

Shue, H. (1996) *Basic Rights: Subsistence, Affluence and US Foreign Policy* (Princeton: Princeton University Press).

Sidgwick, H. (1962) *The Methods of Ethics* (London: Macmillan).

Smaje, C. and Le Grand, J. (1997) *Ethnicity, Equity and the Use of Health Services in the British National Health Service* (London School of Economics, Health Discussion Paper No. 5).

Smith, J.L. (2006) 'Policy Briefing Paper No. 1, May 2006'. Available at: www.ahpi.health.usyd.edu.au/research/publish/ivfbrief.pdf (Accessed: July 1, 2006).

Soskolne, C. L. (2004) 'Public Health: Methods' in *Encyclopedia of Bioethics*, ed. S. G. Post (New York: Macmillan).

Starr, P. (1982) *The Social Transformation of American Medicine* (New York: Basic Books).

Taylor, C. (1989) 'Cross Purposes: The Liberal-Communitarian Debate' in *Liberalism and the Moral Life*, ed. N. Rosenblum (Cambridge, MA: Harvard University Press).

Ter-Minassian, T. (1997) *Fiscal Federalism in Theory and Practice* (Washington DC: International Monetary Fund).

Terreblanche, S. (2002) *A History of Inequality in South Africa 1652-2002* (Pietermaritzburg: University of Natal Press).

Thiede, M. (2005) 'Information and Access to Health Care: Is there a Role for Trust?', *Social Science and Medicine*, 61 (7).

Thiede, M., Akweongo, P. and McIntyre, D. (2007) 'Exploring the Dimensions of Access' in *The Economics of Health Equity*, ed. D. McIntyre and G. Mooney (Cambridge: Cambridge University Press).

Thomas, S., Mbatsha, S., Okorafor, O. and Muirhead, D. (2003) *Financing and Need Across Health Districts in South Africa* (Cape Town: Health Economics Unit, University of Cape Town, and Johannesburg: Centre for Health Policy, University of the Witwatersrand).

Thomas, S. and Muirhead, D. (2000) *National Health Accounts: The Public Sector Report* (Cape Town: NHA Consortium).

Thomas, S., Okorafor, O. and Mbatsha, S. (2005) 'Barriers to the Equitable Funding of Primary Health Care in South Africa', *Applied Health Economics and Health Policy*, 4 (3).

The Times (2006, April 19) 'NHS can't afford drug that transforms lives'. Available at: www.timesonline.co.uk/article/0,,8122-2140963,00.html (Accessed: May 2, 2006).

The Times (2006, April 27) 'Rogers v Swindon Primary Care Trust: judgement in full'. Available at: www.timesonline.co.uk?article/0,,200-2131065.html (Accessed: April 27, 2006).

Ubel, P.A. (2000) *Pricing Life: Why It's Time for Health Care Rationing* (Cambridge, MA: MIT Press).

Ubel, P.A., Arnold, R.M., and Caplan, A.L. (1998) 'Rationing failure: Ethical lessons of retransplantation' in *Classical Works in Medical Ethics*, ed. G.E. Pence (Boston, MA: McGraw-Hill).

UNGASS (2006) *Scaling up HIV Prevention, Treatment, Care and Support* (Geneva: United Nations General Assembly).

Veatch, R. (1986) *The Foundations of Justice: Why the Retarded and the Rest of Us Have Claims to Equality* (Oxford: Oxford University Press).

Wagstaff, A. (1991) 'QALYs and the equity-efficiency trade off', *Journal of Health Economics*, 10 (1).

Wailoo, A. and Anand, P. (2005) 'The Nature of Procedural Preferences for Health Care Rationing Decisions', *Social Science & Medicine*, 60 (2).

Walzer, M. (1983) *Spheres of Justice* (New York: Basic Books).

Webster, C (1988) *The Health Services Since the War Volume 1: Problems of health care and the National Health Service before 1957* (London: HMSO).

Webster's Third New International Dictionary (1965) ed. P. B. Gove (Springfield, MA: G. C. Merriam Publishers).

Welsh Assembly (2005) *Inequalities in Health: The Welsh Dimension 2002-2005* (Cardiff: Welsh Assembly Government).

Whitehead, M. (1992) 'The Concepts and Principles of Equity and Health', *International Journal of Health Services*, 22 (3).

Whitlam, G. (1985) *The Whitlam Government 1972-1975* (Ringwood: Viking Press).

Wiggins, D. (1987) *Needs, Values, Truth: Essays in the Philosophy of Value* (Oxford: Blackwell).

Wikler, D. (2002) 'Personal and Social Responsibility for Health', *Ethics and International Affairs*, 16 (2).

Williams, A. (1997) 'Intergenerational Equity: An Exploration of the "Fair Innings" Argument', *Health Economics*, 6 (2).

Williams, A. and Cookson, R. (2000) 'Equity in health' in *Handbook of Health Economics*, ed. A. Culyer, J. Newhouse (Amsterdam: Elsevier).

Williams, A. and Kind, P.(1992) 'The present state of play about QALYs' in *Measures of the Quality of Life and the Uses to Which Such Measures May Be Put*, ed. A. Hopkins (London: Royal College of Physicians)

Wiseman, V., Mooney, G., Berry, G. and Tang, K.C. (2003) 'Involving the General Public in Priority Setting: Experiences from Australia', *Social Science & Medicine*, 56 (5).

Wittgenstein, L. (1953) *Philosophical Investigations*, trans. G. E. M. Anscombe (New York: Macmillan).

Woolhandler, S., Campbell, T., and Himmelstein, D. (2003) 'Costs of Health Care Administration in the United States and Canada', *New England Journal of Medicine*, 349 (768).

World Health Organisation (2004) *Consultation on Ethics and Equitable Access to Treatment and Care for HIV/AIDS* (Geneva: World Health Organisation / Joint United Nations Programme on HIV/AIDS).

Xue, J., Ma, J., Louis, T., and Collins, A. (2001) 'Forecast of the Number of Patients with End-Stage Renal Disease in the United States to the Year 2010', *Journal of the American Society of Nephrology*, 12 (2753).

Index